HANK WILLIAMS

Country Music's Tragic King

HANK WILLIAMS

Country Music's Tragic King

JAY CARESS

STEIN AND DAY/*Publishers*/New York

The author wishes to thank the following for permission to reprint selections from their works:

Jerry Rivers, for excerpts from his book *Hank Williams: From Life to Legend*, edited by Thurston Moore. (Denver: Heather Enterprises, 1967.)

Roger M. Williams, for excerpts from his book *Sing a Sad Song: The Life of Hank Williams*. (New York; Ballantine, 1973, 1975.)

Harper & Row, Publishers, Inc., for excerpts from *The Country Music Encyclopedia* by Melvin Shestack. Copyright © 1974 by KBO Publishers, Inc.

and to the proprietors of the photos acknowledged in the captions. All photos not otherwise credited are the author's.

First published in 1979
Copyright © 1979 by James M. Caress
All rights reserved.
Designed by Ed Kaplin
Printed in the United States of America
Stein and Day/*Publishers*/Scarborough House
Briarcliff Manor, N.Y. 10510

Library of Congress Cataloging in Publication Data

Caress, Jay.
    Hank Williams, country music's tragic king.

    Bibliography: p.
    Includes index.
    1. Williams, Hank, 1923-1953.   2.   Country musicians—
United States—Biography.
ML420.W55C4   784'.092'4 [B]   78-23942
ISBN 0-8128-2583-7

To my wife and to the memory of my mother.

Acknowledgments

I am deeply indebted to all those who cared enough about this project to give their time and wisdom to it. Among these: Hank Williams, Jr., Billie Jean Horton, Irene Williams Smith, Lycrecia Morris, Wesley Rose, Jerry Rivers, Bob McNett, Don Helms, Sammy Pruitt, Hillous Butrum, Taft and Erleen Skipper, M. C. Jarrett, Jim Owen, Corky and Barbara Adams, Aaron Shelton, Jimmy Lockert, Nick Tosches, Paul Schrader, Red Sovine, Johnny Wright, Minnie Pearl, and David Stone.

Without the willing contributions of these and other friends and relatives of Hank Williams, this undertaking would have been impossible. I hope this book measures up to the high caliber of cooperation I received.

My thanks also to the *Nashville Banner* and *The Tennessean* for opening its files; to the Country Music Foundation Library and Media Center for the treasures of information it provided; to my editor, Benton Arnovitz, for his patience; and to Arlene Magnuson for her superefficient preparation of the final draft.

Special thanks must go, finally, to retired Sheriff Swann Kitts of Union County, Tennessee for unlocking after a quarter-century his knowledge of the events leading to Hank Williams' death. This book is for these who made it possible, with a hearty toast to the future of American music.

Contents

Introduction

It was a hot night in July of 1977 and I was spending late hours worrying on the balcony of my Nashville motel room.

Looking out to the south toward the brightly-lit tall office buildings of downtown Music City, I watched the semis and the tourist station wagons speed down toward town on a long hill of freeway flooded by eerie amber-pink vapor lights.

The view was partially obscured by a forest of high-vaulting signs from the gas stations and motels clustered around the intersection of I–65 and Trinity Lane. Business was brisk, even at 1 A.M. That's typical for Nashville in the summer. A couple of miles to the east, Opryland, the beautiful new "Home of American Music," was romping into its sixth year of operation. The enormous new Opryland Hotel hadn't opened yet. Summertime Nashville has long been chronically short of hotel rooms. The new building would be welcome.

"You're a fool," I told myself. "You think you can hang around here and get a feel for a man who died twenty-five years ago—for a performer who played this town when it still had a personality of its own, not an identity merchandised by multinational corporations and high-powered promotion men from both coasts? You're crazy."

I was convincing myself. What *did* any of the hoopla about "Acres of Opryland Free Parking" and "Bus Tours of Music Row" and nearly a dozen slick nationally-syndicated television shows, what did any of this late-twentieth century mass-culture flab have to do with Hank Williams?

Not much. You can't find Hank Williams in Nashville, just as you can't find your own childhood when you try to go home again. All that's left here is the Hank Williams Museum on

ix

Music Row, which displays Hank's car, some clothes, and other memorabilia. There are the memories, of course, of those who knew him. But so often in Nashville the memories have the ring of what Norman Mailer calls "factoids," facts remembered as the people want to remember them, not necessarily as they happened.

Actually you're lucky to even get an honest attempt at Hank Williams memories in Nashville. Life does go on, after all. There's hay to be made while the sun shines: folks to turn out records for, folks who pay good money for food and rooms and liquor, yes, and now it's a whole New South out there.

"Hank Williams is history," says Nashville, "so what? Let's make us some money *now!!!*"

Nashville in the late seventies is ol' boy money. Ol' boys with dry-sprayed hair, black-with-red-leather Continentals, and creased, tanned, country faces cushioned over Qiana-cloth shirts and fifty-dollar belts, sliding through nonstop telephone conversations like this one:

". . . yeah, he played Pittsburgh the other night . . . shoot yeah! We got fifteen grand and a cut. Got drunker'n skunks too! Yeah? Hell you say. Hold on, Buck. . . .

"Hello . . . no, he's busy that week. No. No. Next week too. Naw, buddy, we booked through November. OK. 'Bye.

"Hello, Buck . . . I'm back . . . you gonna play golf this evenin'?"

Country music is basically not an art form for purists. It has no real standards, which may explain why there is almost no such thing as a country music critic. There's a simple reason for this. Country music waited a long time for the kind of exposure and recognition it enjoys today, and along the way developed strong protective feelings about its artists. They got enough barbs from outsiders; who needed criticism from within?

At any rate, the country music industry is concerned with pleasing masses of people. That concentrated effort doesn't leave a whole lot of time and energy for history or for introspection. Whether or not something important could be getting lost in the commercial shuffle is hardly anybody's concern.

"They've got fans in Austin," Waylon Jennings once told a

reporter, "but they don't have no good studios." So when even a "pure" country singer like Jennings or Nelson wants to make a good recording, he must fight his way past the Nashville establishment into a Music City studio to make his own music in his own way.

Well, ol' Waylon was surely talking about more than just a heavy backbeat's difference when he wrote an autobiographical hit in 1975 entitled, "Are You Sure Hank Done It This Way?"

Because whether you talk musically, culturally, or technically, the answer to his question must be a resounding "No."

What I concluded in Nashville was that I'd have to get out of Nashville to find Hank Williams. I'd have to come back to the full-to-busting motels and Music Row secretaries later, when the time came to single out old friends.

So taking one last look down the pink freeway and another look up to the stars, I came in out of the sultry night to the sealed-in whir of an air-conditioned room. It was time to rest for the drive to Alabama.

I first became aware of Hank Williams through an old Travler radio on my parents' farm in 1954 or '55. At the age of seven I was already becoming quite a country music fan. Most often it was a colorful name—Hawkshaw Hawkins, Slim Whitman, Little Jimmy Dickens—or a particularly fancy western outfit that attracted me to a performer, but with Hank Williams, it was his music.

In the words of Jerry Rivers, Hank's fiddler, the man's songs "grabbed me." I was later to find they never would let me go.

I spent a lot of winter evenings listening to that old radio. The station was usually WKLO in Louisville, then one of the more popular country music stations in the country. Jimmy "Ya'll Come" Osborne, when not singing his own songs live, would play 78 rpm records from his record shop on Broadway, and a lot of the records he played were by "the late, great Hank Williams."

That description didn't mean much to me then. I really didn't understand that Hank Williams was dead. After all, he was one of the most-often-played artists on the radio. But a couple of years later, Jimmy Osborne shot himself in the head and was found in the bathroom of his home in Louisville, and by that time I knew from a country music fan book that Hank Williams had also come to an untimely end on January 1, 1953.

WKLO was never the same without Jimmy; and besides, the times were changing. There was a kid from Memphis who was drawing a lot of attention to a new kind of rhythmic sound. Rock and roll was a wild dark fruit that had grown out of the intertwined hillbilly and black blues vines.

In 1958, a new station, WAKY (WACKY RADIO!), hit the airwaves in Louisville playing raucous sounds by people like Chuck Berry and the Coasters and Jerry Lee Lewis.

Good-bye cowboy hats and Hello, Mary Lou . . . by the time I got to be nine or ten, I was already too cool for country music—and Hank Williams. Later, passing through most of the standard and some of the optional sixties-type musical changes, I tried on everything from Ray Charles to young Michel Legrand, plus all the button-down folkies and some of the chambray cloth folkies.

Come 1966, I was an aimless undergrad at Indiana University and into Dylan, Lou Rawls, and college-weekend beer parties. One weekend of that fall, I was hitchhiking from I.U. up to Greencastle, Indiana, to visit a friend at DePauw University. The chill of a Friday evening sundown was just beginning and I was standing outside the tiny hamlet of Cloverdale. An old farmer in a 1950 Chevy pickup stopped to give me a ride.

The old man greeted me as I got in; there was music in his truck. Under the dusty dash was a shiny new eight-track tape player playing Hank Williams' album "Lost Highway." We rolled northward through the hazy hills and valleys toward Route 40, watching the stars come out and listening to "Ramblin' Man," a Hank Williams classic of the Road, the Drifter, and the One Left Behind. I was hooked all over again.

At a party a year later someone slipped Hank's "Men With Broken Hearts" onto the turntable. I'd never heard it before. The homely sincerity of that powerful spoken lyric cut across the years that night like a prophet screaming into my soul. At the same time I knew clearly that I was listening to a plain ol' country boy, who with a crying steel guitar to help him, was simply making a point about how one should treat a man who's down and out.

I listened to Hank regularly in the years that followed, and to Fred Neil, Traffic, Taj Mahal, and some other personal heroes. Before long, I plunged into the music business myself, trying to make a name as a singer and songwriter.

Some of the pressures and proddings that plagued Hank in his day began to nip at my own bootheels: agents, producers, hangers-on, and a gnawing restlessness about what really lay at the end of my efforts. Finally I quit the ladder I'd been trying so desperately to climb. I left the west coast, went back to the Midwest, got married, became a Christian, and went back to school to begin a new life. That was in 1971.

I still love Hank Williams' music. Some of his songs still bring a mist to my eyes. A lot of people I've talked with confess to those tears, too.

I see Hank Williams in a different light these last few years. He is a sadder, more life-size figure, but not really less intriguing. Neither does his life story seem less worthy of retelling.

HANK WILLIAMS
Country Music's Tragic King

1

A Background of His Reign

One morning in the second week of August, 1952, Hank Williams answered the telephone in his rented house off Natchez Trace in suburban Nashville. The tall, lanky singer looked bad, especially for a man who had become the undisputed monarch of country music. He hadn't shaved for days, and his face was scraped up from a fall he'd taken through his screen door. The Grand Ole Opry star had been on a bender for two weeks straight and now Jim Denny, Manager of the Opry's Artists Service Bureau, was on the line.

As Denny's voice crackled into his receiver, Hank heard what he must have known would be said.

"You cain't fire me!" he shouted back into the phone as he straightened up to his full six foot one, "I quit last week!"

A few sentences later Johnny Wright, who had been sitting around Hank's place, got on the phone with Denny and confirmed the information. Hank Williams was fired from the Grand Ole Opry. His last spree of absences had finally been too much. Denny asked Wright if he would make sure Hank got his final check. And when the phone conversation was over, Hank asked Wright if he would help him get his stuff out of Nashville.

Hank was in considerable pain from his chronic back problem, so when Johnny Wright agreed to pull Hank's trailer home to Montgomery, he also had to agree to put a lounge chair from the singer's living room between the seats of Wright's 1951 Chrysler limousine. This would ease the agony of the long drive south.

1

When the equipment trailer was securely hitched to the Chrysler and Williams himself installed in the lounge chair, Wright drove downtown to the WSM offices. The "Lovesick Blues Boy" was about to receive his last pay from the Grand Ole Opry, where he had debuted just three years before. Those three years had seen Hank Williams quickly become the hottest property in country music, a compelling singer who sang from his guts and a songwriter whose songs were being made into nationwide hits by the biggest pop artists. But the same sensitivity that had made Hank irresistible as an artist was also fast becoming his downfall.

Johnny Wright picked up Hank's check and started out of the WSM offices. Roy Acuff and Owen Bradley stopped him in the hallway.

"They tell me you got Hank Williams out in the car," said Acuff.

"Yeah," Wright answered. "He's leavin' town."

Acuff and Bradley wanted to say good-bye to Williams, so they followed Wright out to the alley where the limo was parked and both wished Hank the best. There wasn't much to say.

"We gotta cash this check," Williams told Wright as they pulled away from the WSM back door, "and we gotta get a bottle, too."

So Johnny Wright dutifully drove to the liquor store at 16th and Broadway and went inside. He handed the clerk Williams' $200-plus check and ordered a fifth of whiskey.

Meanwhile, a small crowd was gathering outside the store, drawn by the gaudy trailer with the words "Hank Williams and the Drifting Cowboys" lettered on it. They were peeking in the windows for a glimpse of the hot-eyed, shy-smiling boy from Alabama. Hank could draw a crowd anywhere.

Wright returned with the bottle and the change and they started off for Montgomery, Alabama, Hank's home town. Johnny remembers steering the Chrysler down old Highway 31 while Hank sat back in the living-room chair where the jump seats would have been, joking, singing, and drinking.

By the time the limo arrived in front of Hank's mother's

boardinghouse in Montgomery that night, the long-legged troubadour had passed out.

Johnny Wright carried him inside, and together he and Lillian Williams pulled off Hank's clothes, put some pajamas on him, and put him to bed in his old room. He'd be back to normal by morning.

Four and a half months later—at the age of twenty-nine—Hank Williams would be dead.

Hank's story begins in a simpler America. That America had no interstate highway system, no counterculture (although Kerouac, Cassidy, and Ginsberg were beginning to experiment along those lines), no color TV (the television industry was still an infant), no pill, no appreciable white awareness of a civil rights movement nor of any need for it, and very little grassroots skepticism about God and country.

It was another time. And what's more, it was the South. Transportation was still dominated by the railroads: The great lines sent sleek passenger specials and long freights on antlike crisscross journeys through Dixie. Whole townsful of ordinary people never left their home county more than once or twice in a lifetime unless forced to by hard times.

This other America of the South had its own music, brought over by Anglo-Saxon stalwarts who stayed back in the Appalachian "hollers" and passed down songs that had been Elizabethan folk ballads and Irish jigs. But over the centuries the music didn't remain the same—it was influenced by Wesleyan hymns and black field laments, just as Southern society became a mixture of European class structure and Christian conviction, always with the shadow of Afro-American anguish and resentment troubling its peace.

This Southern stage set for Hank Williams to tread had only just begun to send its thousands of workers from Georgia fields and Alabama lumber camps into the steel mills, freight lines, breweries, and auto plants of the urban North. The workers would take their music with them to neighborhood juke boxes in Detroit and Cleveland.

Southern music, by the 1940s, was generally known as

Country Music, or more cynically, "hillbilly music" and was often called "country and western" as it still is today. To the public, the boundaries must have appeared vague between southeastern mainline country music, southwestern "western swing," and the songs of the Hollywood singing cowboys.

Beyond the South, America was waiting out a dry spell in popular music that lasted from the end of the Big Band era in the early forties until the onset of popular rock 'n roll in the mid-fifties. This era was dominated by what rock music writer Charlie Gillett calls "melodrama/sentiment/trivia" songs, "pleasant" music that reflected the Tin Pan Alley philosophy. They were unmeant, unphysical, unprovocative love ditties whipped up on order for Broadway shows, Big Band balladeers, and radio crooners.

Between 1946 and 1953, smack in the middle of these pop music doldrums, Hank Williams burst out of Alabama and onto the Grand Ole Opry stage in Nashville. He sprang from there into the history of American popular culture, establishing a permanent beachhead in pop music for a host of hillbillies who would follow.

Between 1949 and 1953, Hank Williams made eleven records which sold over a million copies each. But more than that, he put the capstone on American country music as a popular art form. Before Hank's time country music had a long history of experimentation and growth; afterwards begins a period—still in progress—of over-sophistication, self-imitation, and an artistic numbness brought on by too much formula songwriting.

Country music has become a giant industry. Where once its audience was predominantly rural, poor, and unsophisticated, it is now urbanized or suburbanized, middle-class, and much more a part of the overall American pop scene. The audience has moved out of the South into all areas of the country, creating listening markets for supersuccessful country radio stations in the major population centers of the North, East, and West.

Hank Williams stands apart from the hillbilly legacy he inherited. "Before Hank, most country songs were about somethin' to eat," says one Nashville musician. He was an artist whose art does not dovetail with the traditions of his own time nor with the slick trappings of ours. He wrote and sang about timeless things in a way neither generation can forget.

Why is Hank Williams the King of popular country music? It's possible to construct an impressive theory to explain it, bringing in all this relevant data concerning post-war America: urbanization in the South and Midwest, migration of a southern work force into northern factory towns, and the advent of electronic technology in country music. (The electric steel guitar, one of Hank's trademarks, was still an innovation in the forties.)

So many forces intersected to bring this "music of the people" off the front porches of the South and into newly-furnished living rooms in Akron and Milwaukee that quite an elaborate chart could be drawn showing how all these influences came together to create a "golden age" of country music in the decade after World War II, the decade during which Hank perfected the art.

But this theorizing cannot explain why people—then and now—can be brought to tears by one of Hank's songs. It doesn't explain why Hank Williams' funeral on January 4, 1953, has been called "the biggest emotional plunge" in Montgomery, Alabama, "since the inauguration of Jefferson Davis." Hank Williams' success did not depend on the mere facts of socio-economic progress. He sang to the people and the people loved him, period.

They still love him. In 1977, Wesley Rose, President of Acuff-Rose Music, showed me a gold double album entitled "Twenty-four of Hank Williams' Greatest Hits" which was hanging in the Acuff-Rose building in Nashville. It had just gone over the half-million mark in sales that spring. This kind of impact for a recording artist who has been dead a quarter of a century is unmatched in American music.

Hank Williams? There are still some Americans who hear the name and think you must be talking about a baseball player they can't qute place, but many, many others know exactly whom you mean.

In New York, former Columbia Records executive Mitch Miller calls Hank "another Stephen Foster." In California, his cult following among country-rock groups includes Linda Ronstadt and Glenn Frey of the Eagles. In Nashville, Hank Williams is still the man, the artist, you compare anyone else to and see if they come anywhere near.

Even among the people least knowledgeable about country music, those who don't know Hank Williams from Hank Mancini, the eyes light up and the smiles spread out with recognition when you name a couple of Hank's songs.

"Oh, yeah . . . 'Your Cheatin' Heart'. . . Did he write that?"

"You mean he wrote 'I'm So Lonesome I Could Cry'?"

"'Jambalaya' was a Hank Williams song?"

And so on. After a quarter century, there are precious few Americans who aren't familiar with some of Hank Williams' songs.

This phenomenon shows up in the figures at Acuff-Rose Music. Wesley Rose doesn't give out exact figures about how much money Hank's estate has collected for his songwriting, but he'll not deny that these songs have earned *between one hundred thousand and a quarter of a million dollars, in Williams' royalties alone, every year since 1953, the year of Hank's death.* Total royalties paid on Hank's songs were estimated at $5 million in 1972. The figure today may be close to $10 million.

Record sales over the years comprise a whole other fortune. No other American recording artist has such a durable posthumous sales performance of singles and albums. There are more than thirty Hank Williams albums in print on M-G-M records, and in many country music record stores all of them are on prominent display.

But it's not just the songs and the intensely delivered Hank Williams performances that keep this phenomenon going year after year. Hank Williams was not merely an artist—he was an enigma. He was a mysterious "sad troubadour," a haunted genius, a boisterous yet lonely man who died at the age of twenty-nine of "too much living, too much sorrow, too much love, and too much drink and drugs."

He deserves to be called the King of Country Music if for no other reason than that he assured forever the cross-over of country songs and artists into the broad American pop market.

The trail he blazed was wide enough and permanent enough that it never fell into disrepair, and a veritable stampede of gifted and decidedly ungifted country artists have galloped along it in the years since his passing.

Still, Hank's real kingship is neither a matter of record sales nor his contribution to the growth of the country music industry. Like Elvis Presley, another southern performer whom in many ways he foreshadowed, Hank Williams' reign is a matter of near-idolatrous love and respect felt by hundreds of thousands of people for him and his music.

History, literature, and art tell us stories of many tragic kings. Great King Saul of Israel went mad with jealousy over his successor David. Shakespeare's King Lear slid into a pitifully unstable condition amid the intrigues of his court and family. Van Gogh, the master of modern impressionistic painting, was a tormented suicide.

There is always an aura of mystery surrounding the memory of these men to whom greatness came easier than contentment. In the case of Hank Williams, this magnetism is only matched by the almost universal uncanny sense of identification which his audience felt, and still feels, with the man and the bittersweet life he sang about.

2

Roots and Ramblings

A few hundred miles south of Nashville, and light-years away from the spectacle that Opryland would become, Hank Williams was born in a sharecropper's two-room log house in south Alabama. A dirt road ran in front of the place, and a three-acre strawberry field adjoined the side yard.

That humble dwelling stood in Mount Olive, a tiny community in southwestern Butler County, sixty miles or so south of Montgomery. The year was 1923, and although the Williams family's poverty was acute by today's standards, it was nothing shameful in that time and place.

Not much has changed in that corner of Butler County. The same kind of farms are still there—the sort that were struggling when Lon and Lilly Williams moved out to Mount Olive in the spring of 1922 and leased the house and some land for eight dollars a year.

The house is standing no longer. There's a rutted, grassy trace where the old dirt road used to run, and some small, aged fruit trees that once shaded the back yard. On a summer evening on the small hill where that house stood, you can smell the good smell of country grass and Alabama pines. There's no sound of industry, no traffic down on the "new" blacktop road— just the rustle of the wind and the kind of peace that some people never want to leave.

South Alabama had two basic industries in 1923 and it has the same two today: logging and farming. The railroad served both with a vigor it since has lost. Hank's father, Elonzo H. Williams, worked in all three worlds. Lon grew up in Lowndes County, where he quit school after the sixth grade to work in the logging camps. Eventually he became a locomotive driver

8

and ran logging rigs all over the Southeast. He often sharecropped on the side.

In 1918, Lon married Lillian Skipper, whose family was from near Georgiana, Alabama. Lilly brought with her a more stable heritage than Lon had known; her family was then and still is well-respected around Georgiana.

Lon and Lillian's was not a glamorous courtship. He was an average-looking young man who would bald early in life; Lilly was a large and rather serious young woman. Lon entered the Army shortly after their marriage and saw action in Europe during the closing days of World War I. This was to be a crucial development.

"Lon was shell-shocked and gassed in World War I," recalls Hank's cousin, Taft Skipper, who still lives in Georgiana, "and ever after that he had bad nerves. I can remember Lilly always keepin' a pot o'coffee on for Lon because of his nerves, and sometimes she'd tell us kids to hush up, because Lon was tryin' to rest." No one, least of all Lon himself, ever disputed this explanation for his inability to take charge of his young family in the years following the war.

No one, that is, except Hank Williams himself.

"You think I'm a drunkard?" he once blurted out to a friend. "You shoulda seen my old man!"

In August of 1922, Lilly bore a daughter, Irene. Then on September 17, 1923, not long after they moved to Mount Olive and went into the berry business, a son was born. Poor or no, Lon later bragged that he hired both a doctor and a black midwife to be in attendance. The lady who served as midwife still lives in a sturdy farmhouse just a mile or so from where the Williams' house stood.

So a musical legacy now controlled by a giant Dutch corporation—Polygram—and by two of America's foremost publishing firms, began in the piney Alabama hills ten miles back from anywhere. And if more than fifty years later most of the nearby residents have still never been out of the state of Alabama, Hiram Hank Williams and his music made an awesome leap. Then again, if Hank hadn't started where he started, he probably never would have gone where he went.

"There's so much we could tell if it hadn't been so long ago," says Taft Skipper wistfully. "If we'd knowed Hank was gonna be famous, we coulda wrote some things down . . . a lot of things."

Taft is just a little older than Hank would be now—though his hair is jet black, he confesses to being sixty—and he can remember back to the days when Hank was a baby.

"Lon Williams was a good man, a fine man," he says generously, "but like I said, he had a problem with his nerves."

As Lon drifted from job to job, the Williams family moved to several communities in Butler County: to Garland, to Chapman, to McWilliams, and then into Georgiana.

Although Lon always worked, it seemed he never could hold a job very long. That weakness, coupled with the fact that times were rough anyway, meant that Lilly—a husky and resolute woman—soon had to prove herself a good manager. She even contributed to the family income with various jobs and enterprises. Lilly tried berry farming, canning, and later worked for a time as a practical nurse.

She also played organ at the Mount Olive Baptist Church, giving young Hank the opportunity to do his first public singing standing on a bench beside his mother while she pumped out hymns for the services there. More about that later. The old church is now the "Mount Olive Community Club," but the bench is displayed like a holy relic on the platform at the front of the new church next door.

Lon's problem with his "nerves" came to a head in 1930 when his son was seven. He was committed voluntarily to a veterans' hospital in Biloxi, Mississippi. Lon Williams would stay there ten long years and his marriage to Lilly would dissolve in that time. Hank, who by now was a frail and scrawny but active and "plucky" young boy, was going to be virtually fatherless for the rest of his life.

Nobody knows how much it hurt him. The boy never seemed to grieve outwardly about his loss, yet there are other signs that Hank was seriously scarred by this misfortune. Not the least of these was his early and persistent interest in liquor.

When Lon went to the hospital, Lilly took up the care of her small family. She worked at it.

"I don't believe there was anything she wouldn't have done to make us happy," says Irene Williams. "She worked hard for us, went without ever buying new clothes for herself so that she could make sure we were taken care of."

Her efforts were noticed. "Once when we lived in Georgiana," says Irene, "the welfare department refused to give us aid because Lilly's kids were *too clean*."

From the time of Lon's departure from the family scene, young Hank worked too. Taft Skipper remembers him selling peanuts and shining shoes down at Georgiana's cotton gin. The rundown old building is still standing, though the porch where Hank worked is caving in.

According to Roger Williams, the story goes that soon after his father's hospitalization Hank and Irene went out to make some money while Lilly stayed home with a new boardinghouse venture and her garden.

> Irene roasted some peanuts and put them in little paper bags. Hank took them out on the streets of Georgiana. He also took a can of shoe polish and a rag, and anyone passing up the peanuts was offered a shine instead. Each sold for a nickel. No one recalls just how good a seller or shiner Hank was, but by the end of the day he had made thirty cents. With it, he bought stew meat and rice (ten cents each), potatoes and tomatoes (five cents each). He presented the food triumphantly to his mother and exclaimed, "Momma, fix us some gumbo stew. We're gonna eat tonight!"

Hard work became a constant in Hank's life. There were to be others: strong-willed females, alcohol, and music.

There were a few good years of growing up ahead for Hank. The folks around Georgiana remember him as a skinny kid always on the go. Hank wasn't much of an athlete, but he'd try anything. He often got hurt trying, though, so he took his energy to the streets.

"The family didn't always need what little money Hank could provide," reports Roger Williams, "but Hank himself needed it if he was to have any of the good things a boy wants." Friends and neighbors remember Hank gallivanting around Georgiana in cowboy clothes, gladly running small errands for a nickel or a dime. It was then, too, that his interest in music began to develop.

"As a child, he got to laugh," says Irene. "He loved us. We loved him. And Hank and I were loved very much by our mother."

But it was not a normal childhood. Over it hung the shadow of Lon Williams' virtual disappearance. Much like the young products of today's matriarchal urban ghetto communities, Hank simply had no stabilizing masculine model for his life. His identity had to come instead from the southern culture itself, which taught him how to talk, how to view the world, and how he might be able to earn a living.

But the same culture that eventually made Hank its model son—Hank has been called the "prototypical hillbilly"—still wouldn't let him forget that he was poor and that he had no heritage to offer as collateral for complete social acceptance. A glimmer of resentment was born in those days spent kneeling with a shoerag, and it festered into lifelong bitterness and distrust toward people of wealth and position.

The strong presence of Lilly Williams, with no counteracting father-figure, also worked a curious warp into the weave of young Hank's personality. He never made the normal childhood psychological transfer from what psychologists call *dependent* mother-love to assertive, *independent* (father-emulating) mother-love. The result was what is commonly called a love-hate relationship. Years later, it would be said of Hank's relationship with his first wife Audrey that "he couldn't live with her and he couldn't live without her." This also vividly describes his relationship with Lilly: Audrey merely stepped into the role originated by Hank's mother.

Hank always had plenty of friends, if not close buddies. His cousin J. C. McNeil was one of them. Hank lived for a year with J. C. and his parents over in Monroe County so that J. C.'s sister could go to school in Georgiana. Such trade-offs between relatives were not uncommon in those years.

Hank was eleven in 1934, and in some ways, it was probably the happiest year of his boyhood. Although the McNeils lived in a "camp car"—a couple of old boxcars made into a rude house— their situation, by Alabama Depression standards, was quite comfortable. They had enough to eat, a little bit left over, and a built-in community life as part of the railroad camp where they lived and where Walter McNeil worked.

Walter McNeil actually took a rather fatherly interest in Hank while the youngster stayed there, a welcome interest. It was a much more stable home life than Hank had been used to.

Mrs. McNeil, like Hank's mother, was a church-going woman who made sure Hank and J. C. went with her every Sunday morning. Taft Skipper suggests that "a lot of Hank's wisdom came from the church . . . the timeless things that the Christian Church teaches—things that have lasted thousands of years—had a deep effect on him."

No doubt there's some truth in that, but there's also evidence that Hank learned early a lot more about talking the Christian faith than living it. Christianity has always been very influential in southern culture, but so has a strong predilection for hellraisin'. Anyone who has lived in the South can tell you that if the byword is "Jesus Saves" on Sunday, it's also "Raise Hell!" on the Saturday night before. And the Saturday night gospel is usually more wholeheartedly pursued by most good ol' boys than the Sunday morning variety, the nature of which seems all too vague and feminine to be comprehensible to them anyway.

Hank Williams is only one of hundreds of country singers who, as the emcees inevitably put it, "got started singing in church" or "first showed a unique talent while singing Gospel songs in the choir." It's a commonplace and an almost obligatory apprenticeship for country music stardom.

Yet if it was "Amazing Grace" sung by a down-home congregation that helped to deliver Hank to music and "Peace In The Valley" sung by his friend Red Foley that said goodbye to Hank at his funeral, there was little in between these milestones that relates easily to the sentiment of either song. And that, for an old-line country musician, is just about par for the course.

The year that Hank spent with the McNeil family was significant in two respects, both related to the railroad-and-logging-camp custom of frequent Saturday night dances.

It was at these hoedowns that Hank Williams first began to experiment with liquor—at the age of eleven. It wasn't an unusually early initiation for that place and time. But how did children his age get their hands on booze? The flexible morality of rural southern society made it simple.

According to the unwritten code, public drinking was frowned upon—well, obvious public drinking, that is. First off, it had to be, at least from 1919 to 1933 it had to be. There was that matter of Prohibition. But the social pressure against "showing a bottle" persisted for decades after.

So liquor was almost never carried into the camp dances that young Hank attended. It was usually hidden outside, either left in the car or in the crook of a tree or under a bush, anywhere that was reasonably secure and easily accessible.

And while the fiddle music echoed into the south Alabama sky, the loggers and farmers got progressively drunker as the evenings wore on, though no one was actually seen taking a drink. People just ducked out for air every so often.

Meanwhile mischievous tow-headed youngsters like Hank and J. C. watched to see where the stashes were kept and helped themselves when the coast was clear.

"We'd watch where they hid the stuff," J. C. McNeil reports in Roger Williams' book, "and we'd dig it out and get as drunk as hoot owls on it."

Many parents were concerned about this behavior of their offspring, but few were concerned enough to change their own style of having fun.

For most youngsters, perhaps, this type of lark can be relatively harmless. Certainly not every kid who has early and regular access to alcohol grows up to be an alcoholic as Hank did; but there are two sad side-effects that this situation helped to foster in that young man.

First, Hank learned to equate alcohol with fun. Like millions of sons of the South (and North and East and West) he grew up in a subculture where people were very often withdrawn, passive, and emotionally repressed during the sober workweek, storing up resentments and pressures until the weekend. In this case, the ol' boys were piling up the Depression Blues right good and high week by week, only to let 'er rip when they'd got a good pint or so of corn under their belts at somebody's Saturday night to-do.

Then all of a sudden there was laughter and good feelings and occasionally even a spark of real joy: "Whooooeeee! Let's make up for lost time!" And of course that much pent-up emotion coupled with five or six stiff drinks was an explosive one-two punch. People invariably got out of line, but that was to be expected and put up with. It was all in fun.

In his teens, though, Hank picked up the ancient tribal habit of saving his "fun" for the weekends when the booze flowed and the music played and it was okay to let fly the feelings bottled up inside.

The second result of his early access to alcohol was that young Hank never really learned to live sober. His drinking progressed so quickly from the weekend-spree variety into a compulsion that there was virtually no normal, sober period he could look back on as an adult in order to regain his bearings. Hank's norm just had to include drinking.

When a drinking person or an alcoholic "learns" that life, that coping, that even delight is possible without alcohol, he is often really *remembering* it. Some faint signal from childhood or adolescence flickers across the dim stretch of years—a memory of how good the wind smelled on a certain night, or the excitement of fighting through that first football game—something comes back to remind him that life's greatest joys don't have to be chemically induced.

But for Hank Williams, who was later to wage war with his thirst, the memories of life before liquor were dim indeed. His memories of facing adult or even adolescent pressures without help from the bottle were almost nonexistent.

If Hank met his greatest nemesis in 1934 when he lived with the McNeils, that was also the year he took his first steps on his road to immortality—country music. The same dances at which he stole his first gulps of trachea-torching bootleg whiskey were also the places where he first heard an old-fashioned "string band" play a whole night of hoedown music.

The musicians were just a cut above amateurs. Paid to get a group together and come to somebody's house for a shindig or play at a local dance hall, they were mostly just farmers or tradesmen who also played an instrument.

There were actually plenty of country music styles in the

thirties. Many young musicians aped the "blue yodels" of
Jimmie Rodgers and sang sad ballads with bluesy guitar
breaks. Groups with names like the "Skillit Lickers" or the
"Gully Jumpers" specialized in super-speed fiddle tunes and
novelty songs about various delicacies or the right way to skin a
mule. Others mixed Negro country blues or centuries-old
ballad/laments into their repertoires.

Still, varied as it was, this music had some strong com-
monalities: it was straightforward, distinctly melodic, and
strongly rhythmic. These three traits were the essence of its
appeal, and they became the simple formula of the music made
by Hank Williams, who was to become the greatest country
music songwriter of them all.

Forty-three years later, I find myself down in Red Level,
Alabama, at a place called The Barn, where I've been invited to
spend the evening with some of Hank's kin and a lot of other
folks. I'd wanted to see what had and hadn't changed about
Saturday nights in rural south Alabama.

Red Level is even farther from anywhere than Georgiana and
getting down there is quite a drive. First across a hilly back
road, past straw-hatted black farmers in their fields, from the
town of Garland through a dusky pine woods evening over to
Route 31. Then south on 31 down to McKenzie, where highway
55 forks off from that old main road to Mobile. A few minutes
down 55 and the traveler begins to feel that the rest of America
is far away.

Red Level, like Georgiana, has lost residents in the past few
decades. Its "downtown" stands graying with empty store-
fronts that tell of earlier, busier times. New buildings are
scarce.

The Barn's owner, Ron Taylor, has created his dance hall by
simply erecting a modern, aluminum-shell barn in a hillside field
along a country road about a mile or so out of Red Level. Ron
Taylor's Barn, then, unlike thousands of watering holes with
similar names across the country, is truly what its name
promises.

Perhaps because Red Level locals have seen enough old
buildings, or maybe because of economics, there's been no

attempt to make The Barn "rustic." It's a simple, stark, metal structure set on one expansive slab of concrete. There are no decorations, no niceties, no frills. The patrons park their pickups and cars in a sand lot outside the door, bring their own bottles inside, and buy ice by the bucket and their mixer by the quart. They pay a couple of dollars admission to sit on folding chairs at long plain tables and to hear the music offered up by Ron and his house band. Ron the Owner is also Ron the Lead Singer.

In a sense it's different from days gone by, but in another way it's really the same. Those "colorful" barns where country dances used to be held were simply the ordinary barns of their day, with little or no alteration. And since an "ordinary" barn built today is usually an aluminum one like Ron's, his approach to staging Alabama country entertainment is authentic.

There's plenty of time to get acquainted and meet the folks around the long table before the show starts. Most of the men near us, Taft Skipper's daughter informs me, either work with or for her husband, who is a foreman at a local lumber mill. The mill is now part of a conglomerate corporation that owns mills all over the South. One of the men begins to talk with me across the table.

"Don't you want a drink?" he asks, eyeing my glass of unspiked Coke.

"No, thanks," I answer him.

"Well," he says conspiratorially in a lower voice, "they'll be turning the lights off pretty soon. Then nobody'll notice if you have one." Having gotten me pegged, he takes a gulp from his own glass.

Soon the lights go down, the band takes the stage and begins to play, and the people get down to the business of swilling and dancing. The place is comfortably full by the time the music starts, with a few younger men on the prowl, some girls with the same notion, and many couples of all ages, most of whom appear to be married.

Several people warmly encourage me to dance—my friend from across the table reminds me that my wife is far away—but I elect to keep mostly to the business of observation while trying not to appear to be a snob for all my polite refusals.

The band plays standard modern-seventies country hits hot off the radio, nothing less and nothing more. (This summer's big song—dutifully dished up—is Waylon's "Luckenbach Texas.") The boys aren't bad musicians and the same smooth unpretentious renditions probably would have still been chosen for them if a New York market research outfit came down and ran a sample of audience taste in The Barn on any given Saturday night.

There are no fights tonight, not even near-ones; The Barn is not really your tough honky-tonk type of establishment. It's more a place where solid, hard-working south Alabama folks come to drink, to laugh, to forget the week's drudgery, and to dance with each other's spouses in a weekly ritual of self-imposed temptation. Perhaps the dances young Hank was taken to in 1934 were more innocent, perhaps not.

"He picked up his music real well," says Taft Skipper of his cousin Hank in a classic bit of understatement. "He could play the fiddle, piano—just any kind of instrument—himself.

"It's a talent he picked up somewhere—I don't know where," Taft continues, "except he might have inherited some of it from his Grandpa John Skipper. John was a blacksmith, and he'd make up songs and sing 'em without any music while he was resting from his blacksmithing."

To be sure, Hank Williams did "pick up his music real well." And real quick. Wherever it came from, there was plainly a lot of anxious, warm, raw, musical talent pulsing through his bony young frame.

He probably learned his first guitar chords from Mrs. McNeil, J. C.'s mother, during that year he spent with them. By the end of 1937, when Hank was fourteen, he was an established country music radio personality on Montgomery's WSFA with his own twice-weekly fifteen-minute show. From eleven-year-old towhead to fourteen-year-old professional musician—how did he do it?

Hank worked at it. "A man has to know what he wants to do, and then do it and keep your mind on it, and don't let nothin' else get in the way to clutter up your life," he once told an interviewer. "Singin' songs comes naturally to me the way some folks can argue law or make cabinets. It's all I know. It's all I care about."

From the time he was able to get his hands on a guitar, music was life for Hank Williams. His first instrument might have come from any one of several sources, but this much is sure: Hank had his own guitar at twelve and was doing everything he could to learn to play it well.

His mother Lilly, who is only one of the people who claim to have given Hank his first guitar, later wrote that Hank was so excited when he received it that he ran out of the house, through the front gate, and jumped onto the back of a young calf, which promptly threw him off, leaving Hank with a broken arm. According to Lillian, Hank was wiggling his fingers out the end of a cast and trying to chord the guitar three days later.

Hank took his first real lessons from a man named Cade Durham, a great fiddler and "a real well-known feller" round Butler County. Durham was a Georgiana native and string band veteran who often played music down at the Rhodes Brothers Dry Goods Store. He also gave lessons to young hopefuls like Hank in his sitting room, the walls of which were hung with fiddles, guitars, and violins.

Cade Durham's method was simple: he'd show a boy how to place his fingers on the fingerboard to make certain chords, then he'd saw out a popular melody on the fiddle while his pupil played a rough rhythm with a flat pick on the newly-learned chord.

"All I done," Durham told Roger Williams, "was just start him off on guitar. He had the talent."

If Hank was inspired by the string bands who played the dances and schoolhouses in his area, he was even more intrigued with the black street singers he would sometimes see hanging around Georgiana. These men, who were usually also handymen or short-job laborers, would roam the sidewalks of the South on weekends and other days when there was no pick-up work. They'd stop at any gathering place to sing a few songs and collect some small change in a battered hat.

"Back then," remembers Taft Skipper, "there was a Negro in

Georgiana . . . they called him 'Big Day.' His name was Connie
McKee. Where he got his nickname . . . well, anytime there
was somethin' to do, he was sure to be there.

"Big Day played guitar kinda like Jimmie Rodgers style.
That 'Kansas City Blues' was one o' his favorites," Taft recalls.
"Lot o' times where white boys gathered around, ol' Big Day'd
be there, playing his guitar. He'd put his hat down for the boys
to throw money in. 'Course he played for the colored peoples'
to-dos, too. If they had a big meetin', he'd be on the outskirts of
the crowd, and he'd get him a little bunch around and play and
pick for 'em and they'd throw him money.

"I think," says Taft, "Hank picked up some of his first guitar
stuff from him."

In 1935, Lillian Williams moved her small family to Greenville, just up the Louisville & Nashville railroad line toward
Montgomery. By this time she had settled onto the business of
running boardinghouses; she had managed one with fair success
her last few years in Georgiana. Greenville, the Butler County
seat and four times the size of Georgiana, seemed a more
promising place to set up shop.

Once in Greenville, young Hank quickly looked up another
street singer he'd met in Georgiana, a little gray-haired, good-
natured, black man named Rufe Payne. "Tee-tot" was the name
he was known by. A lot has been said about Tee-tot's influence
on Hank Williams' life and sometimes the story has been
exaggerated. In *Your Cheatin' Heart*, for instance, the 1964
movie of Hank's life, there is a purely fictional scene in which
Tee-tot dies in Hank's arms.

Nevertheless, there was probably no other individual more
responsible for shaping and encouraging Hank Williams' talent
than Rufe Payne. It's unlikely that Hank could have been a
professional performer at fourteen if not for the friendship and
tutorage of Tee-tot when his young protégé was twelve and
thirteen.

The little man with the silver hair and the slouchy hat used to
walk the streets of Georgiana and Greenville in the warm
evenings, usually with a couple of other musicians, often a
harmonicist and a washtub bass-player. They'd stop in front of a
house and play awhile, hoping to get a few coins for their effort,

then move on to the next house. After his family moved to Greenville, young Hank took to unabashedly following Tee-tot and his friends around whenever he could find the time.

"Little white boss," Tee-tot would sometimes warn him, "these here white folks won't like me takin' so much keer o' you." If this worried Hank, he never showed it. He learned everything he could from the old man, sometimes in the form of lessons for which Tee-tot was paid with meals from Lilly's table. But Hank learned mostly by osmosis as he followed the old man up and down the sleepy streets of Greenville.

"There was a bunch of fellers in Greenville named the Beelam Brothers, and they ran four [cotton] gins in Greenville back in those days," remembers Taft Skipper. "Hank had more shoes to shine around those gins than he could keep up with, and he sold more peanuts than his Momma could parch for him. But whenever he got an idle moment, he'd set around with Tee-tot and learn guitar."

One theme that Tee-tot etched into Hank's mind was timing. This skinny kid (who during this period wore wire-rimmed glasses hooked onto his protruding ears) would never be a guitar soloist, but he was going to be able to carry a mighty strong rhythm for a group of backup boys to latch onto. His ability to do that was learned and practiced and learned again with Tee-tot.

There was important psychological chemistry involved in Hank's musical education. First, there were the genetic gifts of intelligence, shrewdness, an artistic heritage of sorts, and a body unsuited to a life of wrestling logs. Hank was already destined to make his living with his wits, although he might as easily have become a store clerk as a musician.

Then there were the years spent tramping southern country fields; and long, pine-shadowed, dirt roads that wound through his fertile young mind just as they traversed his world. They touched wellsprings of natural joy that could give birth to songs and other life-reflecting expressions. He had thousands of barefoot days and lamplit, small-town nights to rub against each other, producing positive feelings, toughness, and the will to feel. Hank was a country boy, a young man whose soul was close to the seasons, cycles, and the intensity of nature in a way he'd never lose. His logic would be reckoned "down-to-earth," developed in a time of social stability that he could believe would last forever—the L&N railroad whistle lulling him to sleep at night and the scent of Alabama pines greeting him in the early morning. Hank was a country boy and a poet.

Finally, bring up this poet in the guise of an unschooled boardinghouse matron's son, "skinny as a buggy whip," with a quick-witted, brash, older sister and a weak-willed absentee father whose influence can scarcely be called paternal. Let him wonder forever how men become men and why he feels resentment toward women. Let him look for male friendship among tobacco-spitting clutches of sidewalk ne'er-do-wells, with the blustery old boys who've brought their cotton to Georgiana and who get a kick from sticking a go-to-town shoe up for some po' white urchin to shine; Hank's sensitivity will be forged and shaped in a real world of cussing, swearing, drinking, sweating, horse-trading, tale-telling, and what must have seemed like centuries of peanut-selling. Hank's adolescence was as stifling as the small towns he lived in; you can bet he was looking for a ticket out.

The first strong male in his life, then, was Tee-tot, a worldly-wise old black street minstrel with whom young Hank had a lot in common. Neither was inclined toward the kind of gut-busting, survival-wages jobs that characterized the southern work market in the thirties; neither of them was on the "inside" of Alabama society, and neither knew or cared much about the simple pleasures of domestic contentment. That left young Hank Williams and Tee-tot with their guitars, with feet that fairly itched to be tapping out a beat, and with somewhere inside the both of them a kind of gregarious longing to be heard and understood . . . soul brothers, for sure.

And the elder brother, across a cultural fault line barely perceptible then, passed on to his student the tools Hank needed to forge his strengths and talents into a career. Forget the poetry for now, let's learn to draw a *crowd!* Tee-tot's entire style was based on the grim fact that he rarely had a captive audience; he had to be able to stop people on the sidewalk, to grab 'em with an infectious delivery, to mesmerize 'em with bold, frank eye contact, and to pull 'em along with the rhythm of a boogie beat thumped out of an unamplified guitar. Furthermore, he had to keep his audience for at least two or three songs, so they'd feel they owed him something, something they'd drop into his hat before they went on about their business.

To Hiram Hank Williams, fresh up from Georgiana, too frail for sports, too smart for farming, too poor for politics, and still a bit too young for girls, performing with Tee-tot was the challenge of his young life. He knew what kind of hunger put ol' Tee-tot out there on the streets day after day. He knew what the blues was already—from the inside out—and he knew, just as a spawning salmon knows to swim upstream, that he had found his own quest.

By now Hank was growing up. He was taller than his classmates in school, with a bony frame and a serious stare that accentuated his deep-set, brown eyes and thin, shy mouth. His manner had become serious and withdrawn, and friends remember him as a loner, not one to get excited about a ball game or an adventure with a gang of boys. School was still a necessary evil and there was still some pressure to help with the family's expenses, but Hank's real schooling, his real work, and his real adventure was to be found on the streets with Tee-tot. What Hank learned were intuitive lessons that only an innate talent can apply: the feeling of a song, how to communicate not only with the voice and with the body, but how to speak soul to soul.

In these two years in Greenville, Hank learned all or nearly all of the chords and chord progressions he would ever use; he learned a few bass runs and a handful of rhythms that he could put behind most any song and make it move.

"All the musical training I ever had was from him," Hank said later of his friend Tee-tot. It was all he would ever need.

3

Montgomery

In that summer of 1937 when the Williams family moved there, Montgomery was still a slow-moving Southern town of 75,000, but it was a metropolis to Hank. In Georgiana, the one tiny radio station had broadcast from Johnson's grocery store; here in Montgomery there were two major country music stations, WSFA and WCOV, which together blanketed most of Alabama and the lower Southeast with their signals.

Hank wasn't quite fourteen. On hot summer evenings of that first year in the city, he'd venture down to Kiwanis Park with his guitar and trade songs with the boys he met there.

"People talk about that ol' man Tee-tot," says Leo Hudson, a Montgomery musician and acquaintance of Hank's, "but Hank still had some to learn when he came to town. Feller by the name of Skeet Simmons taught him a lot right there in that ol' park."

Determined now to make his living as a musician, Hank enlisted his mother's aid. During the next years Lilly Williams made her son's career the chief motivation of her life.

Shortly after the family moved into a house at 114 South Perry Street and Lilly went into the boarding business, she helped Hank trade in the $3.50 guitar she'd bought him in Greenville for a good Gibson with a sunburst finish.

Montgomery was a music capital of sorts. Besides the two country radio stations, it boasted a dozen or more honky-tonks and theaters where country music was showcased, and it was a booking center for bands who played all over south and central Alabama. The town had more than its share of professional and semiprofessional musicians who formed a loose local fraternity of sorts.

Fourteen-year-old Hank's talent was only budding then, and he couldn't easily break into this glittering grownup world of dance halls, schoolhouse dances, roadhouses, and private parties. He had the guts, but he needed a break.

His ticket into professionalism turned out to be an amateur night. The Empire Theater downtown held them regularly, and Hank decided to make his Montgomery debut there with a song he'd written called "WPA Blues."

Hank had seen enough Tom Mix and Hoot Gibson films to give him an idea of how he should look: he took the Empire Theater stage as a cowboy for his performance and began that night to become that image. From then on no one would think of Hank Williams in anything but a cowboy hat and boots like those he wore that night. He took the new Gibson sunburst on stage with him, too.

He was a hit. Forgetting his nervousness he belted out,

> I got a home in Montgomery
> A place I like to stay.
> But I have to work for the WPA,
> And I'm dissatisfied—I'm dissatisfied.

The hometown audience at the Empire could identify with the sentiment. And they couldn't help but like this skinny kid with the piercing, gutsy voice. They cheered, laughed, and yelped and Hank Williams won first prize that night—fifteen dollars. Hank took the money and went out with his friends to celebrate; the next morning the money was gone.

With good timing, Hank rode the crest of his little triumph at the Empire Theatre into the studios of WSFA and asked for an audition. He won a spot on a program that featured Dad Crysell's band and was promptly named "The Singing Kid."

It wasn't long until Hank had parlayed this break into a show of his own, fifteen minutes twice a week, where he got to thump his guitar and sing country songs. He was on his way. Just turned fourteen, he was appearing twice a week on the biggest country music station in Alabama.

It was time to form a band.

At first, his group was a team effort—at least he sometimes

shared the billing with a singer/guitarist/harmonicist named Smith "Hezzy" Adair. "Hank and Hezzy," they were called.

But Hank had another name for his band (no one knows for sure how much he actually allowed "Hank and Hezzy" to be used as a moniker anyway), and that name was the Drifting Cowboys. The very first group of Drifting Cowboys was assembled for radio performances on WSFA and thereby—though they're long forgotten as musicians—have earned themselves a small piece of glory in the history of country music.

Shorty Seals, a well-built young man with arms like tree trunks, played bass. Boots Harris, another boy close to Hank's age, played steel or "Hawaiian" guitar, and two men who probably were well out of their teens rounded out young Hank's first group: "Indian Joe" Hatcher on lead guitar and "Mexican Charlie" Mays on fiddle.

When the Drifting Cowboys gathered around the microphone for their first radio show, fourteen-year-old Hank Williams—with a broad cowboy hat pushed back on his head, a pair of fancy trousers, and cowboy boots—already seemed a born bandleader. He had already grown up to his adult height of six foot one and stood almost a head taller than the rest of the boys in the band.

As strong as Hank's leadership proved to be, the name he chose for his group proved even stronger. The Drifting Cowboys became the name of every Hank Williams band that ever toured with him. Even today, the Drifting Cowboys from the great years—Jerry Rivers, Don Helms, Hillous Butrum, and Bob McNett—are still performing Hank's songs together to eager and appreciative audiences.

Hank needed a band to help him when he went out on the personal appearances his radio show was generating, but the radio shows themselves he still did mostly alone. Together, the two weekly shows paid fifteen dollars.

"I was Hank's first booking agent," Irene Williams Smith claimed on the phone from Dallas. Mrs. Smith is now an office manager for a chemical company there.

Hank's sister credits their mother as a major supportive force for this young singer with nerve enough to front a band before he was old enough to drive a car.

"Mother's desire was to help her son make his dreams come true," says Irene. "Who fed and clothed the musicians when Hank was playing with his first bands? He surely couldn't do it. This was during the Depression. My mother took care of the boys and made sure they had enough to eat. She went out and booked shows for Hank, too. Why? Not to feed her own ego as so many people think, but simply because she wanted to help Hank with his dream."

Hank's musical abilities—he'd been playing only a couple of years—could barely keep up with his ambitions. He idolized Roy Acuff, who with his "Smoky Mountain Boys" was just beginning to build his own career on WNOX up in Knoxville, Tennessee. Later Roy had a song called "Don't Make Me Go To Bed and I'll Be Good"; it's been said that that song could bring tears to Hank's eyes.

Acuff's stock-in-trade was emotional sincerity in his singing, an intensity that made his music altogether different from that of the more lackadaisical Jimmie Rodgers style. Roy Acuff was changing the course of vocal country music, and Hank understood.

But Hank himself was not yet really an innovator. The stage shows that he and the boys put together were straight from the unwritten book of country music tradition. Hank acted as M.C. as well as singer, while the comedy came from Shorty Seals, the bassist. Tradition made it obligatory that the bass player be the band's fool, so he dressed himself in baggy pants and blacked out a couple of his teeth.

The music was old ballads and waltzes, Roy Acuff numbers, some up-tempo tunes, and a few songs of Hank's, mixed in with patter between Hank, Shorty, and the boys. During this period Hank gained a rough mastery of the fiddle and steel guitar, so that he could contribute to the band's versatility. He also learned piano somewhere in these years, but he never played piano onstage.

So the Drifting Cowboys began playing the south Alabama circuit of schoolhouse dances, rough honky-tonks, and dance halls. "The places we played," says Don Helms, "were the kind of places where they sweep up the eyeballs every morning."

Hank, however, took it all in stride, displaying self-containment and savvy beyond his years. A loner, more serious than his peers, the adolescent moved into an adult professional environment with almost total absence of awe or fear.

Lillian began to assist Irene in her booking duties then, and finally took them over herself. She traveled a lot and lined up jobs for the Drifting Cowboys elsewhere in the state; then she'd go along on the jobs to take admission herself or stay near whoever was handling the money so she could make sure the boys were paid fairly for their work.

Admission to a schoolhouse stage show was fifteen or twenty-five cents, and fifty people was a good crowd; so the band's cut, after paying for the facilities, could be as little as ten dollars for the entire group to split among them. Honky-tonks and dance halls paid better, but with them came the hazards of booze and violence.

Lilly also drove the boys to their first gigs, beginning a pattern that would last throughout Hank's life—he seldom if ever drove himself anywhere, even after he could afford the pleasure of a Cadillac steering wheel in his hands.

"Hank didn't drive because he'd never driven as a boy," says Irene, "and also because he had problems with his eyes." His wire-rimmed glasses were never worn now, though Hank probably still needed them. This was characteristic of his attitude toward his own physical well-being. The sleep he missed because of the late nights in the honky-tonks was already taking a physical toll. Hank's high school teachers remember him as an unimpressive student who often fell asleep in class. He never did finish, and finally dropped out of high school in 1942 at the age of nineteen.

I drove into Montgomery in 1977 on an interstate highway that a few years ago made necessary the tearing down of Hank's mother's boardinghouse on Perry Street. Driving down-town toward the capitol building and up Madison Street, where Jefferson Davis paraded to his inauguration as President of the Confederate States of America, I was struck by the number of black citizens on the streets. Montgomery holds memories of Martin Luther King as well as Hank Williams.

A man I met in a Nashville motel lobby had told me about a

painting contractor named M. C. Jarrett who played with Hank in the Montgomery days. He said talking to Mr. Jarrett would be worth my time. Not a few locals have fabricated crucial roles for themselves in their memories of Hank Williams' life, but a brief phone call to Mr. Jarrett convinced me that he knows what he's talking about.

M. C. Jarrett lives on a quiet back street in an older residential section of Montgomery's southeast side. His house is almost hidden from the street by lush trees and bushes in the front and side yards. It looks like what it is, the home of a self-respecting working man.

M. C. Jarrett is a small, wiry man with one of those low, meaty, almost metallic voices aged with decades of coffee and cigarette smoke.

"I first met him in 1939 down at the WSFA studios in the Jefferson Davis Hotel," he tells me after we're settled. "I wasn't lookin' to meet Hank Williams, but I had a friend who thought he could play git-tar and he wanted me to go with him 'cause he was gonna audition for Hank's band."

M. C.'s friend didn't get the job, but the incident made Hank aware that M. C. could play steel, and what began was a long "part-time" acquaintance: M. C. would fill in on steel for Hank and played quite a few jobs with him, but he never really became a full-fledged Drifting Cowboy.

"I'm a workin' man," he says proudly. "And even though I was young, I was a workin' man then, too. I always worked. Music was just somethin' I done on the side." M. C. Jarrett played with Hank on and off for the next half-dozen years.

"Starting out, we played mostly schoolhouses, like the one down in White City," he says. "It was a three-room building in the daytime. But it had big French doors that pushed back and turned the building into one big room with a stage at one end.

"The schoolhouse stage shows didn't pay hardly anything," M. C. remembers. "Sometimes I'd buy beer and sandwiches for the boys on the way down to a show, and I'd barely get enough back from the job to break even."

But soon the Drifting Cowboys could get themselves booked at some of the big dance halls, and the money got a lot better.

"The two big dances we played were at Opp, Alabama—that

was Jerry's Tavern, where I met my wife—and the Riverside Inn down at Andalusia," says M. C.

"The Riverside Inn was the biggest dance hall in the South. They charged fifty cents a person and seventy-five cents for a couple and they'd regularly get 600 people out there on a weekend."

According to M. C., Hank had a seventy/thirty split deal with Bob Lindsey, who owned the Riverside Inn. The band got seventy percent of the night's take. Lilly'd be there to make sure everything went all right.

What's M. C.'s opinion of Lillian Williams?

"She was a good woman," he says. "She had a big heart. But she was a mean woman. She could be rough. And she loved a dollar bill like most people do that came up the hard way."

But M. C., like Irene, doesn't think Lillian pushed Hank too hard or caused him undue anxiety.

"His problem was always drinking," says M. C. flatly. "He was gonna drink. He loved beer with a passion. Beer was his drink. He loved it." This was true early in Hank's career, while his taste for whiskey grew stronger as well.

"I used to sometimes play with Hank on the radio real early in the morning," M. C. tells me, "and Hank would always first thing buy him a pint of whiskey from the bellhop at the Jefferson Davis Hotel. It cost him three dollars for a buck and a half bottle that way, but he was too young to go buy it at the state store.

"Hank's mother did everything she could to try to stop Hank from drinking," M. C. remembers, "but it was no use. Sometimes we'd walk downtown to the movie theater together from his house, and Miz Williams would watch to make sure Hank wouldn't duck in the saloon on the way to the movie theater. She'd watch until we turned the corner right by the theater.

"But Hank had a system to get around this," M. C. continues. "Y'see, by the time we got to the saloon door on the way to the theater, we were out of Lilly's *hearing* range even though she could still see us. Hank had it worked out with his buddies so he'd yell out for a bottle of beer before we got even with the saloon door, and as we walked by, somebody'd hand him a bottle of beer and he'd throw a quarter through the door—all slick as a whistle. He never missed a step. Then he'd just hold the beer in front of him till we turned the corner by the theater and drink it down as soon as we were out of Lilly's sight."

"My mother didn't even know Hank had a drinking problem," says his sister Irene, "until one night the boys carried him in not only drunk, but badly hurt from a fight."

"Without a few drinks, Hank felt inferior," says M. C. "That's why he liked to drink when he sang. He'd get a few drinks in him, and his confidence would come to him and he would actually get better because he began to believe more in himself.

"But what a gift he had. He could express what his audiences felt! He could feel what an audience wanted and what they were feeling, and give it right back to them. I have to admit. . . ." M. C. pauses. "I have to admit it took me until after he was dead and I began to think on these things to realize he had that gift. I mean it wasn't something that him or anybody else talked about. But I'll tell you something: He'd do whatever it took to satisfy an audience, even if it meant makin' up a song on the spot.

"Hank never handed out praise when you played for him," M. C. continues, "and neither did I. I remember one time we did a number and when it was over I said, 'That was pretty good. Let's do it again,' and Hank said, 'God damn, it must have been good, 'cause that's the first time you ever told me I done anything good!'"

This line turns out to be one of the few bonafide quotes that M. C. can remember from Hank.

"Lookin' back," he says, "and I've done it many a time, the thing is, he never did *say* a whole hell of a lot . . . except when he was on the radio or in front of an audience. Then he would crack jokes and talk along all night.

"I told Hank one time," says Jarrett, "that I thought we was gettin' as good as them guys on the Grand Ole Opry. He said, 'Hell, we ain't half as good as they are.'"

Hank was building a personal following all over Alabama through his radio show and his stage shows were often well-received. Yet more than a couple of people have testified that he always had a bad reputation in Montgomery.

"It wasn't just his irresponsibility," says Montgomery musician Leo Hudson. "He didn't treat his band right. He'd take in a hundred dollars on a show and pay them a dollar apiece."

Whether or not this is true—M. C. Jarrett simply says there was "no set policy" on paying band members—it is true that Hank was not really any kind of hometown hero until he made it to the Grand Ole Opry. Some of this was due to drinking, some to rumors of wild living and alleged shady dealing, but one suspects that much of Hank's poor image in Montgomery was a matter of society's coolness to his unpolished rural ways and his lack of any social credentials.

Leo Hudson recalls, for example, that Hank "didn't talk in a 'decent' way." Hank once spoke of someone who had a cold, and "he said, '*Snot was runnin' out of her nose.*' Now you know he could of said *mucus* or somethin' without talkin' like that."

"I was criticized for playin' with him," M. C. Jarrett remembers. "People'd say, 'You playin' with that damn drunk?' or 'I heard you on the radio with that drunk Hank Williams.'"

Jarrett wasn't swayed. "I said to hell with 'em. I played with Hank for enjoyment, and he always done right by me."

Even if Hank really "done right" by the boys in his band, it was still a wild affair to play a dance date with him once he had settled into his drinking habit. "He could be staggering on the stage and still he'd invite hecklers to step outside," says Jarrett.

"I remember one night in Rutledge, Alabama," M. C. continues, "and there was so many people there, they was standin' in the windows. Hank was so drunk, we had to start the show without him. About halfway through, Hank staggered in and took over.

"Somebody hollered, 'Aw go on back outside, you drunk,' and Hank answered him, 'I'll see you after the show, young man,' and he went right on with the show. The fiddler had to hold him up with his shoulder."

Both of Hank's reputations—the musical and the liquid—grew fast in the Montgomery years. By the time of the war, he was a "star" on WSFA, receiving fan mail from all over Alabama. The first Drifting Cowboys were replaced and the band reshuffled several times. Among the musicians who played with him out of Montgomery were guitarists Redd Todd and Louis Brown, steel player Jimmy Webster (who replaced M. C. Jarrett and was killed in a car accident before Hank left Montgomery), "Little" Ed Rawlins and Bubba "Cannonball" Nichols. Lum York became one of Hank's bass players along with Eland Smith and stayed with him off and on until Hank moved to Nashville to join the Opry in 1949.

Hank's late teens came and went in an endless circuit of dances—Fort Deposit, Andalusia, Opp, Rutledge, back to Montgomery—schoolhouse stage shows, and occasionally a stint with a medicine show. The band went on the road in old Chevies and Buicks; piling themselves and their instruments in was an art in itself.

First they put the bass in through the back doors and ran it lengthwise through the car, then they fit themselves in around it, piling guitars, fiddles and amplifiers under their feet or in the car's trunk. When the weather was good enough, they carried the bass on top.

When Don Helms and Sammy Pruitt joined Hank's band in 1943, Hank issued them blackjacks to defend themselves. "We needed them," says Helms. "Some of those places we played during the war . . . well, some'd be on the outside shootin' in and some'd be on the inside shootin' out. . . ."

These years occasionally took Hank back to Georgiana where he played at Fred Thigpen's Log Cabin, one of the more popular roadhouses in the state, and sometimes when he and the boys played Evergreen, Alabama, he stayed with Taft and Erleen Skipper, but his Georgiana roots were very weak. He was totally taken up in what he was doing.

The lifestyle he established in those years never changed much: It was high-gear-full-speed-ahead-play music-get-drunk-book-some-more-shows-fight-off-drunks.

And so on.

What else was there to do? He had no other skills. He had no conception of what a settled-down lifestyle might be like, and he had no friends outside the world of honky-tonks, music, and WSFA. Hank chose and maintained the pace of life he did because he knew no alternative. If he'd lived twenty years longer, he'd still have found no alternative . . . without a miracle.

There was only one departure from this pattern in the years between 1937 and 1942. In the summer of 1940, when Hank was not quite seventeen, he decided to become an authentic Drifter of the West. He ran off to Texas, presumably with Lilly's permission, and got a job with a rodeo.

Hank talked the rodeo promoters into billing him as a *real* singing cowboy, but this meant that Hank had to take a crack at bronc-riding, which he had never done. In fact, it's not established that he'd ever been on a *tame* horse in his life, let alone a bucking bronc.

"He drew this horse called Ol' Dan or something like that," a friend recalls as he repeats Hank's account, "and he was supposed to climb up in the chute, drop down on the horse, and come out riding while the announcer gave him a big build-up."

Hank looked down from the top of the chute and saw that Ol' Dan was fairly bristling. The would-be bronc rider decided he needed a moment to think and jumped down from the chute, grabbing a handy bottle of corn liquor to help him cogitate on the matter. Then up the boards he went again, only to freeze once more above the horse's back. Clearly he needed more time and another pull on that bottle. This cycle was repeated several times before young Hank was ready for Ol' Dan.

Finally he dropped down on the bronc's pitching back, the cowboys opened the gate, and the announcer told the crowd, "Here's Hank Williams, the Singing Cowboy!" But almost before the words were out of the loudspeaker, Hank was off the horse's back. He was thrown about fifteen feet in the air and landed square on his tailbone.

The result was a back injury which would come back to plague Hank years later just at a time when he could have done without any more troubles. At any rate, his rodeo career was quickly over.

So Hank came back to Montgomery, kept on idolizing Roy Acuff, kept on writing his own songs—though not all of them were good enough to get on the air at WSFA—played every dance hall, saloon, and schoolhouse that he could book, and continued drinking.

By 1942 he was the best-known country music personality in Alabama, but he still hadn't graduated out of the minor leagues.

Nobody was ready to take on Hank Williams the Talent, because you also had to take on Hank Williams the Drunk.

There was no doubt about his talent. That he compared favorably with nationally-known stars was obvious when he'd open an Opry show at the Montgomery City Auditorium.

Says M. C. Jarrett, "I heard many Opry stars say after a show, 'If this boy could just leave the drinkin' alone, he could be the greatest.'"

As it turned out, he left booze alone just enough to be the greatest. Because of phonograph records, a short time was all he needed.

But to be the greatest, he was going to need one more catalyst.

4

Audrey

Hank Williams' married life can be compared to that of Abraham Lincoln. Though Lincoln loved his wife Mary and she loved him, their relationship was perhaps the stormiest that the White House ever saw.

Lincoln, like Hank Williams, suffered no little amount of depression over his marital woes and both couples shared the experience of full-scale, top-volume, watch-out-for-the-furniture battles in houses that were too public for comfort.

Both men married long before prominence came to them, and both wives may have had a lot to do with assuring that prominence. Abe and Hank were very private men, yet each would disclose to friends how hard it was to live with his spouse.

One major difference between their marriages was that Lincoln married out of his social class, while Hank Williams fell in love with a girl not a hair more sophisticated than he was.

Audrey Mae Sheppard came from the little community of Enon, near Banks, Alabama. Hank met her in 1942 and he never was the same again. Neither, for that matter, was she. Audrey had been raised on a poor south Alabama farm where her father, Charles Shelton Sheppard, grew "cotton, peanuts, cows and hogs" and somehow got by.

She was not delicately beautiful, but she was striking; tall and well-built, with large expressive eyes, high cheekbones, and a spirited personality. Hank was infatuated from the start, and it wasn't long until it was obvious that Audrey had captured his total social attention.

"I met Hank one night in 1942 when he played for a medicine

show in my home town, Banks, Alabama," Audrey told the *Montgomery Advertiser* shortly after Hank's death.

"Someone introduced us after the show and I knew immediately that here was the one person in the world who could make my dreams come true," she remembered. "Prior to meeting Hank, nothing very exciting had happened to me."

It was an instantly strong relationship; friction entered almost as quickly, too. According to Audrey's description of their courtship, Hank was talking marriage almost from the start. "Hank and I had a date the night after I met him, and the second night he proposed. I didn't believe he was serious, of course, but I was attracted enough to join his band a few weeks later as a singer. Pretty soon, he said, 'I love you,' so often that I got to believing it. I had wanted to believe it a long time. We were married about a year after our first meeting."

Audrey was already a married woman when she met Hank. She had met and married a young man named Erskine Guy while still in her mid-teens. She had had a daughter, Lycrecia, by him, but the marriage was already an abandoned issue by the time Hank came onto the scene. A divorce was impossible for Audrey and her husband, however, because he was overseas in the war. Not until he returned to the States could they sign the divorce papers.

Hank's love life before Audrey is a subject on which not all memories agree. Some friends have painted a rather promiscuous picture of the young singer, while M. C. Jarrett maintains that Hank wasn't much for "makin' dates and so on—like the normal average musician—to go out after the show."

Nearly everyone, however, agrees on the style of love life that Hank and Audrey soon inaugurated; there was never a dull moment.

Audrey didn't like Hank's drinking habit. "If you're going to go with me," she told him, "you're going to have to leave whiskey alone."

But she had no more luck at curtailing his drinking than his mother before her. By that time Hank had already settled into the classic "spree drinker's" pattern.

"He might stay dry for months, then one day he'd take one

drink and it was off to the races," remembers steel guitar player Don Helms.

Audrey, then, became a part of the Hank Williams retinue: she sang with the band despite a dearth of singing talent, traveled with the boys, and began to help out with booking and ticket-taking.

Lilly's reaction, by some accounts, was less than enthusiastic.

According to Hank Williams, Jr., when Hank first brought Audrey home to meet his mother, Lilly snorted, "Where'd you get this whore?" Whereupon son and mother instantly engaged in physical combat in which each pummeled the other while they rolled on the floor.

Others say that Lilly liked Audrey at first, and only began to have disagreements with her later. The two women fought for control of the band's nightly receipts while Hank lay passed out in the car.

"Audrey was a connivin' type of woman," says M. C. Jarrett. "I don't say she didn't love Hank, but she loved that dollar bill and I think she could see the potential—even though Hank wasn't big time, he almost invariably made good money."

So Audrey began to share Lillian's role helping Hank along in his career. From the beginning they teamed up to keep Hank sober as much as possible.

"Audrey and Mrs. Williams," says Jarrett, "kept him dry till intermission time, then they let him have a pint. By midnight, the show was over and they had all the money. He'd be drunk . . . and they were in charge. They never failed to pay me, though."

According to Jarrett, this was standard operating procedure. "It happened that way almost every time I played with Hank, except when the take was too small to worry about," he says.

Jarrett adds one more claim to his memory of Hank's first years with Audrey:

"He was livin' with her while she was still drawing an $80 allotment check every month [from Guy]," he says. "I know it. I seen 'em cash the checks too many times."

Evidently it was easier to live together in Montgomery than to risk Hank having a run-in with Audrey's father. Mr. Sheppard, apparently, didn't care too much for Hank.

"That ol' man told Hank he'd kill him if he ever came around the farm," says M. C. "I've been with Hank when we picked up Audrey a mile from her daddy's house. I would walk down the road whistling . . . that was the signal. Then Audrey would [leave the house and] meet Hank. And then they'd pick me up about a quarter mile down the road on the other side of the house."

But the relationship was legitimized and the Sheppard family hassle presumably pacified one Saturday night in December, 1944, when Hank and Audrey were playing a show date down in Andalusia. According to Roger Williams, it happened like this:

> The ceremony was performed in a rural filling station by the station owner, who served as a justice of the peace on the side. A couple of the Drifting Cowboys acted as witnesses, and the whole party had to pool its funds to pay the J. P. Lilly Williams wasn't along on that trip, so she knew nothing of her son's wedding until the couple returned to the boardinghouse the next day.

That brawl mentioned by Hank, Jr., may have taken place on the day after the wedding instead of earlier, as Lilly realized that someone else had legally and permanently stepped into the picture between her and her son.

Technically, the marriage ceremony was invalid, because court records show that Hank and Audrey were married only ten days after her divorce from Erskine Guy became final, and in Alabama a sixty-day waiting period is required. But Alabama law also allows common law marriage status for a man and woman who live together openly as husband and wife, so one way or the other, Hank and Audrey were legally married from December, 1944, until May 29, 1952.

"Hank and I didn't have much in those early days," Audrey has said. "I washed his clothes—and later when we could afford it—I designed his stage clothes."

"The Williamses took up residence at Lilly's boardinghouse in Montgomery," reports Roger Williams . . .

It was an old, two-story frame house at the edge of the

downtown area. Sparsely furnished but inexpensive, it attracted the usual cross-section of boardinghouse clients. There were single girls, with and without visible means of support. There were loners and losers and rummies.

Lilly ruled this brood with a firm hand, taking no crap from nobody. One of her boarders recalls her as being "a heavy Marjorie Main. She was loud and a little overbearing, and she had a kind of fanatical religious crust."

When Audrey married Hank she may have "seen his potential," but Audrey Mae Williams can't be accused of merely grabbing onto a good thing. The south Alabama circuit of honky-tonks and dances was a grind, and Hank wasn't always easy to live with, even sober.

"We was goin' down to Andalusia one night—down the Mobile highway," remembers M. C. Jarrett, "and Audrey began to harp on Hank. 'You're not gonna get any beer tonight' she was sayin'.

"Well, none of us were sayin' much," says Jarrett, "Bubba Nichols was in front with Hank and Audrey, and he was just watchin' the road and drivin' that ol' Buick. Me, Sammy Pruitt, and Little Ed Rawlins was sittin' in the back. We'd been through this before."

But that night was going to be a little more interesting than usual.

"About sixteen miles down the highway," continues Jarrett, "was a place called Mose's. Shortly before we got there, Hank told Cannonball, 'Stop the car,' and I swear he just opened the door, snatched Audrey out by the hair of her head, got back in, and said, 'Take off,' and left her there in the ditch.

"Then we stopped at Mose's and Hank got four or five Falstaffs," says Jarrett. "And we stopped a couple more times for beer. When we got to Andalusia, Audrey was already sittin' there waiting for us . . . and they got back together and everything was all right again."

So it went.

"Hank was often misunderstood because his emotions and his thinking and his feeling were so much deeper than the average person," Audrey was to say years later in his defense.

"But his love was even deeper. It can never be written on paper," she added. "Words won't express him or his life."

Yet Hank had genuine magnetism and love, that, if it is caught nowhere else, is frozen in the wax of the records he made. The sheer force of his feeling for Audrey practically leaps into the room when you listen to "Cold, Cold Heart." He loved Audrey with all his heart. Everyone who knew him is sure of that, and though his friends' accounts may provide little hard evidence, he surely showed that love to her.

For Hank, this intense new feeling of romantic love had to shove itself into the already hectic, fast-paced fabric of his personal race with time. By the time he married Audrey, he was on the upswing of his career, though no one knew it yet. He was pushing with new energy toward the good days that were coming with the end of the war. People were already using up all their gas ration cards to get up from Panama City and Pensacola to catch Hank Williams at the Riverside Inn in Andalusia; when the war ended, those fans and many others would be "free and ready" to hear and see a lot more of Hank and the Drifting Cowboys.

The demands of his career notwithstanding, Hank was determined to make the best of his roles as husband and stepfather.

"It used to hurt him when I called him 'Hank,'" Lycrecia Guy Morris remembers from her early childhood. "He wanted me to call him 'Daddy.'"

Williams never himself told the child of his feelings. "Finally mother told me that Hank would like me to call him 'Daddy' so I started then and I have ever since," says Lycrecia. "I didn't mind. I'd taken to him right away and I really liked him." Yet although Hank loved Lycrecia as if she were his own daughter, he never did legally adopt her.

His relationship with Audrey made Hank as complete as he was ever going to be. The exhilaration and frustration of loving her began to transform a good country singer into an artist. Hank now had an awakened heart from which to write and a flesh-and-blood audience of one to whom he would sing.

"Hank always used to say he wrote his songs for me," Audrey has told reporters. "'You are my inspiration,' he said."

She was that. She was his positive inspiration, his negative inspiration, and the catalyst for all his songs that spoke of teetering on that brink between intense joy and equally intense frustration.

Years later Audrey was hospitalized for a minor ailment. Hank brought the children to see her and gave her the first fur coat she ever owned, but he and Audrey were on the outs so she never spoke to him throughout the visit. On the way home, he told their housekeeper, "She's got the coldest heart I've ever seen." So began a song about a "cold, cold, heart."

"I've heard Hank say things that ought not to be repeated about Audrey," reports M. C. Jarrett, "but there's no doubt in my mind that he loved that woman better than he loved life."

5

Bad Breaks, Good Breaks, and the First Great Songs

By 1942, nineteen-year-old Hank Williams was a seasoned veteran of the Alabama country music circuit, with five tough years of drinking, brawling, back-seat-sleeping, and straight-ahead country music-making already under his size thirty cowboy belt.

Steel player Don Helms describes the music Hank was doing when Helms first became a Drifting Cowboy about that time:

"He was doin' a lot of Roy Acuff songs and Ernest Tubb songs back then . . . whatever was current . . . he did a little Bob Wills. Hank hadn't written all that many songs yet," remembers Helms. "And Audrey didn't travel with us at first. She had her own band and a radio show on another station [WCOV]. But later, while she and Hank were engaged, she disbanded her group and traveled with us some."

Hank's appearance had matured; the softness and some of the sensitivity of adolescence had already disappeared from his features, leaving him with the frank, haggard, serious visage he took with him to stardom. The face was dominated by the eyes—"deep-set, very brown, and very tragic," in the words of Minnie Pearl—and by the wide expressive mouth, which could be set in a hard line, flicker into a winsome half-smile, or open up into a broad, straight-toothed country boy's full grin.

43

It was the face of the South. Hank looked as much the part of the hillbilly's hillbilly as he could sing and talk the part, and this was to be just one more factor in the explosive equation of his eventual success.

He was learning and growing as a performer, as fast and well as any performer has done—but then, so much of it seemed to come natural. His rapport with an audience could be uncanny, as M. C. Jarrett reiterates:

"He could just *tell* if an audience was in the mood for a happy song or a sad 'un."

Hank could keep up a laid-back, homey string of song introductions, dialogues with band members and philosophical throw-away lines throughout an entire evening's performance—if he didn't get too drunk—or for a fifteen-minute radio show. He was fast growing into a personality, a *presence*, in today's terms. At least he was a *persona*. But the image was not like the private Hank Williams. He came alive in front of an audience in a way he never could in normal social interaction.

Offstage Hank was still a "loner," even in a crowded Buickful of people. He was often pensive and quiet, and was never a great talker. His style was maximum action, minimum talk.

Hank was moving into the same kind of pattern established a little later by Marilyn Monroe. Just as Marilyn fabricated several cinematic roles—sexpot, waif, comedienne—while failing to deal with a yawning emptiness of her *real* self, Hank Williams seems to have directed much of his energy toward the creation of a person who in fact did not exist.

All of his good country memories and cowboy aspirations figured into this supremely romantic character that the public would know as Hank Williams. Building on the tradition of the great Jimmie Rodgers, Hank Williams would become a "rider of the rails;" he would be a drifter, a lonesome cowboy who can't settle down, can't be understood, needs love, but can only give it on the run.

That's a classic part, but in the absence of open range, background strings, and Technicolor sunsets, it doesn't bring much substance into the actor's life. It may serve to make the actor himself a more intense performer, but less of a man.

But this is, after all, how legends are created. Hank Williams the wandering cowboy, tall and lanky in boots and a wide-brimmed hat, with a tear in his voice and an almost fierce lonesomeness in his eyes, was going to usher in a new era in country music—the era of the heartthrob male performer.

Without conscious effort, Hank was adding a new dimension of romantic intensity, with strong sexual overtones, to the art of "hillbilly" performing. Jimmie Rodgers had skimmed the surface of this psychological pool with his blues yodels and his funky little guitar breaks, but he'd lacked the physical intensity to communicate sex appeal. Roy Acuff had plenty of intensity all right, but there was no subtlety to Acuff, no mystery. It was either train songs or I-love-you-will-you-love-me? He was skirted all around the sex-market, yet still kept his own worshipping market.

But this Hank Williams character—unlike the simple, one-woman, Hank Williams person—would develop by the mid-forties into something else . . .

There was something vaguely more complex in the way he put across the most basic lyrics. Instead of *I-love-you-will-you-love-me?* it was more like *I-love-you-in-my-way-take-it-or-leave-it-but-don't-do-me-wrong.* And the last part of Hank's message—*Don't do me wrong*—was it an order or an impassioned plea? Women couldn't make up their minds. There was an alarming ambiguity in what he was saying to them. It was different from what they were used to. It was upsetting. It was dynamite.

But the development of a magnetic *persona*, no matter how intriguing that role may be, is no substitute for coming to grips with the person one really is. Perhaps no one can do both; as the tension of the unresolved selfhood is what creates the need for a highly-developed stage role to be created.

So Hank grew as a performer much more steadily than as a person. To have done the latter at this or any time in his life would have required a contemplative slow-down that he never got around to. His was now and would continue to be an anxious, restless existence whose rare moments of relaxation would often be spent writing songs, preparing to reassume the legendary part he had created for himself.

In 1942, though, the fun of the honky-tonk rat race wasn't

compensating for the frustrations of trying to keep a country band going in wartime Alabama. Roger Williams explains:

> For Hank Williams . . . it had to be more than fun. He'd been a serious performer, a professional, for several years, and he was trying to make it big. Proceeds of a couple hundred bucks in Andalusia or Enterprise didn't look very big. He was popular on WSFA, but apparently not popular enough to propel him on to greater things—the Louisiana Hayride in Shreveport, say, or the Barn Dance in Chicago or the Mecca of country music, the Grand Ole Opry itself. He was drawing as many as three hundred fan letters a day, but they produced neither money nor job offers. "You can't eat fan letters, Mama," he complained, "not even with ketchup on 'em."

Hank in 1942 was at the lowest point of his musical career; he knew it and it bothered him deeply. He had developed some of the confidence of a veteran, but that just made worse the knowledge that his career was going nowhere. Besides, he couldn't keep a band together; too many musicians were getting drafted, among them young guitarist Sammy Pruitt and handsome Don Helms.

So with characteristic swiftness, Hank dropped out of Sidney Lanier High School and the music business both. He offered his services to Uncle Sam, but was turned down by the Army because of the back injury he'd suffered in his short-lived rodeo riding stint in 1940.

There were no jobs to speak of in Montgomery, so Hank headed south to Mobile and landed a defense job at the Alabama Drydock and Shipbuilding Company. It wasn't very glamorous being a shipfitter's helper for sixty-six cents an hour, but it was steady.

Hank eventually went through on-the-job training and became a full-fledged welder, but his heart was still in show business. He played all the dates he could scare up in the Mobile area, working small clubs not even worthy of what he'd already accomplished. He piloted a 1935 Ford sedan around Mobile, and a local musician named Freddie Beach remembers that he drove like he was "practically blind." According to Irene Williams, Beach's diagnosis may have been close to the truth, but Hank would have been the last to admit it.

Beach has also some memories that grate against Irene's. Whereas she has offered us a wholesome picture of Lilly's devoted efforts to help along Hank's career, Beach says Hank told him he had to put money in postal savings while he was in Mobile to keep it away from his mother.

Hank had a pretty good wartime situation going—working at the shipyard, playing the Mobile juke joints at night, and living cheaply with an aunt—but at one point in this period, probably toward the end of it in 1944, came an episode that proves how the anxious wanderlust of the real and the legendary Hank Williams could sometimes come together.

Before I even met M. C. Jarrett, I was told that he had "taken a trip out west" during the war and had worked in a shipyard with Hank. Since this story had never surfaced before, I checked with one of the other parties whom Jarrett mentioned as being along on this adventure—Leo Hudson, the Montgomery saxophone player who would later be one of the last people to see Hank Williams alive.

Hudson said, Yes, Jarret's story was true. Here's what happened:

"Hank and I left Montgomery one time during the war," says Jarrett, "and went out to Portland, Oregon." The boys had signed up with a special program sponsored by Kaiser Ship-building Corporation which offered a drydock job, free training and lodging, and a free train ticket to Portland. This was probably in the summer of 1944.

"We didn't even know we was on the same train until we got to Chicago and changed trains," remembers Jarrett. "There was four of us from Montgomery—Hank and me and a feller named Bill Brown and Leo Hudson."

They'd all decided to take a crack at welding on the Liberty Ships that Kaiser Shipbuilding was frantically producing.

"Once we got to Portland, I believe Hank went to school about one day . . . maybe two . . .," Jarrett says. "At night, Hank and I would go out to the honky-tonks . . ."

The would-be Liberty Ship welders were housed in barracks,

and the opportunity immediately presented itself for Hank to pick up some extra cash.

"The first day I got to Portland," says Leo Hudson, "I heard this commotion in the barracks area. I come around a corner and here's Hank with his guitar and a crowd gathered 'round him."

"We were all drunk," says Jarrett, "especially Hank. We sat on the grass outside the barracks and Hank sang while I played and Bill Brown passed the hat.

"There was one guy there—a bartender—and he could play one song on the fiddle—'Over the Waves.' So Hank would sing a song and Bill would pass the hat; then this guy would play 'Over the Waves.' Then Hank'd sing another song and Bill would pass the hat again . . . and the fiddler would say, 'Lemme play again.' And it went on that way all afternoon."

But Hank's days of barracks life in Portland were few.

"Pretty soon Hank moved downtown to a hotel and he began to go around to the honky-tonks with his guitar. He'd play and pass the hat and people would contribute," says Jarrett. "He made it all right.

"It wasn't long, though, before he called his momma," M. C. adds, "and she wired him some money and he went back home."

The Portland experience may or may not have been Hank's last attempt at non-musical employment. Jarrett places the episode in the summer of 1944. The records at the Mobile shipyard show him working there on and off from November of 1942 until August, 1944. Hank could have taken off from Mobile early in the summer and returned to work a while longer before going back to Montgomery. But the most probable scenario is that he quit at the Mobile shipyard in August, went out to Portland, and returned directly from there to Montgomery, where he picked up again the struggling career he had left behind.

So Hank spent just under two years out of the music business; but not completely out of it, since everywhere he went he performed. Not much is known of his relationship with Audrey during these years, but it's fairly certain that they carried on their romance despite separations. Perhaps, since Audrey was still married, both were comfortable to play a waiting game until the end of the war . . . when Hank would come home from the shipyards and Erskine Guy would come home from overseas to sign the divorce papers.

Hank and Audrey probably made frequent trips between Mobile and Montgomery to see each other. But exactly how their love affair grew and developed during this time is open to speculation.

The exact circumstances of Hank's return to Montgomery, too, are clouded by time. There is no lack of explanatory stories; Jarrett gives Hank himself the credit for charting his comeback course.

"Hank buckled down and began to book more shows. I came back from Portland, too, and we played Friday and Saturday nights at the Riverside Inn in Andalusia and Thursday nights at Jerry's Tavern in Opp." These were the same dates Hank had played before, but the crowds were getting bigger and more responsive.

Lillian Williams, however, says it was her initiative that got Hank out of the Mobile shipyards and back on the south Alabama honky-tonk stages. This version is found in her booklet, *Our Hank Williams*:

I believed in Hank. I knew he had what it took with his singing. So I rented a car and went to every schoolhouse and night club in the Montgomery area. I booked Hank solid for sixty days. Then the third week he had been "out of the music business," I went to Mobile and got him and put him back in it. When Hank saw the datebook for those shows, he gave me the sweetest smile I've ever seen and said, "Thank God, mother. You've made me the happiest boy in the world."

As Roger Williams has noted, Lilly is slightly confused about time. She puts Hank's period of musical unemployment at three weeks' length, when it actually lasted almost two years.

However, it is probable that it was at least partially her initiative that brought Hank back to Montgomery to resume his career.

He got his job back at WSFA, and a Hank Williams songbook published by the station near the end of the war treats his career there as if it had never been interrupted:

"Since 1936," its biography begins, "Hank Williams and his

Drifting Cowboys have been among the top-ranking favorites of the listeners of Station WSFA in Montgomery. . . ."

This "Deluxe Song Book" also relates that "Hank has traveled throughout thirty-eight states and hopes to visit the ten remaining states in the Union before very long. He has appeared on dozens of radio stations and also in several rodeos out west. He is happily married and he and 'Miss Audrey' are already famous as a team."

So late 1944 was an eventful time for twenty-one-year-old Hank Williams. He got back into show business, managed to renew his relationship with his large radio listening audience, and married Audrey in December.

It's hard to pinpoint exactly when Hank started turning out mature songs. He wrote songs almost continually after his "WPA Blues," composed when he was twelve or thirteen.

But Hank Williams started so young that it took a long time for maturity to develop in his songwriting, as well as in his singing. M. C. Jarrett has a tape taken from home recording sessions he did with Hank in Montgomery. It's a scratchy collection of primarily gospel material with Audrey and Hank singing many duets.

"I always pitched him high in A," Jarrett recalls, and on a couple of these songs, it seems Hank was pitched almost too high. His young voice strains for the high notes on "When God Comes and Gathers His Jewels," yet still he stubbornly puts the song across. He was learning his limits the hard way, but it would pay off later in artistic growth.

It was not until after his 1944 return to the music business that this maturity evidenced itself in Hank's performing and writing.

His first song to win any notoriety at all was sold to Pee Wee King and recorded by him.

"I was playin' a show down in Dothan, Alabama, with Pee Wee," Minnie Pearl remembers, "and that's the first time I saw Hank Williams." Williams was pitching a patriotic song to King called "Prayin' For The Day When Peace Will Come." Perhaps out of pity for the skinny young songwriter in the threadbare suit, the established star paid Hank Williams ten dollars for the rights to the number.

The lyrics reflect Hank's emerging talent, still bogged down in sentimentality and clichés. There are wives and sweethearts "so dear" who are waiting for the time when their "loved ones" can return. And won't the world be happy when that day comes, etcetera, etcetera.

Both the song and its fate show how far Hank still had to go in 1944 and '45. His songs did not yet possess the diamond-like quality of later years, and once written they could only be peddled to better-known singers. There were no publishers of music in Montgomery. The lyrics to thirty Hank Williams songs are printed in that little WSFA "Deluxe Song Book," yet neither the songs nor the book itself were copyrighted at the time it was published.

Out of these thirty songs, most are chaff and only a few are genuine wheat. One, however, would become an all-time hit. "Honky-Tonkin'," the first of Hank's good fast blues tunes, appears in the book, uncopyrighted, under the title "Honkey-Tonkey."

Several other early compositions are included that Hank would record a couple of years later when he got the opportunity. Among them: "Never Again Will I Knock On Your Door," an old-fashioned country waltz tune which at one point rhymes "o'er" and "before"; "When God Comes And Gathers His Jewels," a religious ballad about a boy who's lost his mother; another gospel number, "Calling You," which remains as one of Hank's best recordings and one of his most straight-forward evangelistic gospel lyrics; and "Six More Miles," which is a spare, cutting lyric about the death of a sweetheart, made quite plausible and palatable by a simple mournful melody and a trotting-speed rhythm. The mood of the song is haunting, like a New Orleans funeral parade, and it foreshadows the many Hank Williams classics which will seem to be forged out of not one emotion, but several conflicting ones.

Also included in the WSFA songbook are quite a few numbers which Hank would eventually leave behind, presumably with a blush. Among them, "Grandad's Musket," another war tune that seems to have been a south Alabama favorite:

Grandad with his musket in the days of yore

Could knock off a squirrel at a hundred yards or more;
So give me Grandad's musket and I'll march to war
To join with MacArthur and even up the score.

Other forgotten and forgettable early tunes were "I Bid You
Free To Go," "Back Ache Blues," and "My Darling Baby Girl,"
which was written by Hank and Audrey for little Lycrecia, her
daughter by her first marriage.

Hank Williams was merely getting the bad stuff, the soph-
omoric sentiment, the experimental clichés, and corny phrases
out of his system. Once his career got rolling, he would record
very little junk, even though the pressure to merely produce
would be intense. These songs are all important because they
are a record of how Hank Williams felt his way into country
writing. Although some of them are syrupy by today's standards, they are not really more so than some of Roy Acuff's
biggest hits of that period.

Slowly but surely, Hank Williams was building up a port-
folio of original songs. This too, was important, because when
his recording break came, he had lots of his own material to
draw from—enough to see him through until initial success
brought new confidence. Then a whole truckload of new songs,
ripe and full-grown, would be fertilized into fruition by that
confidence.

As he experimented along traditional lines in his writing,
Hank was also experimenting in his performing, into areas not
so traditional.

"A lot of the things we did on dance dates were like nothing
you'd ever expect Hank Williams to have done," remembers
Don Helms. "He'd do some of the dirtiest, low-down blues
numbers you can imagine—old Blind Roy Fuller songs,
"Matchbox Blues," that type of thing—real old blues numbers
he'd picked up."

Perhaps the most significant comment from Helms on Hank's
blues singing is this one: "He did it his own way."

"I think," says Helms, "Hank Williams was the originator of
what became rock 'n roll. Back then there was pop and there
was hillbilly, two separate kinds of music. But Hank came along
and began to put pop-type lyrics with hillbilly instruments and
a heavy, bluesy beat."

The beat, according to Helms, did not always come just from hillbilly instruments.

"When we played dances," he remembers, "we used drums, tenor sax, trumpets—sometimes two or three extra men along with our band."

So with the extra instrumentation, with Hank's love for the blues, with a half-dozen beers inside him, Helms recalls that on Hank's big-band era dance dates, the audience might be treated to "some of the raunchiest blues things you ever heard."

"Hank was an original," says M. C. Jarrett, but Hank didn't become an original overnight. The key to his success, once he got the exposure he needed, was a distinctive style. The style was something he'd been working on for years—copying, listening, trying out new licks, resurrecting old licks—through night after night of saloon stages, fistfight encores, crowded sedans, and country music. The music made the rest of it worth going through.

"People don't come to honky-tonks to listen to music," Hank once told his mother. "They come to fight."

But if no one else was listening, Hank was. On the nights when he kept control of himself, the innovative possibilities of the music provided the only break from what had become a mere routine.

"It was after I started with Hank," says Don Helms, "that he arrived at his style. Before that, he'd sing like Roy Acuff on a Roy Acuff song, like Ernest Tubb on an Ernest Tubb song, and so on."

Hank told Helms, "I'm gonna get my own style—right between those two [Acuff and Tubb]."

"And that's what he did," Helms concludes.

Things, then, were picking up. Sammy Pruitt and Don Helms rejoined Hank after the war. Hank's following continued to grow. Now he regularly joined the Opry headliners when they played Montgomery, and he was quite capable of stealing the show from them.

"He'd stretch out one of those big long legs, buckle his knees, close his eyes and let go a moan, and women would go nuts," remembers one musician from that era.

Roger Williams records this anecdote from Hank's year in Montgomery:

When Hank sang his "Me and My Broken Heart" on a show with headliner Ernest Tubb, Tubb was so impressed he told his manager: "That kid was the best thing in the show, including me. Let's sign him for the rest of the tour."

But Ernest Tubb's manager knew about Hank Williams' reputation as an unreliable performer. Hank's behavior pattern was consistent—he always missed some shows now and then. He would leave the bottle alone for months by now, but his sprees when he took them became worse and worse.

"He got so heavy into drinking along about '45," says M. C. Jarrett, "that he couldn't control it at all. He had to go to the hospital up in Prattville, to dry out. Audrey arranged for a bunch of us to fill in for him at the dance over at Andalusia."

According to Jarrett, Hank Williams at age twenty-two was already in the advanced stages of alcoholism.

"He'd done that [gone to the hospital to dry out] before," says Jarrett. "He'd get the d.t.'s and all. It'd get so bad that his mother'd put him in the hospital.

"The reason that he had to go to Prattville that one time in '45 was because they wouldn't take him anymore at the hospital in Montgomery," Jarrett continues.

Besides drinking, Hank's unreliability in other ways was a red flag to the Opry representatives who knew him late in his Montgomery years. When an Opry show was coming to town, local performers like Hank often handled and sold large blocks of tickets.

"Once before a show in '44 or '45," says Jarrett, "Hank was given 500 tickets to sell. But when he got the tickets, he went on a drunk, traded them all off for whiskey or gave them away to friends. By the night of the show, most of Hank's tickets were unaccounted for."

Since Williams was the home-town headliner, the Opry people had to let him on the stage for that night's show, but Jarrett believes this episode is one big reason why it took Hank Williams four more years to make it to the Grand Ole Opry.

With all his obvious shortcomings, young Hank still possessed a magical quality that inspired loyalty and professional respect from those who knew him best.

Don Helms was only fourteen when he first played with Hank Williams, but he remembers he went home and told his mother, "I'm working with an ol' boy now that's really gonna be somethin' someday."

"I didn't know what it was about Hank," says Helms, "but it seemed like all of a sudden I felt different about the music business. He wasn't all that great a singer and he wasn't that good lookin'. He just knew what to say to the people and how to say it."

A pattern was being born then that continues to this day among the friends and fans of Hank Williams: people who identify with Hank so strongly that they're willing to overlook his weaknesses. Perhaps like Judy Garland's, Hank's appeal was made even stronger by his weakness.

"A lot of people would alibi for him," remembers Don Helms. "They'd say, 'So what if he gets too drunk? Let him drink if he wants to.'" After all, they'd felt like goin' on a bender themselves a few times.

Hank Williams performed a tribal function for the South. He had absorbed, in his short life, a lion's share of the common experience of its people. He had known poverty and hard work, had learned to think of fried chicken as a Sunday delicacy, had loved the trains, the trees, the traditions of the southern land, got choked up over Momma, fought with his woman, struggled to pay bills, fell hard in love, fought hard when challenged, and drank hard when he couldn't take it any more.

Moreover, Hank had been given the gift of recreating his experience for an audience; that is, recreating *their* experience for his audience. At first, he did it by joining in with the flow of country music as it had been, because he was not the first hillbilly to speak for the hillbilly to the hillbillies.

The phenomenal twist in this pattern, though, has to do with the way Hank's maturing process brought a new personalization into his music. More and more, his songs would be drawn not from what he felt songs should be, but from just what he was going through. And the more he told what he was going through, the more the people identified.

This gift was so strong that Hank Williams would have been a success no matter what his obstacles. By 1946, his music, his

style, his on-stage personality, and his songwriting skills were
so well-developed that nothing was going to stop him. Like
some charismatic political candidate who by sheer grassroots
popularity can topple the party powers, Hank Williams
possessed the country music audience even before he was given
the opportunity to sing from the Grand Ole Opry stage. And the
drinking, regrettable as it was, could not yet slow him down
because its possession of him only increased his empathetic
possession of his audience.

Hank gave the people a picture of their pain, a reminder of
their faith, and an enactment of their escape. Struggle, heartbreak, drowning sorrows at the roadhouse, soberly remembering what Momma used to say about Jesus, corny jokes and ol'
boy laughter, proudly fighting with the woman and proudly
defending the right to fight with the woman, frustration,
anxiety, relief, hope, conviction . . . does it sound like merely a
regional encyclopedia of story themes?

If not, then you can understand why this Southern performer
could not be held back from becoming an American legend,
known and loved as well in Minneapolis as in Mobile.

Acuff-Rose Music occupies its own building on Franklin Road
on the south side of Nashville, clearly the most impressive
edifice in an otherwise undistinguished neighborhood. It is
geographically aloof from the comings and goings on Music
Row, where most of the publishing companies, management
agencies, and record company offices are clustered together like
a crowd of Southern politicians at a Washington cocktail party.

Acuff-Rose owns a margin of independence from the pressure
to be anxiously scurrying to find and produce new talent. The
million-dollar building is only one sign of that independence.
The gold records from country music standards that line its
hallways are the best evidence. Acuff-Rose probably owns the
rights to more timeless country tunes than any other house in
the country; it takes in many hundreds of thousands in yearly
revenues whether or not it has a current hit.

The Hank Williams catalogue is the trump suit of Acuff-Rose.
Without it, the building could certainly not be so imposing, the
credit so good, the furnishings of the president's office so plush.

And the whole thing started with an interrupted ping-pong game in the fall of 1946. Hank Williams had come to Nashville.

He came with Audrey on the bus to try to get a hearing from the people at Acuff-Rose. It was probably the Acuff name that drew him, but it was Fred Rose he needed to see. Fred Rose was the songwriting, record-producing, cofounder of Acuff-Rose, who along with country legend Roy Acuff had determined that too many country songwriters were not getting the breaks they deserved from the New York song publishers. So in 1942, Acuff and Rose had gone together to form the company. In 1945, Fred's son Wesley left a job as chief accountant for a Standard Oil refinery to come and run the day-to-day publishing operation for his father and Acuff.

"Hank and Audrey came up to WSM and wanted to sing some songs for my father and I," remembers Wesley Rose. . . . "It was lunchtime and we were playing ping-pong. At that time we were looking for some songs for a girl singer named Molly O'Day—the 'female Acuff,' they used to call her. So, since we were looking for material anyway, we thought we might as well give a listen."

So Fred and Wesley Rose led Hank and Audrey to an empty studio and sat down to hear the tall kid from Alabama.

"Hank didn't say much that first day," Wesley Rose remembers, "Audrey did all the talking; he did the singing." Williams seemed bashful and self-conscious, remaining quiet throughout the audition.

"He apparently didn't think that we'd even listen to him," says Rose. "Maybe he'd been turned down in so many spots that he felt this was just a wild gamble. In any case, it was Audrey who was the salesman that day."

Wesley Rose can't remember exactly the songs Hank sang, but says that probably "When God Comes and Gathers His Jewels," "Six More Miles," and "My Love For You Has Turned to Hate" were among them.

Fred Rose, who had seen a lot of composing talent come and go, signed Hank immediately to an exclusive songwriting contract with Acuff-Rose. He bought the songs Hank had sung that afternoon, hoping to get them recorded by Molly O'Day. Thus began one of the most profitable publisher-songwriter partnerships in the history of American popular music.

The elder Rose's career had been a long and interesting one.
Born in St. Louis in 1897, he had been writing songs profession-
ally since 1919, when "Alashan," which he wrote with W. Duke,
was published. In his early years, Rose wrote "Red Hot
Mama," for Sophie Tucker, and several other hits including
"Honest and Truly" and "'Deed I do."

Fred Rose left the Ohio River town of Evansville, Indiana, at
fifteen, perhaps inspired by another young songwriter from the
Wabash River valley, Paul ("My Gal Sal") Dresser. He settled
in Chicago and soon began an active career as a songwriter and
vaudeville performer. His early credits include work with
Fibber McGee and Molly and playing piano for the great
bandleader Paul Whiteman, Gershwin's popularizer. Rose also
had a Chicago radio show in the twenties called "Fred Rose's
Song Shop."

The story goes that Rose landed accidentally in Nashville
during the Depression when his vaudeville group took a wrong
turn on their way to Evansville. He settled into work at WSM
and into the world of country music. Though Nashville was not
the popular music mecca then that it is today, Rose's songwriting career was not damaged by his choice. He would leave
Nashville only for a short period of time, going to New York,
then to Hollywood in the late thirties to write and produce
songs for Gene Autry, including "Be Honest With Me," "Yesterday's Roses," and "Twiddle O Twee." Then he returned to
Nashville and went into the publishing business with Acuff.

In 1946, Acuff-Rose was already a healthy young business.
Rose had written several hits for Acuff, Roy himself had
penned a few songs worth a few hundred thousand sheet sales
apiece, and the organization was building up a strong bullpen of
younger country songwriters. Pee Wee King and Redd Stewart
("Tennessee Waltz"), Jenny Lou Carson, Mel Foree, were
among those in the Acuff-Rose stables.

Though Fred and Wesley had an ear for talent, they could not
have guessed that young Hank Williams—who so trustingly
was putting his future in their hands—would sell more songs
than the rest of their then-active crew combined.

On the other hand, as Hank Williams signed up for a standard
songwriting contract with Acuff-Rose, he scarcely could have

known how perfect a team his genius and Fred Rose's crafts-manship would make. For the second time in his life, Hank Williams was brought into a crucial professional relationship which gave a strong boost to his creative abilities. First there was Tee-tot, who passed down to Hank a blues-singer's mantle of stridence, wit, and controlled mournfulness. Now there was Fred Rose, who brought all of the pop-music savvy and the know-how of his Chicago, New York, and Hollywood experiences to bear on Hank Williams' songs and career. If Hank Williams had been a young millionaire, he could not have bought two better influences to help him make his musical-songwriting talent into all it could be.

Fred Rose was not merely an old pro songwriter. He was a man inspired to contribute to the world of popular music. While in New York, Rose had become a devout Christian Scientist. This experience encouraged him to find a new and worthy goal—presumably higher than mere pop songwriting—and move toward it. The goal he chose was to become a publisher of music, with a bent toward gospel material. Acuff-Rose, then, was the fulfillment of a dream for the veteran songsmith now in the autumn of his career.

After Acuff-Rose was established, Rose found that he could work well and comfortably with other songwriters, and so began his twelve-year stint as a publisher-songwriter-record producer specializing in helping other songwriters and artists with the nuts and bolts of turning a new song into a hit. Over the years, Fred Rose's name appeared on a long list of country hits, and countless other songs for which he took no credit bear his unmistakable imprint. One song he wrote in 1945, "Blue Eyes Cryin' In the Rain," became a monster hit with Willie Nelson in 1975, twenty-one years after Rose's death.

Hank Williams was destined to become a partner with one more musical touchstone, but that would come just a bit later.

For now, it was enough for Hank to have a songwriting contract with Acuff-Rose. He and Audrey returned to Montgomery with renewed hope and enthusiasm for his career. The strong hope of success helped Hank to put down the bottle then and leave it alone for awhile.

In the early years, the liquor had helped; or so Hank had

thought. There was the boost it gave to his confidence and the songs he could produce while holed up in a room in Lilly's boardinghouse with nothing but a guitar and a bottle for company. But now, real success—tangible, honest, untainted, and big-time as could be—was flickering its awesome luminous shadow over Hank Williams, and something in him began to respond with the instinct of a professional that was stronger than his emotional and physical addiction to alcohol.

The best years were about to begin, and even Hank's thirst seemed to sense the importance of rising to the occasion.

6

M-G-M and the Louisiana Hayride

The discovery of talent is a curiously ironic business. Every great and popular artist has been an unknown at one point: the new name turned over in someone's mouth to see how it sounds, the face that will become so familiar clenched in anxiety while a Mr. Big of some sort decides its fate; yet what does Mr. Big know? What can he predict or cause to happen? Public reaction could fool him either way: He may have a strong positive reaction to an artist who will be a commercial bomb, or he may remain unmoved by a performer who is destined to become a sensation.

For that reason, it is only a recent phenomenon to find a major record label or a major talent agency discovering and hyping an unknown artist. There have always been other ways to approach the testing of new talent.

In the country music industry, as well as the recording industry as a whole, it has often been the small record label that introduces a performer to the public. And though that label's share of the mass audience might be small, it can be an accurate barometer. If you press a few thousand records and they sell off the shelves pretty quick, you've got something. It may be a fluke or a fad or the only good song that artist will ever do, but you've got *something*. *Somebody* out there besides you and the artist's mother likes it.

So you press a few thousand more and if *they* go too . . . well, in fishing terms, you know you've found the right bait.

Many country artists have begun their careers on small

labels: Loretta Lynn on Zero; Jim Reeves on Abbott; and, of course, Johnny Cash, Elvis, and Jerry Lee Lewis on Sam Phillips' accidental gold mine in Memphis, the Sun label.

In the late fall of 1946, six months or so after Hank Williams signed with Acuff-Rose as a songwriter, a man named Middleman contacted Fred Rose from New York. Mr. Middleman owned a small record company called Sterling Records.

"He was looking for a western group and a hillbilly group to record," Wesley Rose remembers. "To fill the western slot, my father decided to use the Oklahoma Wranglers (also known as the Willis Brothers), and I suggested we bring Hank Williams up from Montgomery to be the hillbilly act Sterling was looking for."

Although both elder and younger Rose had been impressed by the skinny kid from Alabama, they were not without reservations about him.

"We could tell Hank had singing talent," says Wesley, "but his biggest problem, we felt at that time, was that he had too much Acuff in him . . . because he idolized Roy Acuff."

(Years later Hank Williams would try to explain Roy Acuff's magic to Californian Ralph Gleason in an interview: "He's the biggest singer this music ever knew," Williams would rave. "You booked him and you didn't worry about crowds. For drawing power in the South, it was Roy Acuff and then God!")

Acuff fixation notwithstanding, Hank's singing had been strong enough that Fred Rose agreed to give him a shot at recording.

"We offered him the Sterling deal," says Wesley, "and he came in and did a four-song session. It was cut at WSM's radio studios, because at the time, there weren't any recording studios in Nashville."

Hank rode into Nashville from Montgomery on a bus with his guitar and his song sheets, wearing a battered cowboy suit under his overcoat. Fred Rose, perceiving that Hank could use a psychological boost, bought him a new stage uniform to wear for the recording session.

So on December 11, 1946, Hank was ushered into Studio D in the fabled WSM studios. The studios were housed in the offices of the National Life and Accident Insurance Company, parent company to the Grand Ole Opry. Studio D was a room about thirty-five by thirty-five which could handle the recording of small groups and soloists and doubled as an on-air studio for WSM. It was nothing overly impressive, but to Hank Williams, it must have seemed like he was entering the Holy of Holies.

The Oklahoma Wranglers did their stuff first, recording all together in one take while the big stylus cut the lacquer master disc right on the spot. When the western group was finished, it was lunchtime. Hank joined them for a sandwich at the Clarkston Hotel coffee shop just down the street from WSM. The Willis Brothers remember two things about their conversation over lunch that day. First, that Hank was not getting his hopes up about the results of his session, and second, the remark he made when asked if he'd like a beer with his sandwich:

"You don't know ol' Hank," he replied. "Ol' Hank don't have just *one*."

According to those in attendance, Hank was rather awe-struck and anxious when his turn came, but his part of the session flew by smoothly. Four songs were recorded, all of them tunes Hank had sold to Acuff-Rose back in the summer: "My Love For You Has Turned to Hate," "When God Comes and Gathers His Jewels," "Never Again Will I Knock On Your Door," and "Wealth Won't Save Your Soul." Hank laid down the songs with the Oklahoma Wranglers providing his backup music; the Drifting Cowboys had stayed in Alabama.

The Willises were not impressed with Hank's rawness and his fundamentalist lyrics. "We hadn't been used to hearing a country singer who was as country as he was," they told Jack Hurst years later.

This first session was, in Wesley Rose's words, "pretty good—no hit records, but pretty good." Aaron Shelton, one of Nashville's recording pioneers, was there that day and offers a more enthusiastic recollection. He and his partner Carl Jenkins engineered the session.

"We were real impressed with Hank," says Shelton. "Very seldom did we feel that way about a new talent, but we felt Hank had a great potential right away. Carl and I both came to that conclusion."

The songs were new to Shelton and Jenkins, but they weren't affected by the material as much as by the singer and his performance. "The pure magnetism of the guy's presentation," says Shelton, "was what we couldn't help but notice."

That magnetism, though some of it was visual, is captured in the masters that remain from that session, especially in the two religious numbers, where Hank's intensity was particularly apparent. That voice, that gutsy, reedy instrument that has been described as something akin to a buzz saw cutting through a pine log, made its recording debut in forceful and mature ripeness. You've got to go back to earlier recordings, ones made in Montgomery practice sessions, to catch Hank Williams' voice sounding boyish.

Of the songs on this first session, "Wealth Won't Save Your Soul" stands out as the most intense if not also the most impressive. Hank puts it across with all the conviction of a southern tent-revival preacher on his last night in town. He also gets some able backup singing from the Oklahoma Wranglers on the choruses.

Hank was paid ninety dollars for this first session. At this point in his career the money didn't make much difference. He had begun to smell success in the form of his songwriting contract, and he would probably have been glad to pay Sterling ninety bucks for a chance to prove himself. The Sterling people, on the other hand, were not obligating themselves to Hank beyond this one session. He was not signed to the label in any long-term sense; hence the flat-fee arrangement.

So Hank Williams had now worked his first Nashville recording session. This was significant historically in more ways than one, because Nashville was not yet what it is today. Until after World War II, Nashville was home to the Grand Ole Opry and a country music hub of sorts, but it was not *Music City USA* as it now has become. There were no record company office-buildings and there weren't any recording studios. Country artists at that time were often managed out of Nashville—if they were Opry regulars, they had the help of the Opry's own booking agency—but the record companies still did business from New York. To get into a bonafide studio, a country performer had to travel at least as far as Cincinnati or Chicago.

Hank Williams arrived on the scene just in time to get in on the ground floor of what was to become a multibillion dollar enterprise: the recording of country music talent in its natural habitat, with its own people at the controls as well as in front of the microphones. Aaron Shelton and Carl Jenkins, who engineered that first Sterling session for Fred Rose and Hank Williams, were already playing a crucial role in getting Music City USA off the ground. Together with their partner George Reynolds, they had set up the Studio D facility in WSM's studios right at the close of the war. They paid rent to WSM for the studio and in turn collected fees for studio time from the performers who recorded there.

In 1946, Shelton and Jenkins opened the first recording studio in Nashville in the old Tulane Hotel. Castle Studios, they called it, after WSM, which was known as the "Air Castle of the South." Hank Williams would make most of his great recordings in that studio. At the time Hank first recorded in Studio D, Shelton and Jenkins were running both operations simultaneously.

Glenn Snoddy worked as second engineer on many Hank Williams recordings, and remembers when WSM bought the first two professional tape recorders in Nashville in 1949.

"They were Ampex 200s, numbers thirty-one and thirty-two," he says with a technician's memory. Snoddy, who now manages Woodland Sound Studios in Nashville, relates that Castle also bought its first Ampex 200 (Number 34) at about the same time.

"But it took us a while to get used to the tape machines," he remembers. "We'd still cut a disc as well as a tape, just to make sure we got a recording . . . and usually we'd use the disc, not the tape, for the playback after a song was cut."

Shelton, Jenkins, and Reynolds were mighty proud when they had set up the Castle Studio. By 1949, they had the new Ampex 200 and also the first Scully master cutting lathe in the Southeast. For the first time, Nashville could offer professional quality recording as good as anywhere in the country.

This technical breakthrough was a sign of things to come.

Today Nashville, along with the new Osmond complex in Salt Lake City, is one of only two cities in the country which can attract network television productions away from New York and Hollywood. And the recording, of course, has grown a bit. In 1973, there were 15,877 recording sessions staged in Nashville. By the mid-sixties, there were a half dozen major record labels with Nashville studios and offices, along with the hundreds of small labels and independent studios that make up the scene today. (One of the best descriptions of the entire new Nashville milieu is Paul Hemphill's book *The Nashville Sound*, which offers an impressive array of facts as well as numerous illuminating glimpses of current Nashville personalities.)

"It wasn't long after the first Sterling session," says Wesley Rose, "that Middleman called back and wanted Hank to do another one." It seems the boy had sold some records. Hank, who was still playing, slugging, and dodging around the Alabama honky-tonk circuit, was overjoyed. And the record sales, even more than a few shots of whiskey, did something positive for his confidence.

When he went back into Studio D to make his second Sterling session, he loosened up a little. Whereas the first group of songs could all have been Acuff numbers, he now stepped out into new territory all his own.

This session included "Calling You," a spirited gospel number, "I Don't Care If Tomorrow Never Comes," a stock ballad, and the train song Hank wrote from memories of his childhood, "Pan American." But the important song he cut that day early in 1947 was an infectious little old number called "Honky-Tonkin'." It wasn't Roy Acuff style, it wasn't Ernest Tubb . . . it was all Hank Williams.

Or rather it was Hank Williams singing out of his own roots. "Honky-Tonkin'" is a lively, bluesy invitation to join the singer for some fun on the town. Its boldness—the song addresses a girl who already has a "baby," giving her an option should she "have a fallin' out"—is straight from the black blues tradition of Mississippi John Hurt; Leadbelly; and McKinley Morganfield, better known as Muddy Waters. In country music it was unheard of to write songs asking women to leave their present partners and come along with you. But Hank did it. And he put the song across just as easily as sippin' from a jug.

He also gives us a hint of things to come in the way he plays vocally with the words "honky-tonkin'," throwing the short second syllable of "honky" up into the falsetto range after holding and bending the first syllable: "hoooonk-*ee*-tonkin', honky-tonkin'." Hank's falsetto was not to show up in another song for a couple of years, but when it did, the yodeling, moaning effect of it on a song called "Lovesick Blues" was going to be historic.

"So 'Honky-Tonkin'' established a style," says Wesley Rose, "and from that point on, Father decided to place Hank on a major label."

This decision by Fred Rose turned out to be more than a mere business deal; it eventually amounted to an adoption of sorts.

"This was the beginning of what was almost like a family relationship between Hank and Acuff-Rose," says Wesley. "A strong relationship began to grow between Hank and my father, especially." Hank called Fred Rose "Pappy" as Wesley did, and trusted Rose to guide his career into its next phase, whatever that meant. Yet, there was no contract between them regarding management, not even a very formal agreement. It was just more or less understood. Fred Rose would produce all of Hank's recording sessions throughout his career. He would help Hank choose material, he would help him write songs, and he would become a very close friend in a paternal kind of way. Hank, for his part, would heed Rose's advice and would do whatever Rose told him to do.

"You really didn't need a piece of paper with Hank," recalls Wesley Rose. "He stayed loyal to Acuff-Rose even later on, when other people tried to tempt him to leave."

At the time when Hank Williams recorded "Honky-Tonkin'," there were no mobs of publishers and record companies beating down his door. He was still just a local radio personality from Montgomery recording on a tiny label. Fred Rose, though, sensed something in Hank's delivery, in that magnetism that Aaron Shelton remembers; the future of this kid was in his hands, and he began to realize it could be a big future.

Fred Rose knew what to do. A friend of his named Frank Walker had just founded a record company for M-G-M. Walker was a former president of RCA Victor records with an amazing career already behind him. Born in 1889, Frank Walker had started working in show business in the early twenties and became a personal manager for the great operatic tenor Enrico Caruso. He had entered the record business in 1919 with the Columbia Gramophone Company [later to become Columbia Records] and had been with RCA Victor from 1939 to 1945. Walker had been interested in country music since the days when he had to literally ride a horse into the woods in pursuit of musical talent. Along the way he had been involved with the careers of Al Jolson, Gene Autry, Bessie Smith, Artie Shaw, and Eddy Arnold, to name a few.

Fred Rose went to New York, found Frank Walker, and played him the Sterling recordings of Hank Williams. Walker liked them. He came to Nashville and signed Hank to a contract with M-G-M.

"You'll get the standard three percent per record," he told Williams.

"I don't understand percents," was Williams' reply. He was wary.

"Well, let's make it three cents a record, then," said Walker. It amounted to a somewhat better deal.

"That I understand," Hank said. He grinned and signed on the dotted line.

So once more Hank Williams had a strong ally in his corner. First the old minstrel Tee-tot, then Fred Rose, and now a record company executive who had worked with the greatest talents of the century. Hank Williams, had he known who to go to, could not have found a better pair of show-biz mentors than Fred Rose and Frank Walker. Yet, in a sense, he didn't find them at all—rather they found him. As it was, Hank Williams was just grateful for the breaks.

Hank joined a fast-growing stable of recording artists at M-G-M. Bob Wills, the Texas-Swing king, had been the first country performer signed by Walker when he formed the company. In the pop field, Walker had Art Lund and his new popular ballad, "Mam'selle." He also had signed Blue Barron and Art "I'm Looking Over a Four Leaf Clover" Mooney. Hank's record sales would soon outstrip them all.

The arrangement between Frank Walker, Fred Rose, and Hank Williams was incredibly loose by today's standards and quite casual even in those simpler times. All of Hank's recording would be done in Nashville, with Fred Rose supervising all sessions. Rose would be responsible for deciding on material and producing the records independent of M-G-M's control. After a session or sessions were completed, Fred Rose would send the masters to New York with instructions concerning what should be released and when it should be released. Frank Walker and M-G-M would then handle all promotion and merchandising details. As Roger Williams has noted, "It was a sensible plan, and it worked beautifully."

From the beginning, there seems to have been a strong mutual respect between Williams, Walker, and Rose. Though he had his social shyness and his distrust of businessmen, Hank could "fit in with anybody if they met him on his terms," according to Don Helms. Walker and Rose seem to have done just that, not expecting Hank to be something he wasn't. This vote of confidence was to inspire Hank Williams now into the best professional years of life. His loyalty was put to the test quite early:

> The trust Hank had in Fred Rose quickly became apparent. Before making the deal with M-G-M, Rose showed Hank's Sterling sides to an executive of another major record company. The executive said he wasn't interested. Then, when Rose left, he called Hank long distance and said he'd like to sign him to a contract.
>
> "Get hold of Fred Rose," Hank said.
>
> "I'm not interested in Rose," the executive snapped. "He's just out for himself. Besides, *he* can't do anything for you."
>
> "He got you to call me, didn't he?" Hank asked angrily, and hung up.

This vignette from Roger Williams' research shows the

almost childlike trust which Hank Williams put in Fred Rose, the same kind of trust that can be read in his eyes in a later photo of Hank signing an M-G-M movie contract, looking up at Frank Walker with a heartbreakingly vulnerable smile.

While there was something almost wistful going on inside Hank as he responded to the approval of these new friends, there was nothing unbusinesslike about his professional response to the situation. Just as if he had been the coldest, slickest hack in the songwriting world, he gave M-G-M a hit with his first record for the label.

"Move It On Over" became one of the big country songs of 1947 and 1948, selling several hundred thousand copies. Nothing misty-eyed about this particular tune, either. It was, like "Honky-Tonkin'," a piece of brashery of the kind that would make Hank Williams a country music trendsetter.

Songs in a canine vein were nothing new to country music; however, usually they had been ditties about Old Blue or some great huntin' pup or the like. But Hank wrote "Move It On Over," and created the industry's first *doghouse* song right out of his own experience. Throughout their marriage, Audrey's standard reaction to a Hank Williams spree was to lock him out of the house, and with his musical bemoaning of that sad fate— asking the "little dog" to "move it on over" and make room for the "big dog"—Hank Williams touched a nerve in the country music audience. This song wasn't some drippy pledge of love meant to fan to flame an affair gone cold. It wasn't a doodley-woo "happy" love song, either, though it sure did *move*. And though it had a comic twist, it was much more than a Little Jimmy Dickens-style novelty song.

It was Hank's first record to capture a widely-known experience. And it began his long string of hits that came about because the audience knew from the gut what he was talking about. Who hasn't had the wife get mad when he's had a few too many? Who hasn't stumbled home a time or two to find himself bolted out of his own house?

"Hank came along and began to sing about where people *were*," says Don Helms. And with "Move It On Over," he discovered that that was a pretty sure-fire formula.

Now Hank Williams was a singer-songwriter with a major hit on a major label, but on the other hand he was still playing the same Alabama bars he'd played for years: the Riverside Inn at Andalusia, Jerry's Tavern at Opp, and the Journey's Inn in Camden. These would not do as any kind of catapult to stardom.

"Someday I hope to have some real money rollin' in," he told Journey's Inn owner H. B. Hawthorne, but Hank and Frank Walker and Fred Rose knew he was going to have to have a better showplace for his live performances than the south Alabama dance circuit.

In the late forties there were still umpteen barn dance-type radio programs around the country: the National Barn Dance on WLS in Chicago; the WWVA Jamboree from Wheeling, West Virginia; the Renfro Valley Barn Dance from Renfro Valley, Kentucky; and the WOWO Hoosier Hop from Fort Wayne, Indiana, to name a few. In the thirties and forties, these shows were instrumental in putting many personalities over the top and into national prominence. Gene Autry and George Gobel both got their starts on the National Barn Dance, country music great Hawkshaw Hawkins was a WWVA veteran along with Grandpa Jones, and the Renfro Valley gang included Red Foley and Homer and Jethro at different times in its long history.

In May of 1948, station KWKH in Shreveport, Louisiana, reinstated its own barn dance show, the Louisiana Hayride, and it—like the shows mentioned above—became a training ground for country talent and a showcase that could move a performer toward the Super Bowl of country music broadcasting, the Grand Ole Opry.

Hank Williams' ability to entertain audiences needed a proving ground, and the Louisiana Hayride, it seemed to Fred Rose, was the perfect place for that to happen.

"My father and I discussed the whole matter—Hank's recording career, his possible future on the Opry, everything—and decided he should go to KWKH," says Wesley Rose. One reason the Hayride was chosen was because of its pure country orientation. Some other barn dance shows mixed in pop talent, and Rose was afraid Hank's style was too strong for an audience used to its "folk" music in small, watered-down doses. The Hayride audience was a country audience, and it was their reaction to Hank Williams that Fred Rose wanted to measure.

Another boost to Hank's career that would come with Shreveport would be the booking services that KWKH provided for Hayride artists. With a great sigh of relief, Hank could say goodbye to the days of scrambling for dates with his sister's, his mother's, or his wife's help.

By 1948, Fred Rose's weight in the country music world was such that one phone call to KWKH's manager Henry Clay was all it took to get Hank Williams onto the Louisiana Hayride.

"We'll send him down for a Saturday night guest shot," Rose told Clay. "Then you let us know if he's a regular."

On the day following this guest shot, Fred Rose received a call from Clay. "He's a regular, all right," said the station manager.

So in the summer of 1948, Hank Williams joined the cast of the KWKH Louisiana Hayride. He took Audrey with him to Shreveport, but Lum York was the only one of the Montgomery musicians to follow Hank Williams to Louisiana. Hank tried to get his steel guitarist Don Helms to come along too, but Helms thought he had a better deal going with another group.

"He told me he'd let me off this time, but that one of these days he was going to the Opry," says Helms, "and when he went, he was gonna want me to go with him." Helms agreed, figuring that'd be fine if it ever happened.

Even with the success he had so far attained, it must have taken some blind faith for Hank to make such a confident statement about the Opry. The pace of his ascendancy was not picking up. It had taken him nine years to be discovered as a songwriter, and another year or two before his first records began to make any impact.

"Move It On Over" had taken off, but Hank Williams had not. One thing still working against him, of course, was alcohol.

"Some people just drink and they can't tell you why," says Don Helms thirty years later. "I don't think Hank knew why he drank. I'm sure Hank didn't realize for a long time that he had a problem. For a long time he could pretty much drink when he wanted to and stay sober when he wanted to . . . then it began to catch up with him.

"He'd get dried out," continues Helms, "and get straight and you could set a bottle on the table and he'd leave it alone. But if he ever took that first drink, he was gone for about two weeks."

As it turned out, Hank happened to be "gone" when Harry Stone and Jim Denny from WSM came to Montgomery to talk to him about his move to Shreveport. The very fact that they made this trip is a tribute to the potential they saw in Hank Williams. At the time, Stone was WSM General Manager and Denny was Artists' Services Director for the Grand Ole Opry.

Stone and Denny hung around Montgomery until someone found Hank and, sobered up, he met to talk with them. Against the advice of WSFA's station manager, they still saw hope of Hank Williams making it onto the Grand Ole Opry.

Before Harry Stone died a few years ago he told Roger Williams, "I was used to hillbilly artists being a problem. It seemed like they were drinking most of the time."

Hank's move from Montgomery to KWKH and the Hayride seemed to slow down his drinking. He may have gotten into perspective exactly how success might come: Not never as he sometimes feared and not automatically as he must have wished, but a piece at a time, if he were willing to work hard to earn the pieces one by one.

Hank must have known that his drinking reputation had hurt him in Montgomery. There's no doubt that he felt shame and guilt about drinking, but still he didn't understand why his own personal compulsion was so strong.

Hank Williams, after all, was working in an atmosphere where everyone drank. That's what honky-tonks were for. The boys would roar their Ford V-8s into the dirt parking lots and stay around until they felt good and oiled, then scream back onto the narrow two-lane highways, mud flaps flying, moon hubs glistening, and wide-open pipes roaring Detroit lullabies into the night. Sometimes they even made it home. Quite often they didn't; and someone would have to come and fetch a crumpled but still shiny Harley Davidson Electra-Glide or a

beautiful post-war Olds—nosed and decked and now flattened—
out of a creek bed or off a scarred-up pine tree.

So many of the guys seemed to be able to do it every week—
just get way out there beyond reason or hope or ability to
communicate—and stay that way all weekend. Hank met
hundreds of them, usually in unfortunate circumstances. They
almost always liked to fight.

Maybe it was the psychological release of war's end, maybe it
was the faster cars and looser money and no more ration cards,
maybe it was just progress; but somehow these ol' boys of
Tennessee and Alabama and Texas, these honky-tonk hound
dogs, Mercury-movin' moonshiners, and spiffed-up farm boys
were building up a collective hell-raiser's momentum that was
to raise forever the pitch of socializing in the South to a new
level, wilder and louder and more revved-up than ever. These
relatively innocent hoodlums with their Wildrooted hair and
motorcycle jackets didn't know it, but they and their zoot-
suited collegiate counterparts were setting up the system and
the logical flow of events that would roll right on into the crowd-
bangs of Fort Lauderdale and Daytona in the sixties and
seventies.

So what was so unusual about a honky-tonk hillbilly who got
drunk once in a while? Nothing. They all did it as often as they
could, it seemed. And Hank went right along with 'em. By the
time he teamed up with Fred Rose, Hank Williams was a tough
(if not formidable), wary, street-wise young man who had
dodged a lot of broken bottles and a few knife blades. He had
even had a piece of an eyebrow bit off in one fracas.

Hank would have liked to have had a So What attitude about
his drinking. His response to friends when coming off a bender
was often to joke about it or to grin sheepishly; or else he would
act as if nothing had happened.

Still he knew, as all his friends knew, that Hank was hooked.
He'd never just drink a few, just try to reach some comfortable
plateau; it was always that same sickening slide. Once he picked
up a bottle, he was on his way to Bombsville. He would drink
himself unconscious invariably; and it became part of the
Drifting Cowboys' routine quite early on to carry Hank home to
bed after a show date.

Something though, some vague instinct toward success, some inner resource of self-control—or perhaps some particularly effective effort on Audrey's part—began to give Hank a certain amount of discipline with his thirst during the time he spent on the Louisiana Hayride.

It wasn't instant success that did it, because his move to Shreveport didn't bring instant success. In some ways it was harder than before. The trips were longer, for one thing. Now he and his new bunch of Drifting Cowboys had to meet obligations all over western Louisiana and East Texas. Unlike the old days, these fresh audiences in Bossier City and Lake Charles, in Tyler and Longview, Texas and Texarkana and Baton Rouge, had never heard of Hank Williams. They had to be won over, and they were a somewhat more sophisticated crowd than the South Alabama folks.

So the shows had to be better and longer. The band had to polish Hank's material and play like professionals every night. Still the shows were one-nighters, mainly, sometimes three or four or more of them in a row out of town, with Hank having to make sure his band was taken care of. It was good to be away from the old system of having Momma do his booking and her watching over his shoulder all the time, but sometimes Hank must have wished dearly that he could take the boys back to Lilly's boardinghouse for some free overnights and fried chicken.

Hank paid Lum York and the other band members a flat sixty dollars a week and sometimes it was tough to meet the payroll with all the expenses incurred on the road. At one point he even disbanded the group for a while.

But Hank held on. After all, every Saturday night he got to sing his songs into a lot of folks' parlors and filling stations on the Hayride; that had to be worth something, he figured. Also, the pressure of finding dates was off his shoulders, and it felt good to have it be someone else's job to make bookings for Hank Williams and the Drifting Cowboys.

Then there was his own radio show, which was part of his deal with KWKH. It was an early morning, fifteen-minute broadcast for Johnny Fair Syrup, and the casual music-and-talk format was perfect for Hank's easygoing, friendly stage personality. Hank billed himself as "the Old Syrup Sopper," and before long he was not only soppin' syrup, he was *sellin'* it.

The folks at KWKH remember how poorly the Johnny Fair Syrup company was doing when it and Hank first got together, but within six months Hank had turned the market around for Johnny Fair. He even had the folks buyin' syrup in the summer, which is the slow season for a syrup company.

Between the friends he made as the "Old Syrup Sopper" and the audience Hank reached on the Saturday night Louisiana Hayride, the boy from Alabama began to get himself known in this new territory. The requests for more and better-paying dates began coming in and once more the public's interest in him did great things for Hank's confidence, for his showmanship, and for his creative abilities.

The confidence began to come as strongly as if he were drinking it from a Lone Star beer bottle, but he wasn't. Things were finally looking up. He was still recording for M-G-M, and the records were beginning to pile up sales all over the South though he still couldn't come up with a big follow-up to "Move It On Over." Since Hank wasn't drinking so heavily, he found Audrey much easier to live with; she never had been and never would be much of an alcoholism therapist.

Then in late 1948, Audrey announced to Hank that she was going to bear him a child. That made him happy. He had loved, though not adopted, Audrey's daughter Lycrecia, but now, *he* was going to have a child. Among other things, it confirmed his feelings that things were finally, maybe, gonna get better.

Johnny Wright remembers well the Shreveport days. He and the late Jack Anglin—the pair was well-known for many years as Johnny and Jack—had joined the Hayride cast just before Hank. Kitty Wells, the country music queen of the fifties and also Johnny's wife, was also on KWKH at the time, along with the Bailes Brothers and Curly Williams and the Georgia Peach Pickers.

"It's true that Hank didn't hardly drink while he was working out of Shreveport," says Wright, "but he did fall off the wagon at least once."

A group of Hayride regulars and other friends organized an

Easter egg hunt and picnic on Easter Sunday of 1949. The party was staged out on the shores of Caddo Lake, fifteen or twenty miles outside of Shreveport.

"Hank came to the picnic and brought Audrey, who was pregnant at the time with Hank Junior," Wright recalls. "Well, as the afternoon wore on, Hank got to drinkin'. . . . He got so drunk that Audrey had to drive him home."

Later that night, Audrey called Kitty. The two couples had spent time together before, but this wasn't a normal social invitation.

"Could you two come over here to our place?" Audrey asked her friend. There was a note of anxiety, almost desperation, in her voice. Things were getting out of hand at the Williams bungalow.

"Hank had got to arguin' with Audrey," Johnny Wright remembers, "and was wantin' to break up lamps and things. Audrey, since she was pregnant, was especially scared when he got violent."

So Johnny and Kitty went over to Hank and Audrey's house that night and helped to cool down the situation.

"We stayed up all night with Hank," says Wright, "until he sobered up. Then he didn't drink any more that I know of the rest of the time he was in Shreveport."

Now those Saturday nights at the Hayride became the place where Hank Williams put the finishing touches on his live-audience magic act.

"He was just electrifying on stage," Frank Page of KWKH told Roger Williams:

"He had the people in the palm of his hands from the moment he walked out there. They were with him, whatever he wanted to do."

When introduced, Hank Williams would offhandedly slouch out to the microphone, but as soon as the music began, it was off to the races—a transformed performer held court on the Hayride stage. His body moved with the music, the cowboy-booted toes tapping and the long legs bending with the rhythms. On the fast numbers, Hank began to bounce and bob like a boxer, all the while holding his audience spellbound with

the intensity of his eyes. Those dark, sad expressive eyes
flickered with fun or they pleaded with the sad songs, but they
seemed always to shine with life.

Meanwhile, of course, Hank was singing. And somehow . . .
it was as if there had never been anybody else sing a country
song. *This* was what country music singing sounded like.
Everything else was just an imitation of this original. Haven't
we heard this voice before? It's so *familiar*. But where?
Well. . . .

Even the name, once you began thinking about it, fit the bill.
Hank Williams, the country singer; *The* Country Singer. And
yet, here he was, in flesh and blood, not making any big deal
about it, making half-funny jokes with the band between
numbers, introducing his songs humbly with lines like, "Here's
a little tune we just recorded and we hope you folks like it."

It was incredible, and of course at that time, only a few
people knew what was happening. But if you got down there to
Shreveport on a Saturday night in 1948 or early '49, if you made
it into the 3,400-seat Municipal Auditorium where the Hayride
was broadcast, if you sat down with the tobacco-chewin'
farmhand on one side and the Juicy-Fruit-chewin' Cajun James
Dean with his frilly-dressed girlfriend on the other, if you
waited around through the other acts and then saw this thin
feller up there begin to sing with that got-to-say-it voice and
those eyes that looked right at you . . .

Then you knew.

"I think, in his time, no other performer—country, folk, or
pop—could come within a country mile of Hank Williams," says
Melvin Shestack in his *Country Music Encyclopedia*.

Shestack saw Hank Williams perform in a rural fairgrounds
jamboree near East Bloomfield, New York, shortly after Hank
had signed on with the Hayride. His description of that show
and of the interview Williams granted him after the show—
Melvin was then the entertainment writer for his high school
newspaper—are a must for anyone looking for an insight into
the unguarded personality of Hank Williams. The story appeared in *Country Music* magazine a few years ago and is also

the main attraction of Shestack's biography of Hank in his *Encyclopedia*.

I won't quote the entire story here, but I will stop and dwell on that afternoon in the summer of 1948, partly because Shestack offers one of the best reviews of Hank Williams as a performer during that period, and also because his story contains one of the few extended conversations with Hank Williams reported anywhere. Ralph Gleason is just about the only other person who has captured for us such a conversation with Hank.

Shestack was qualified to make that judgment of Hank Williams the showman. He had seen enough performers in his role as an industrious, self-appointed, entertainment critic to know what was going on in the entertainment world in 1948. And Hank Williams, before Shestack even knew who he was, blew him away.

The scene was a fairgrounds tent set up in the middle of a field in upstate New York, with cars from "as far away as Pennsylvania and Canada" parked all around and "people of all ages, from toothless old grandfathers in faded engineer's caps to healthy kids in well-worn hand-me-downs and Momma-scissored haircuts." The folks had brought their lunches and sat out in the field for picnics before the show, and now they were crowded inside under the hot tent, having seen some of the opening acts:

> "Here's a boy you might be hearin' a lot about," the MC announced. "He was just signed on by the *Louisiana Hay-ride* and you can buy his recording of 'Move It On Over' on the M-G-M label. He's a boy who's gonna go far in our kind of music. Folks, let's give a great big upstate New York hand to that lonesome drifter from Alabama, Hank W-i-l-l-i-i-ams!"

Hank climbed onto the stage and passed out some sheet music to the house band, then turned and faced the audience. He was wearing a "Roy Rogers-style hat, white as snow" and a white suit with padded shoulders and butterflies embroidered on it. He acknowledged the mild applause from the folks and fiddled with the mike.

"My own boys couldn't make it this trip and we haven't had a chance to rehearse. I come here by bus and the roads ain't so good [trickle of laughter]. But I'd like to play you a number to start that I've written and am going to record. It's called 'Lovesick Blues.'"

From the very first crack of "sweet d-a-a-a-a-addy," the audience exploded. They stood on their chairs. They howled at "Howlin' at the Moon" and they screamed at "Why Don't You Love Me Like You Used To Do?" And I was screaming with them. THE MAN WAS GREAT. Nobody has ever successfully explained the quality that deserves the term "great." But whatever it is, Hank Williams had it. He was supposed to have twenty minutes on the program. The audience wouldn't let him go for almost an hour.

When Hank finally left the stage, young Shestack followed him to the screened-off corner of the tent that served as a dressing room. He explained to Williams that he was not merely an autograph-seeker but that he was an editor of his high school newspaper and that he'd like to interview Williams.

"Well, well," he said, looking at me. "How old are you?" I told him.

"Hell's bells," he said. "Writin' for a newspaper at that age. When I was your age I couldn't much write." He enjoyed his joke. He handed me his guitar while he opened his collar and took off his tie and jacket. He was wearing brown, clip-on suspenders and was sweating. His hair was already thinning.

"They sure are nice folks," he said, "that audience." He picked up a half-empty bottle of orange soda. "It's warm," he said. "Why don't you and me go get us a cold one?"

So the cub reporter and the country singer made their way around the fairgrounds, munching hot dogs (New York "white-hots") and drinking pop. As they walked, Hank asked about the local food and tried to joke with his interviewer, who was seriously and hurriedly taking notes.

Finally Hank suggested that Shestack put away his notebook and join him under a nearby tree to relax.

I asked him if he thought country music would sweep America. "I don't know what you mean by country music," he said. "I just make music the way I know how. Singin' songs comes natural to me the way some folks can argue law or make cabinets. It's all I know, it's all I care about."

Next Shestack asked where Williams got the ideas for his songs.

He smiled (he kept smiling—not a nervous smile, but a natural one) and said, "I don't know how to answer that. Sometimes I make 'em up. Other times they just come to me. And other times I listen to people and try to understand how they feel about things. Feelings about things. That's what songs should be about."

The young man and the younger man talked on, and a rapport began to grow. They spoke of the trials of growing up, and of parents and their hopes for their children; how parents had trouble understanding their kids, about Hank's hope that when he had kids, they'd turn out okay.

"What do you mean, 'okay'?" the boy asked Hank.
"Well, if I had a son," he said slowly, "I wouldn't mind if he growed up like you."

The boy shrugged that one off, embarrassed.
Hank talked on with his interviewer, about his growing up: the music he'd learned from black people ("That's real natural music"); about how he had his first Drifting Cowboys at fourteen ("A man has to know what he wants to do, and then do it and keep your mind on it, and don't let nothing else get in the way to clutter up your life"); and they discussed cars, America, people in general—how they seemed the same wherever Hank went—people's quirks, women (Shestack was embarrassed again), whiskey ("Don't you start drinkin' now, just because your friends do it"), and religion.

"Are you a God-fearin' boy?" he asked. It was a question I

didn't expect. "I really don't know how to answer that," I said. "I don't think much about fearing God."

"Well, boy," he offered deliberately. "Don't let it trouble you none. I ain't afraid of God, either."

At that point, the interview was cut short as the jamboree's M.C., anxious and exasperated, found Hank and warned him it was time for the next show. He couldn't believe Williams had disappeared for so long a time just to give a kid an interview.

"He ain't just some kid," Williams said. "We're buddies, aren't we, buddy?" I nodded.

The MC tried to pull Williams away. "Hey, you'll send me a copy of the interview when it's published, won't you?" Williams said to me. He quickly scratched his address and went off. "Next time, *you* buy the white-hots."

Melvin Shestack's teacher/editor wouldn't accept his story for the school newspaper, letting the boy know what she thought of "hillbilly singers" and assuring him that his fellow students at Monroe High would not be interested in his story.

So the ever-conscientious Shestack wrote a long letter to Hank, explaining how he'd not been able to deliver the publicity he'd promised.

Two months later, in an almost unintelligible scrawl, Hank Williams wrote me: "Don't sweat, buddy. The world's not yet lonesome for me."

Shestack tried to see Hank Williams once more, after a concert in Los Angeles in 1950, but the guards wouldn't let him through to the dressing room. Disappointed, Melvin Shestack wrote Hank another letter, telling of his bad luck and how nobody, including Melvin's girlfriend, would believe they knew each other. And not too long later, he received another post card from Hank. In an even wilder handwriting, all it said was: "Buddy, life gets tougher all the time."

This story may be the most revealing piece ever written on

Hank Williams. It's been said more than once that Hank either liked you or he didn't, and he must have liked young Melvin Shestack pretty well. He opened up to him in unusually cooperative fashion. No professional reporter could have gotten this story. Hank wouldn't have trusted him, or wouldn't have cared whether that person got a story or not. But something in the way this kid was writing out of love and respect for country music was irresistible to Hank.

What all does this afternoon interlude reveal?

First, it verifies that Hank Williams knocked audiences dead before they knew they were supposed to be knocked dead. He didn't need stardom to create charisma for him; he had it. In Ralph Gleason's words, "He had that *thing.*"

But the more provocative revelations here are more personal than professional. Here is a picture of a very human, very natural and, yes, vulnerable young Hank Williams. He's a long way from home, probably the farthest he'd been from the South since Portland four years earlier; he's alone with no band-buddies to hang around with, and so he seems to welcome the chance to relax and talk with this cleancut kid from a high school newspaper.

Although Hank is only twenty-five, the relationship between the two young men is as if Hank were much older. Hank himself seems to foster this feeling ("When I was your age . . .") and the awe of the younger man picks up the message. It figures. Hank's radio shows from a year or so later sound like those of a man in at least his mid-thirties. He projected that kind of maturity—as if he were already an old philosopher sittin' on his front porch—and of course it was out of this side of his personality that Hank gave birth to Luke the Drifter, the persona under whose name he would record all of his philosophical songs and recitations.

Hank warned Melvin not to start drinking just because his friends did. *Hank Williams did not encourage drinking.* He could have. He could have bragged about how much he drank, as many young men would have given the same situation. He could have treated it as just one more joy of adulthood that

Shestack had to look forward to, but he didn't. After all, it was no joy to him.

On God, Hank is again probably more frank with this interviewer than with many others. His words, "I ain't afraid of God," are ambiguous, to be sure. But in any case they are not the words of a man who wrote gospel songs talking about his faith to a music critic, telling him what he wants to hear about Momma's Bible, the Church in the Wildwood, the Old Rugged Cross. Yet on a Hayride Saturday night back in Shreveport, Hank would ask that the house lights be lowered while he sang his gospel songs, and he would give these songs a special introduction: something like, "I want you folks to listen to this next song real close." His favorites were what he called the "old shout tunes," "I'll Have a New Body, I'll Have A New Life" and "Where the Soul of Man Never Dies." Hank would get all the boys in his band and sometimes the whole cast to help him out on these special songs.

A new and broader-ranged circuit had been established. Hank and the Drifting Cowboys spent more time than ever in cars, crossing and recrossing the mid-South in big bulgy sedans that flew eighty and ninety miles an hour across the flat lowland highways. Hank had to buy a trailer, but that didn't slow his drivers down, even though the speed limit with a trailer was 35 mph. It wasn't long before Hank bought his first really nice touring car, a blue-black 1949 Packard. He must have felt pretty good—the old-Chevy veteran from Montgomery— watching that big Packard bird on the nose of the car's hood as it ate up the center line of the highways. Things were beginning to click.

7

The Beginnings of Genius

"A man has to know what he wants to do, and then do it and keep your mind on it, and don't let nothing else get in the way to clutter up your life," Hank Williams told young Melvin Shestack.

He practiced what he preached. Except for the tough war years of '42–'44, Hank Williams made a concentrated effort all his life to be the best country performer he could be. From the beginning, he wrote songs. He was even writing things before "WPA Blues." In grade school he came up with a ditty, part of which has remained, that goes like this:

> I had an old goat,
>   she ate tin cans.
> When the little goats came,
>   they were Ford sedans.

But as Hank was getting started, writing songs was just part of performing them. He probably would have resented being called a "poet" as a schoolboy. Hank never knew much about nor cared much about the English language as portrayed in books. Later in life, people would hear Hank say that something was "written like Shakespeare" when he thought it was haughty or too wordy.

Still he made up songs. All the time. He'd write down some words and plunk around on the guitar till he came up with a melody that seemed to fit. Then he had another song to sing. He

85

didn't think of his words as messages; they were lyrics. They were the hooks to hang the song on. They had to be true, of course; they had to be what he really felt, but didn't everybody write that way?

He wrote songs, rewrote them, changed them around. M. C. Jarrett claims that "Move It On Over" was originally the same melody built around the refrain, "That's Your Red Wagon, Just Keep Movin' It Along." The point is, young Hank Williams wasn't trying to be a *literary person,* he had no dreams of an apartment in the Village or of winning a Pulitzer Prize. How can you dream about what you don't even know exists? He was just a country singer who wrote most of his own songs.

The first songs were mostly throwaways. Many times it is the melody, not the lyric, that lifts them above mediocrity. The best of them, "Six More Miles," "Calling You," "My Love For You Has Turned To Hate," offer little in the way of really inventive lyrics or original thoughts. The one possible exception is the inspirational number, "When God Comes and Gathers His Jewels." This is, after all, a metaphor in which faithful Christians (including a mourning boy's dead mother) are compared to "jewels" which God will come and gather someday.

Hank was too busy to think about poetry. If it came, it came. Meanwhile he had shows to book, band members to hire and fire, club owners to talk to, musical arrangements to work out, and a wife to feed and fight with. Whenever he wasn't singing, he was scrambling.

But now Hank had reached his mid-twenties. He had begun to see some results from all his efforts over the years. KWKH was doing his booking. He'd made some records. He had less to worry about, but still a lot of free time in which to think and write songs, especially on the road.

"Sometimes I make 'em up," he told Shestack. "Other times they just come to me. And other times I listen to people and try to understand how they feel about things."

Like most everything else in Hank Williams' life, it was simple. Sometimes you tried to write songs, sometimes you tried to catch things that seemed to be playing through your brain, and in the meantime you kept your ears open to other people. It is unlikely that Ernest Hemingway or Robert Frost would have argued with his regimen.

As the man matured, as his horizons grew wider and his nightly environment not quite so frenetic, the deeper soul of Hank Williams began to surface in his songs. Several of Hank Williams' real classics were written before he left the Louisiana Hayride—among them "Honky-Tonkin'," "I Saw the Light," and "I'm So Lonesome I Could Cry."

"Mansion on the Hill," one of Hank's mini-hits between "Move It On Over" and "Lovesick Blues," is significant because it establishes a genre of country song, the message from the jilted poor boy to the girl who has opted for riches instead of the poor boy's love. This sentiment has been kept going by various country songwriters down through the years and was the theme of the Eagles' 1975 country/pop hit, "Lyin' Eyes."

Several songs of Hank's pre-Opry years grew right out of his experience with Audrey. They announce a recurring theme in Hank's songs—that of the frustrated mate who just can't seem to get along with his wife. "There'll Be No Teardrops Tonight" falls into this category, but the most lucid early expositions of the theme are found in "You're Gonna Change or I'm Gonna Leave" and "I Just Don't Like This Kind of Livin'."

Also in these years, Hank wrote his definitive statement to the public about his marriage. "Mind Your Own Business" is a defense of a husband and wife's right to squabble. Hank warns the listener to mind his own business 'cause he and Audrey have a "license to fight." With this song, Hank borrows a trick from Jimmie Rodgers. He hangs the words on essentially the same melody and structure that "Move It On Over" was built on. No copyright problem here—he'd never sue himself.

These are most of the important songs of this period, but three others—the most enduring—warrant a closer look.

"Lost Highway" is not a monster BMI money-maker like "I Saw The Light" or "I'm So Lonesome I Could Cry," but it deserves special attention for several reasons. To begin with, "Lost Highway" is one of the best examples of how Hank Williams fused black blues and white country music. The song is a straightforward, humble lament of a man who has taken the "lost highway" of sin and is warning the boys he knows not to follow him down that road. Hank uses the blues form to carry this song, choosing the darker and moodier Emaj9 and Amaj9 chords to carry the body of the song, instead of his usual bight open G, C, and D chords. To these chords he adds a recurring blues riff at the beginning of the song and between verses, played in funky harmony by the lead guitar and steel.

The lyric, too, is the Blues. The directness of it, the terseness of it could have sprung out of the old field laments Hank had heard from Big Day and Tee-tot. The entire song is built out of four-word sentences tied in a string, yet somehow it is eloquent.

Hank didn't write "Lost Highway." It was written by a young contemporary of his named Leon Payne. Nevertheless, it is a summation of Hank's feelings about life, just as much as if he'd written every syllable himself. The song, briefly, is a tale of how the singer became a rolling stone, lost and alone. He's sinned and now he's paying for it.

Payne's lyrics recount how this boy started out in life no worse than the next person, but somehow along the way went astray and wound up on the Lost Highway. Hank adds to the words a blazing urgency as he sings in his most forceful style. Clearly he means what he's singing, even if the words aren't originally his own.

Finally comes a warning to the boys not to start down the road of sin, or they'll find sorrow and heartbreak and the sad lonely feeling of walking the Lost Highway with no hope of getting back to normal life.

If we start down that road, we're warned, we'll eventually curse the day we chose to do so.

Well. If Hank (or Leon Payne) chose to "live fast, love hard, die young and leave a beautiful memory" just because life was more fun that way, he sure didn't express it here. Of course, it could be argued that Hank was merely mouthing Leon Payne's words with no particular personal application, but like the power of "Men With Broken Hearts" the dynamic of this song is in the way Hank Williams makes us believe it. It would be impossible for him to be so convincing if he did not also believe what he was singing.

"Don't think I'm unaware of my problems," Hank seems to be saying to the public, while at the same time warning potential lost highwaymen that one of the things they'll have to put up with is a reputation for being what they are.

"Lost Highway," like Hank's own songs, is really no mystery at all. Hank wanted to be understood. He was not, after all, a Bob Dylan.

"I Saw The Light" is the greatest of Hank Williams' gospel songs and perhaps the greatest gospel song in modern country music. It has become one of those obligatory tunes, one that invariably gets chosen when a producer is looking for a rousing, use-the-whole-cast number to top off a TV special or a multi-star benefit concert.

There are a couple of stories on the origin of "I Saw The Light," both of them actually variations on the same story. Roger Williams' version places Hank and the Drifting Cowboys on the way back to Montgomery after a show date somewhere out in the country. Lillian was also in the car. As they approached Montgomery, Lilly saw the airport lights, realized they were almost home, and exclaimed, "Thank God! I saw the lights!"

Then Hank awoke with a start, asking "What did you say, Momma?" Whereupon she repeated her words and Hank sat back to think them over. By the time they reached the boardinghouse, according to Roger Williams, Hank was already on his way to writing a classic song.

However, M. C. Jarrett, Hank's part-time steel player in Montgomery, tells it this way:

"Hank told me the story of 'I Saw the Light,'" says Jarrett. "The Williamses had an old 1938 Shivvalay and they were goin' up somewhere around Rockford, Alabama, where Hank's grandmother lived.

"It was a long drive," M. C. continues, "and it was just ol' dirt roads. You couldn't drive more'n twenty or twenty-five miles an hour. Finally Hank seen a lamp in a window and said, 'I see the light!' Mrs. Williams and Irene were in the car . . . I don't know who else.

"The song has a definite meanin'," says Jarrett, "but the original meaning was, 'I see the light . . . Grandma's house . : . we're home.'"

Whichever story you choose, the conclusion is that the song originated with a catchy phrase, not a spiritual experience. It may or may not refer back to an authentic experience of "seeing the light," but Hank did not write it as a direct result of such an experience.

Nevertheless there is a genius here: the ability to recognize a phrase that could become an unforgettable refrain for a song, then to work on that phrase, get it into a proper context, and build a song around it. Hank was doing instinctively what the Tin-Pan-Alley boys had been teaching each other for years in more sophisticated surroundings. He taught himself the art of creating an entire song from one good "hook line."

In many ways, "I Saw The Light" is nothing special. The words are fairly standard gospel material, describing a dramatic change in the singer's life from wandering in sin, trading the wrong for the right, and getting right with Jesus. But again, Hank is able to string the sparse little sentences and phrases into a whole bigger than its parts.

The song also benefits from one of those patented, simple, timeless, Hank Williams melodies. So many of them have that quality of déjà vu, as if someone somewhere has been singing them for centuries and Hank just happened to overhear and pass the thing on down to us. For that reason if for no other, the song deserves its success.

Finally, there is "I'm So Lonesome I Could Cry." Though in many ways Hank's songwriting talents still had some maturing to do, this song, recorded in 1949 when he was not yet twenty-six years old, may be his greatest poetic contribution. Originally intended for recitation, presumably as one of the earliest Luke the Drifter recordings, Hank got down to the point of putting the song on lacquer before deciding it should be sung, not talked. Among other things, his choice meant that a young singer named B. J. Thomas would get his break with Hank's song when he recorded it and sold a few million copies of it in 1965.

The mood of the song, in literary terms, is almost transcendental, mixing as it does the inner pangs of the heart with images of the natural world in flashes of swift imagination.

It is a very sad song. One line in particular stands out as a foreboding signal of Hank's fate; the one about the robin who weeps when leaves "begin to die." That means, says Hank, the robin has lost his will to live, and Hank, identifying with the bird, repeats, "I'm So Lonesome I Could Cry."

If any of Hank's songs can unquestionably be called diamonds that were squeezed out of his soul under the weight of tremendous pressure, this must be the one. It is a song of straightforwardly-admitted pain, but it holds no self-pity. Hank does not draw our attention so much to himself, but to the reflections in the world and universe of the things he is feeling. The purple sky, the falling star, the dying leaves, the whippoor-will, all tell us far more eloquently than any amount of thought-description just exactly how it hurt for Hank Williams.

What we really don't know, of course, is exactly why.

The question comes to mind: Did God intend some of us to suffer more deeply in order that they might express the feelings all of us have and help us out of our own torture pits? Or was Hank Williams a man beset with problems like any other man and simply unable or unwilling to deal with them? As his pain becomes self-destructive, the question must haunt any narra-tive of Hank's life, "Who is guilty?" Is it God or fate for dealing him too heavy a blow? Is it the friends and family who could not or would not help him? Or is it Hank himself, proven in his innermost soul to be a sensitive yet ultimately irresponsible lightning rod of poetic and musical talent?

In any event, Hank Williams, in the years of 1947 to 1949, began to emerge from the Acuff-imitative mold, out of the more-rhymes-with-o'er lyricism, out of the standard ballad/gospel/juke tune cycle of his earlier songs, and into a true lyricist and composer.

There will still be some standard ballads, he will still write blues tunes without seeming even to have to think about them, but these have been joined now by a new kind of work. It is the Art of Pain.

It's almost as if one night Edgar Allan Poe had delivered by cosmic mail his invisible mantle of pain's dark hidden wisdom to some iron bridge down on some back-country creek between Montgomery and Shreveport. And at midnight when Hank's Packard came brooding its straighteight engine across the narrow bridge, having to check its speed, a demon came from

Nowhere, sweeping the wispy cloak through an open window and over the sleeping form in the big car's rear seat. And if this would have been so, the very frame of the sturdy Packard would have groaned, and the fender skirts sunk three inches with the weight.

8

"Lovesick Blues" and The Grand Ole Opry

In the spring of 1949, Hank Williams is rapidly approaching stardom. He has come a long way as an artist since leaving Montgomery, has seen how a professional country act should be done, and learned with the Drifting Cowboys how to put on such a show. Roger Williams elaborates:

A typical show went like this. The Drifting Cowboys, minus Hank, would open with a couple of instrumental numbers. Then the emcee, Bob McNett after he joined the band, would introduce Hank with appropriate fanfare. Hank would come on, sing a song without saying anything, then introduce each of the band members. He always got some humor into his introductions, and the boys in the band led the audience in yukking it up over his jokes. One of his favorites, which he used in introducing McNett, a farm boy from northeastern Pennsylvania, was to tell how "We had to roll peanuts off the mountain to get him to go with us."

By this time, Hank's program of his original songs, ballads like "Wedding Bells," and his gospel numbers was enough to turn on any country music audience. He and the boys bounced and fiddled and picked their way along skillfully and heartily, playing arrangements that had come into being through sheer repetition and instinct. If a song had been recorded by the group, then the licks on the record became the "official" arrangement of the number.

93

Hank, though he still couldn't read a note of music, kept a close ear to the band. He knew in his head what he wanted to hear on each song, right down to individual riffs.

"I was pretty green when I started with the Drifting Cowboys," says Bob McNett, "and I think Hank kinda let me off easy sometimes because I was so new, but he always spoke his mind about what he wanted from the band. I played simple, and he wanted the music pretty simple, so I happened to fit."

Bob McNett was a farm boy from rural Pennsylvania who joined Hank's Shreveport group in January or February of 1949. He may have been green, but fiddler Jerry Rivers says McNett played the most commercial country guitar Rivers had ever heard.

"When I first joined the Drifting Cowboys playing out of Shreveport," says McNett, "life was easier than it was going to be later on for Hank. We all traveled together in the car and got to know one another. There wasn't so much pressure, and Hank would horse around just like one of the boys."

Hank was a good man to work for, in Bob McNett's eyes. "Sure, there were times when he was very abrupt," he says, "but that was Hank. He spoke his mind. I got to know him well, and I liked him."

When McNett joined Hank Williams in Shreveport, one of the first things he noticed was a particular song Hank was doing around Louisiana and East Texas. It wasn't just the song that struck McNett; it was the crowd reaction. Hank would sing the thing and the audiences would go crazy. Sometimes they wouldn't let Williams off the stage.

At the time, both song and singer were new to Bob McNett, but he was soon to see the significance of both. The combination of Hank Williams' singing talent and a catchy, funky, little tune called "Lovesick Blues" was about to cause an explosion in country music.

"You knew 'Lovesick Blues' was an old song, didn't you?" Nick Tosches asks me. Nick, then a Nashville-based country music writer, has agreed to share some of his knowledge with me at the suggestion of my editor. We're sitting in Nick's apartment after a lunch at one of Nashville's bustling bars not too far from Music Row.

The apartment is a dead giveaway to Tosches' hobby, which is collecting memorabilia—records, tapes, magazines, sheet music—from the country and pop music industries of the twentieth century in America. One whole wall of his living room is nothing but albums, and vintage 78 rpm records fill a bookcase in the hall.

"Yeah, it was an old vaudeville tune or something, right?" I answer, trying to sound like an authority.

"Right," says Tosches. "It was written in New York by Irving Mills and Cliff Friend and first copyrighted on April 3, 1922." He looks up from his notes.

"Would you like to hear the first recording of it?" he asks.

"Are you kidding?"

Tosches disappears into another room and returns with a tape.

"This recording was made on the Okeh label by Emmet Miller," he says as he threads the tape onto his deck, "on September 1, 1925."

He rolls the tape and I hear a needle drop onto an ancient disc and begin its scratchy trip. After a trumpet-clarinet introduction, the song begins. Only it's not the song yet; it's a dialogue:

"I got de blooooooes," a male voice moans.

"What kinda blues?" his partner asks.

"I got de lovesick blooooooes."

And so on, until finally Emmet Miller just can't explain his blues anymore without singing how he's got a feelin' called the blues since his momma said good-bye.

Blackface patter I hadn't expected. Nick knows it and smiles across the table at me. We listen through the song and he stops the tape.

"Emmet Miller recorded the song twice," he says, "the second time was in 1928, again on Okeh."

The second Miller recording was a minor hit, says Tosches. But it wasn't these early recordings that Hank learned the song from.

"It was Rex Griffin's version of the song that Hank heard and

liked," Nick tells me. "You wanna hear it too, don't you?" This
time I hear a yodeling, pop-cowboy sounding singer and a
simple guitar arrangement of the slick, bluesy chord progression that "Lovesick Blues" is built on.

"That's Rex Griffin," Nick says. "He recorded his version in
1939 for Decca. It wasn't a particularly big hit. Nobody knows
for sure how Hank happened to hear the song or why he
thought he should do it. . . ."

Tosches smiles again. "But it was a pretty good idea."

Hank put the song into his act in late 1948 or early '49 and
began to make it his own; perhaps he thought it was in the
public domain. (One wonders if Melvin Shestack's memory is
correct when he says Hank told that upstate New York
audience that he had written the song.) With Hank's lonesome
yodeling ability to put the song across, it soon began to get a
tremendous response from the crowds he sang to.

Hungry for a hit after a year-and-a-half dry spell, Hank told
Fred Rose he wanted to record "Lovesick Blues." Concerning
Rose's reaction to that idea, stories differ. Ed Linn's research
for his story, "The Short Life of Hank Williams," led him to
believe Rose opposed cutting the tune on record:

> For two years, Rose had been telling him to forget about
> "Lovesick Blues." When he finally did let him record it, it was
> only because they needed a number to fill out a recording
> session. Even then, he thought so little of the song that he
> didn't bother to stay in the studio to supervise the recording.
> Hank and the band did it in one take. . . .

Wesley Rose, however, maintains that his father personally
set up and supervised the recording of "Lovesick Blues" after
Wesley had made a trip to Shreveport to hear Hank do the
song.

"Hank had been getting a good response from the song, and
thought it should be recorded. We set up a session in Cincinnati
specifically to record 'Lovesick Blues,'" says Wesley.

In any case, the song was recorded in Cincinnati very early in
1949, and the finished master sent to M-G-M in New York for

distribution. What followed has seldom been matched in the country music industry.

"Lovesick Blues," sung by an almost-unknown singer named Hank Williams, took off for the top of the country charts and stayed there for most of 1949. At the end of the year, it was voted "Best Hillbilly Record" in the *Cash Box* poll of jukebox operators. "Lovesick Blues" was also number one on the 1949 *Billboard* chart of Country and Western records, and its success brought two more of Hank's records onto the same chart. "Wedding Bells" came in at number five and "Mind Your Own Business" at number twenty-eight.

Also at the end of that momentous year, Hank Williams was selected by *Billboard* for the number-two slot in its listing of the "Year's Top-Selling Folk Artist" (right behind Eddy Arnold).

It's only slightly ironic that the song that would make Hank Williams famous and become his trademark throughout his years of performing was someone else's song; because, as Roger Williams has noted, he couldn't have written a song better suited to his own singing talent.

Though its chord progression is more complicated than most country songs and more sophisticated than the songs Hank wrote, the melody line and yodeling breaks are the perfect vehicle for Hank to display his ability to "moan the blues."

That born performer's ability to milk a song for all it's worth seems to sweat from the grooves of Hank's recording. The painful-sounding crack or "tear" in his voice as he switches from low to high falsetto register will become a hallmark of his career and a much-imitated device in the industry. Hank moved through the tricky phrasing and unusual melody with the ease of a meadowlark riding a gust of wind; and, as usual, he kept the tempo of the entire number at just the right speed. The result was one of the classic recording performances in all of modern popular music.

In concert, Hank began to sing the song at the end of every show, and sometimes at the beginning and middle of the show as well. A salesman since his days of hawking peanuts, he knew that you can't oversell a product that's truly in demand.

Hank Williams became "the main topic of conversation" in the country music industry, according to Jerry Rivers, who at the time "Lovesick Blues" hit was kicking himself for not accepting two earlier job offers from Hank. The record was so big that it seemed it would be impossible to keep Hank Williams off the Grand Ole Opry now.

Just as it was becoming apparent that "Lovesick Blues" was going to be a smash hit, Hank Williams was presented with another cause for excitement. On May 26, 1949, Audrey bore him a son in Shreveport: Randall Hank Williams. "Hank Junior" quickly became the object of more tender affection from Hank, Sr., than any other person or object had ever been or ever would be.

Born, as he was, at the very threshold of his father's stardom, Hank Junior spent most of his first year and a half of life in a house with a positive mood. His father soon dubbed him "Bocephus," after a comic character on the radio. The name stuck, and it still appears on most of Hank, Jr.'s, publicity materials.

Becoming a family man was the one thing that might have rescued Hank Williams from oblivion. Through the tangible joy of looking at his baby son, Hank may have gotten a glimmer of what things are truly important in life. Too much else was happening, though, and the old lifestyle had already patterned Hank's behavior. There was the drinking, which had abated but which still hung over his life like a thundercloud unleashing occasional tempests. And the Road was there, the almighty Road which left wife, stepdaughter, and son far away while the crowds, the adulation, and the willing women came so, so close. Finally, the pace—when was there time for reflection? When was there time to think about settling down when he was working so hard to climb up? The pace that had been a part of Hank Williams' soul since he first auditioned for WSFA kept nudging Hank farther down the line to a bitter trade-off with providence. He would master the pace in order to get what he so desperately wanted, but in the end the pace would be his master.

Hank's overall response to his impending success was not, like so many things in his life, simple. "Hank was enthusiastic in Shreveport," says McNett, "and felt as though all of a sudden something was happening—especially after "Lovesick Blues" started selling records."

But as "Lovesick Blues" continued to climb the charts, there was more than gee-whiz excitement going on in Hank's mind.

"The week that 'Lovesick Blues' hit number one on the *Billboard* charts," relates McNett, "Hank was very anxious to get a copy of *Billboard* and see where the song was. We were headed out of Shreveport that day for a string of road shows, and we picked up a copy on the way out of town. Hank got in the car, found the charts as he'd been doing every week, and saw there in black and white that "Lovesick Blues" was the number one country song in America."

Williams seemed hardly to react at all.

"He put the magazine down on the car seat and stared out the window," says McNett, "and didn't say a word for two hundred miles."

Bob McNett feels Hank was awed by what was happening. "I think he was a little frightened. He kept the whole thing to himself and never got enthused with the rest of us. It's as if he was thinking, 'What's going to happen? What will people expect of me? Will I measure up to their expectations?'"

Hank's reaction to stardom and to fatherhood may have been alike: a natural satisfaction and anticipation tempered darkly with the worry that he would not be able to live up to the part being written for him in the script.

Hank's already-stormy marriage, his bent toward instability, and his drinking problems were all known to the management of WSM in Nashville. They had heard glowing reports of Hank Williams for several years from Opry headliners who had been overshadowed when they played Montgomery; they had talked with WSFA management and obtained a realistic estimate of Hank's professionalism, and had helped him to get the job on the Louisiana Hayride.

Harry Stone and Jim Denny now had a real-live dilemma on their hands. Instead of Hank Williams the talented unknown, they were faced with Hank Williams, singer of the hottest record in the country music industry.

Negotiations between Acuff-Rose and WSM officials began as "Lovesick Blues" started its climb up the charts. When the song reached number one, "the Opry people were convinced," according to Wesley Rose. Still the Grand Ole Opry was not ready to bring Hank Williams up into its fold of regulars just yet. Not only was he a risk in terms of irresponsibility, but what would he do to the show's clean fun family image?

A compromise was arranged: Through the strings pulled by WSM manager Harry Stone, who couldn't see that Hank had any worse a drinking problem than many other country entertainers, a guest shot on the Opry was set up for June 11, 1949.

What happened that night can only be compared to events since; no previous entertainment debut in the South, and few in the country, could match it.

It was one of those crazy instances where a song had become a tidal-wave hit and hardly anyone knew who was singing it. Hank Williams was remembered by a few folks for "Move It On Over," but even to them he was a mere voice without face or body. All of that was about to change.

Actually it had already begun to change. There are a couple of clues that lead one to believe that the Opry had really decided on Hank before his Nashville debut. The most obvious clue is that Hank broke up his Hayride band in *mid-May* of '49. The break-up of the unit is reported in the May 21 issue of *Billboard*. There is no reason to think he would have broken up that unit unless it was in anticipation of something else that he'd been promised or that he thought was in the bag.

Bob McNett remembers the night Hank fired the old group.

"Hank came offstage quickly after a Louisiana Hayride appearance," reports McNett, "and said, 'I'm going to Texas tomorrow. If I call you, you have a job. If I don't, you don't.'"

McNett went back to the hotel room he shared with Lum York and Sammy Barnhart. There was no call the next day. McNett, rather angry, went to Hot Springs, Arkansas, then to Pine Bluffs, and then back home to Pennsylvania. It was a busy time of year on his folks' farm, and he knew he was needed there, if nowhere else. Lum York, also discouraged, went back to Montgomery.

"I didn't know of any Hayride shows scheduled for Texas that week," says McNett. "It's my guess that Hank was doing a single act with an Opry package show." He may have worked as a single several times with Opry shows before he officially left KWKH.

Saturday night, June 11, 1949, was a hot night in Nashville. The old Ryman Auditorium was packed out of its 3,400 seats and enthusiastic country music fans were standing in the aisles at the rear of the big room. Through the open windows of the old church building, cars could be heard honking on the Nashville streets between songs as the Grand Ole Opry chugged into its twenty-fourth year on the air.

Backstage it was the usual circus. The Opry has always been a casual affair, with performers, stagehands, musicians and "guests" milling around its wings; and the Ryman had these crazy narrow hallways that led out from the dressing rooms. Sometimes mere navigation backstage was difficult.

Hank Williams had broken up his Shreveport band back in May. He knew that the Opry was a good possibility, but he still had to prove himself to the audience here in the old Ryman. He waited through the thirty-minute segments of the first shows, nervously wondering if the house band would be able to keep pace with him.

Then, suddenly it seemed, he was on. Red Foley was introducing him to the crowd, and he made his long legs carry him out onto the stage and into the bright light that flooded the other musicians. He steeled himself and thought only of this moment and of selling the song he had come to sing. The house band struck up the familiar introduction. Hank Williams planted his boots about two feet apart, leaned into the mike and moaned the first yodeling line of the old song.

The audience reaction was instantaneous. Not many of them had been sure who this lanky kid with the white cowboy hat was, but now they knew. He was that ol' boy who sang that "Lovesick Blues!" A cheer went up that was deafening, and it was none too quick in dying away. The audience rose to their feet between the pews, clapping for Hank.

Hank Williams drank it all in like a healthy chug of pure adrenalin. He bore down now on the audience, rollicking and buckling his knees as he sang and yodeled through the song. His eyes kept the front rows riveted down while his body bounced and the thin mouth turned slightly and naturally upward at both ends; they wouldn't forget him.

When the song was over, it wasn't over. The big crowd wouldn't let Hank Williams off the stage. The South was rising again! They whooped and hollered and clapped and stomped until Hank had performed an unprecedented six encores to "Lovesick Blues." Hank, flooded with emotion and excitement, was only too happy to give them all they wanted.

Finally Red Foley stepped in and said a few words to quiet the audience while Hank walked offstage, and the magic slowly receded. Hank Williams had paid for the right to perform on the Grand Ole Opry stage, and everyone knew it.

The fans knew it best, and the WSM people knew that the fans knew it best. So there really wasn't anything left to do except sign the papers. Hank Williams had bought that stage, and he still owns it today.

Hank became a Grand Ole Opry cast member. It had finally happened, and now he was going to be almost too busy to savor it. Having never been a sit-around-the-house type husband, the Opry road trips were going to keep Hank away from his family more than ever. Meanwhile Audrey, who had been a part of the act in Montgomery, had faded somewhat into the background while Hank starred on the Louisiana Hayride; and then she'd been pregnant and was kept home with an infant son. There were indications that she was not entirely happy with Hank's success. But overall, the security of having made it to the Opry was worth everything else. Besides, Hank had probably promised her a spot on a radio show as soon as he could swing it.

Hank's move to Nashville required more professional attention than personal arrangements. Hank and Audrey didn't have much to move, though their scraping days were over, according to Fred Rose. He'd told Hank that "Lovesick Blues" was making enough money so that Hank would be able to build a new home in Nashville.

But more pressing than the house or the settling in was the need for a new band. In those days, any personality of any importance on the Opry had a band of his own; and Hank was damned if he was not going to have the best group of Drifting Cowboys he could put together.

The first two people he went looking for were Don Helms, the Drifting Cowboy from Montgomery days, and Bob McNett. Helms, remembering what Hank had made him promise over a year earlier, promptly took the necessary steps to join Hank in Nashville.

McNett was a little harder to find.

"I was on the farm in Pennsylvania," says McNett, "and it sounds funny now, but we didn't have a phone."

A friend of McNett's, Ken Blevins (whose stage name was Ken Montana and who was Patsy Montana's brother) drove thirty miles to tell McNett that Hank Williams had called him and that Hank wanted McNett to call him in Nashville. Bob promptly drove to Canton, Pennsylvania, ten miles from the farm, and called Hank.

Nothing was said about what had happened in Shreveport.

"I'm reforming the group in Nashville," Williams told McNett. "Do you want to join me?" Evidently, Bob had had enough farming for one summer. He was on a bus to Nashville the next morning.

To play bass, Hank wanted someone with more polish than his old Montgomery pal Lum York. He found a twenty-one-year-old Nashville musician named Hillous Butrum, who had been playing on the Opry since he was sixteen. Butrum was working with blackface comedians Jamup and Honey on the last tent show out of Nashville when Jerry Rivers called him. Fiddler Rivers had already been hired by Hank a couple of days earlier.

Jerry Rivers had known who Hank was since early 1948, and Williams had offered him a job with his Hayride group. But Rivers had opted to stay in Nashville; all his nineteen-year-old energies were aimed at the Opry.

One night in July of 1949 Rivers was working on Big Jeff's WLAC radio show, which served as an apprenticeship/bread line for many young Nashville musicians in those days. A friend of Rivers named Jack Boles made a point of telling Jerry that Hank Williams needed a fiddler for his new band. Rivers hightailed it over to the WSM studios immediately.

"I saw Hank Williams for the first time sitting on a stool at WSM radio studios," Rivers has written in *Hank Williams:*

From Life to Legend, "while Clifford [the black WSM porter] shined his sharp-toed boots."

"Hank was tall and very thin," Rivers recalls, "only 25 at the time but unusually mature, his black hair already quite thin under his white, broad-brimmed hat." Rivers told Hank he was interested in the fiddling job. When the shoeshine was done, Hank led Rivers and his friend Boles down the hall to an empty studio.

Hank was evidently relishing the moment. Here was this uppity nineteen-year-old who'd been too Opry-happy to come to Shreveport. When Jerry opened his fiddle case, Hank grabbed the instrument and whipped off the old hoedown tune, "Sally Good'n" while Boles played guitar. It was rough but the rhythm was right. Then Hank turned to Rivers.

"Can you play 'Sally Good'n,' boy?" he asked.

Rivers, who knew the tune backwards, played it forwards with all the gusto he could call up; again Boles provided accompaniment.

"When we hit the last note," Jerry remembers, "Hank said, 'Anybody who can play 'Sally Good'n' better than I can is a darn good fiddler. You're hired.'"

But starting when? It was a Friday night. Williams told Rivers that all the other boys were ready and that Don Helms would be in from Alabama the next day.

"We'll work the Opry tomorrow night and leave right after the Opry for a tour up through Ohio," Williams explained. "So why not start right now?"

"That Friday evening in July of 1949," writes Rivers, "I suddenly found myself in a peculiar position. In ten minutes I had changed from the category of a local square dance and schoolhouse musician to the fiddler for Hank Williams, currently America's number one Country Music record seller."

The next day Hank worked hard all day with his new band. Rivers had to get a union card to play on the Opry. And they all needed uniforms, so that had to be taken care of. Don Helms had to be met as he got in from Montgomery. Sometime during the day, there had to be time for rehearsal, too.

When they reached the Ryman that night, all but Butrum

were new to the Opry and therefore were in various stages of acute awe. But they felt ready. They had on their cowboy-style uniforms and white hats and—what the heck—they'd all played to some audiences before. They walked onstage with Hank Williams that night and were comforted further by the good familiar sound of a throbbing ovation.

What happened was almost a replay of the previous week's show. When Hank finished singing "Lovesick Blues," the audience demonstrated a profound conviction that he should stay onstage all night.

"I believe the roaring applause continued for at least five minutes after we finally returned to the dressing room," recalls Rivers.

After the show, Hank and the boys rolled out of Nashville in the Packard, ready for their first road show as stars of the Grand Ole Opry.

The Grand Ole Opry's growth in popularity, if charted on a graph, would be reaching toward its first peak at just about the time Hank Williams joined it. Later, the mid- and late-fifties would see, if not an outright decline, then at least a sluggish plateau.

Several changes would happen to the music industry, most notably rock 'n roll. Of course the Opry would begin to thrive again in the sixties and move into the seventies by announcing Opryland and the new Opry House that went with it.

Back in 1949 no one was visualizing two-hundred acre theme parks and a $15 million Opry House, but a more fundamental dream had been fulfilled. The Grand Ole Opry had become, after two decades or so of competition, far and away the biggest entertainment institution in country music. It had not been easy. The National Barn Dance on WLS in Chicago was an older show, and for many years enjoyed a more prestigious reputation. The WWVA jamboree in Wheeling, West Virginia, the Big D Jamboree in Dallas, and the Renfro Valley Gang up in Renfro Valley, Kentucky, had also vied with the "Grand Ole Uproar" for leadership in presenting live country music to the radio audience.

The Grand Ole Opry, the oldest continuous-running radio show in America, was born in 1925, as any country fan will tell you. Its originator was an Indiana-born ex-newspaperman named George D. Hay. He picked up the name "The Solemn Old Judge" while doing a police-beat radio show in Memphis, then went to Chicago where he helped the WLS barn dance to get off the ground.

No sooner was that task begun, but that Hay was contacted by a new station in Nashville, WSM ("We Shield Millions"), which was owned and operated by the National Life and Casualty Company. WSM was experimenting with the relatively new idea of putting hillbilly music—real up-the-holler-behind-the-ridge mountain music—on the radio. They wanted George D. Hay to announce their show. He brought with him to the show his nickname and an old Mississippi riverboat whistle that he'd blow at opportune times throughout a broadcast.

The most-accepted birthday of the Opry seems to have been Saturday night, November 18, 1925. On that night Hay took Uncle Jimmy Thompson, an eighty-year-old "champion" fiddle player, on the air with him and announced that Uncle Jimmy, accompanied by his niece on the piano, would be playing some old time tunes and that requests were welcome. Almost immediately the telegrams began arriving at WSM, and the WSM barn dance was off and running.

One Saturday night a couple of years later, after the barn dance was already attracting legions of locals, both musicians and spectators, George Hay casually dropped the line that would hang a name on America's best-loved country music show.

Coming, as it did, on the heels of the NBC network Music Appreciation Hour, the barn dance always created a minor cultural earthquake when it hit the airwaves. Those not ready for the changeover could be blown right out of their rocking chairs, knitting and all. On this particular night, it was black harmonicist DeFord Bailey who drew the lot of kicking off the barn dance. The Music Appreciation Hour signed off, Judge Hay signed on with a few choice transitional words, and Bailey took off on an old train tune called the "Pan American Blues."

After Bailey finished, Hay pronounced twenty-six words that would ring through the history of broadcasting: "For the past hour, we have been listening to music taken largely from Grand Opera," he intoned, "but from now on, we will present the *Grand Ole Opry*."

David Stone, announcer on the Opry from 1929 to 1940, reminisces about the years that followed:

"The groups came in from all over central Tennessee," he says. "There was Dr. Humphrey Bate and his Possum Hunters, who were the first group to perform on the Opry, the Crook brothers, and then old Uncle Dave Macon, who would become the Opry's first star performer."

It was a long way from today's production, according to Stone. "Nobody was paid much," he says. "Maybe five dollars or so changed hands now and then. They did it for the glory of it."

Stone's choice of words is not overstatement. George Hay himself was something of a romanticist, especially when it came to country music. He wanted to keep the Opry "homey" for the "home folks," the little people who "do the work of the world." "They win the wars and raise the families," Hay said years later. "Many of our geniuses come from simple folks who adhere to the fundamental principles of honesty included in the Ten Commandments." Hay said the Opry "expresses those qualities which come from these good people."

The "glory" that David Stone spoke of had another equally fundamental side to it in addition to the "good qualities" that George Hay wanted the Opry always to reflect. These people were preserving the traditional music that they had received from their ancestors. Some of the Opry's early performers also made recordings for the Library of Congress.

By the time David Stone left the Opry in 1940, though, the seeds of change had already been sown. Roy Acuff had come down from WNOX in Knoxville with his Smokey Mountain Boys and became the Opry's first singing idol. That same year, Republic Pictures made the first full-length Hollywood movie featuring the cast of the Grand Ole Opry. The star system had arrived at WSM; Ernest Tubb and Eddy Arnold would begin to shine in the mid-forties.

In 1939, the Opry went on the NBC network with its Prince Albert Tobacco segment, and by that time the show had outgrown the WSM studios and operated out of Nashville's War Memorial auditorium. Then in 1943, the show was moved to the Ryman Auditorium, an old tabernacle built in 1886 by steamboat captain Tom Ryman after he was inspired by the sermons of evangelist Reverend Sam P. Jones.

In a curiously complete fashion, the stage was now set for the Grand Ole Opry's greatest natural talent when he arrived in 1949. The show was a national phenomenon, with a large network audience as well as the large southern and midwestern audience within range of WSM's clear-channel signal. It had developed a star system whereby a certain amount of extra oooing and ahhh-ing was accorded to people like Eddy Arnold and Red Foley. The great comedic team of Minnie Pearl and Rod Brasfield had arrived. And the Opry was under the direction of two of the most competent administrators of its long history, WSM Manager Harry Stone (David's older brother) and Jim Denny, Artist's Services (booking) Director and later manager of the Opry. Along about 1940, the Opry people had discovered almost accidentally that Opry road shows could be a big hit, and so they had blossomed in the following eight years into a large separate enterprise.

But with all the changes, two fundamental things remained the same in 1949 when Hank Williams began working the Opry: The show still included the contributions of the "Solemn Old Judge" and his ever-present steamboat whistle (though George Hay was beginning to suffer from "fits of despair" that would plague him through his sunset years), and the Opry was still music for the common people. Urbanization had begun, but it had not yet done its damage to the American rural heritage. The Grand Ole Opry and country music in general still possessed the original mystique which had brought it into glory: Through all the fiddle-sawing and guitar-thrumming could be dimly heard the strength of the pioneer spirit, the wonder of unspoiled nature, and the pure and boisterous energy of the common people.

It is no wonder, then, that Hank Williams came out of the Alabama pines to become both the Opry's last authentically rural headliner and also, in Jim Owen's words, "America's first superstar." But even with such a well-set stage, no one else could have played his part.

9

Fast Climb to the Top

Not long after their first tour together, Hank invited the Drifting Cowboys over to his new house on Franklin Road for the band's first publicity photo session.

"When we got there," remembers Hillous Butrum, "Hank was sittin' in the middle of the living room floor. One boot was off on one side of the room and his other boot was over on the far side. Hank was in between readin' the paper."

Naturally the boys asked why Hank was sprawled on the floor when he'd just bought a houseful of new furniture.

"This durned furniture," he replied. "I'm afraid to sit down on it—'fraid I'll break it!"

Stardom wasn't changing the fact that Hank Williams was just an ol' country boy. "We called him 'Gimly-ass,'" songwriter Vic McAlpin has said. "He was one of these guys who was so thin that he didn't have no ass at all, so that one back pocket would hit against—and even lap over—the other one. . . . There were several of us that called him 'Gimly' all the time. We'd leave the 'ass' part off around the public."

Though Hank was still plain ol' Hank when he began appearing with the other Grand Ole Opry personalities, the power of "Lovesick Blues" was such that he began outdrawing them almost immediately. If anyone was jealous, there's no record of it. Hank seems to have made as good an initial impression with the Opry regulars as he did with the public. He couldn't help but be unassuming; and besides, it never really seemed to get through to him what a hit he had become.

In the next year and a half following his Grand Ole Opry debut, Hank Williams was going to become the biggest country music star—both in record sales and box office clout—of his time. This phenomenon was neither easily accomplished nor logically predictable.

Hank, with his voice as rough-hewn as his manners, was bucking the already-snowballing trend toward "smoother" country music. Red Foley, Eddy Arnold, and others were charting a new course for country music that would lead away from the kind of raw passion and energy that Roy Acuff had brought to the Grand Ole Opry. Hank Williams, however, had no intention of becoming any less country than he was. It's doubtful that he could have, anyway.

Hank and the Drifting Cowboys were on their way to developing one of the best country bands of their era. Soon the band's success with Hank would bring them offers to record with other artists. Hank had matured and become at least a little smoother since his Montgomery days; and the Drifting Cowboys, swelled with new pride and exhilaration, were determined to supplement his Alabama wail with the finest straight-ahead yet up-to-date musical arrangements possible.

It wasn't difficult for Hank to get them to play the way he wanted. They were a flexible group. After all, in that summer of '49, none of the Drifting Cowboys was older than twenty-one.

Wavy-haired steel man Don Helms, who had played with Hank in 1943, became the primary instrumental stylist for the Drifting Cowboys. His piercing intros set the mood for most of Hank's songs. "The lonesome sound of Don's steel fit right in with the lonesome sound of Hank's singing," says Hillous Butrum.

It was no accident. Jerry Rivers remembers how both Hank and Fred Rose urged Helms to use only the highest register strings when recording. "That's what made Don's sound distinctive," says Rivers, "from the way everybody else had been playing steel."

"Also Hank and Fred didn't like me to play on one string," says fiddler Rivers, "which was what most everybody did." Instead, the Hank Williams Sound would always include "double stop" fiddle breaks, where the fiddle plays the melody and a harmony simultaneously on two strings.

Helms on steel, Rivers on fiddle, McNett on electric guitar, and Butrum on bass began to be able to play as if they were one man, sensing and anticipating each other behind the strong, steady rhythms of Hank's steel-stringed Martin.

"'Lovesick Blues' was so hot as we started out," says Butrum, "that our tours were always getting dates added to them." Once the crowds had heard that song, they heard and liked a lot more of Hank Williams and the Drifting Cowboys.

The main product, of course, was the voice. Hank hadn't yet written all the hits he would eventually have, and so he still relied on other people's material to round out his performances. Claude Boone's ballad "Wedding Bells" was one of these that Hank sang a lot early in his Opry years.

But it didn't matter whose song it was; Hank's voice was always a most distinctive musical instrument, instantly recognizable among the other country singers even then.

Instantly recognized, but hard to describe. Henry Pleasants in his book, *The Great American Popular Singers*, takes a crack at it:

> Certain closed vowels as they occur in such words as *could*, *would*, *look*, *love*, *me* and *see* emerge as if they had become lodged between the vocal cords en route from the lungs to the throat . . . then there is the nasality in such words as *down*, *town*, *around*, *want*, *die*, *cry*, *when*, *then*, *heart*, *part*, *shame*, *name*, etcetera, not to mention a curious and characteristic quaver, not quite vibrato and not quite tremolo, suggesting a kind of feedback from overloaded muscles in the throat, which is probably what it was.

It was a piercing, hard-edged, country voice that made no concessions to the pop audience, but the country audience recognized the Real Thing when they heard Hank. This is not at all to imply that Hank Williams was a limited singer; the opposite is true.

"Having no vocal pretensions or vanity," writes Pleasants, "he was free to match voice to song, without worrying about conventionally accepted criteria of what constitutes an admissible vocal sound . . . one feels that he had a different voice for every song."

Pleasants notes how Hank chose the lower register when singing "Ramblin' Man" with its "long, mournful, upward glides." On it Hank sounds "almost like a basso" and "quite a lot like a distant train whistle." On other, faster, numbers, Hank's voice could become higher and brighter, making him sound more like a tenor.

"Actually the voice was a light baritone," says Pleasants, "with an exceptional range of about an octave and a sixth from an A below [the scale] to an F above."

All of this is simply telling us that Hank Williams was just naturally a great singer. Pleasants is especially impressed by Hank's unique yodeling abilities and calls "Lovesick Blues" a "rollicking display of vocal agility, unprecedented, in my experience, in the work of any other singer."

It was unprecedented. The country music audience didn't need an expert in the field of vocal music to tell them that they'd never heard anything like Hank Williams before. That's what made Hank such a smash, that's what was causing those first road trips to get extended by the crowds who wanted to see and hear the "Lovesick Blues Boy." Hank's kind of standout talent barely needed promotion. Anyone who heard him was an instant, walking, raving advertisement.

So now, with a groundswell of public acclaim reaching up to meet him, Hank Williams was taking his Drifting Cowboys out to meet America. Hank's very first Opry tour sent him and the boys into Ohio and the Midwest. Before long, the package shows were taking them all across the continent. The supply of Hank's stage shows could barely keep up with demand.

"We finally got some uniforms tailored for us," says Hillous Butrum, "when we went with Hank on his first West Coast tour." In those days there were no places yet to buy cowboy clothing in Nashville, so most bands went to specialists like Nudie's Rodeo Tailor in Los Angeles, where Hank and the boys bought their outfits.

Once on the road with Hank Williams, the Drifting Cowboys quickly learned that their boss had a special talent.

"Hank had this incredible ability to hypnotize an audience," says Butrum. "He could get 'em laughin' and fallin' out of their seats, then turn around and on the next song bring tears to their eyes." Hank didn't merely perform; he literally took control of his audiences and led them anywhere he wanted to.

"He knew how to start it," says Butrum, "by getting the audience involved in the songs as he introduced them."

"I got a little song . . . like to do it for you now," Hank would drawl. "You all listen close to this one. This ol' boy in the song really had the heartaches. His ol' lady really gave him a hard time. . . . I'm thinkin' about releasin' this as a record. Like to see what you folks think of it."

Then he'd do the song and the folks would hang on every word.

"I'd stand on stage and watch our audiences when Hank was working," Ott Devine of the Grand Ole Opry once remarked. "They were plain spellbound."

Coupled with Hank's natural magnetism was the fact that he never pretended to be anything but a country boy. He was totally and inescapably informal. For example, this is how he'd introduce "Lovesick Blues" in the early days:

"Well, folks . . . like to sing one that's made me a laaahhhhtta taters. Now I just wanna get me another one that'll make me some beans to have with 'em!"

"Audiences could sense that Hank wasn't putting anything on," remembers Hillous Butrum. "They listened to him a few minutes and before long they were thinking 'Why, he's just one of us.' He always had this rapport with an audience."

On the road, Hank quickly came up with nicknames for each of the band members. Jerry Rivers was "Burrhead," called that for his closely-cropped blonde hair. Don Helms was "Shag," and Bob McNett was always introduced as "Rupert Robert McNett from Rollin' Branch, Pennsylvania."

"Hank found out one day that my middle name was Buel," says Hillous Butrum. "And from then on it was 'Here's *Buel* on bass. Let's get ol' *Buel* to drive,' and so on."

In return, the boys always called Hank "*Harm*," which was their colloquialism for his first name of Hiram. The relationship between Hank Williams and his band members steadily grew into one of warmth and admiration.

"The days from 1949 to 1951 were some of the best times of

my life," Jerry Rivers writes in *Hank Williams: From Life to Legend.* "During this time Hank's health was good, his attitude and enthusiasm were at an all-time high and no one ever gained the professional respect and acceptance of the public and the industry so rapidly."

Playing around the country in a Grand Ole Opry troupe was hard work in the late forties and early fifties. It wasn't just the long road trips with little sleep; the shows themselves were a bigger job than nowadays.

"I figure that on an average today," writes Jerry Rivers, "an artist will work approximately twenty minutes on the typical 'package' auditorium show which will probably star from five to ten big names. In the early fifties, two or three stars made a big show, and most shows were played individually by single acts with perhaps a comedian added to the group."

Rivers remembers that during that first year, before Hank's asking price went too high, the Drifting Cowboys played the old Kemp Theater circuit throughout the Carolinas, Virginia, and West Virginia; four to six stage shows a day between feature movies.

None of the band members felt any great sense of loss when Hank got too big to play the theater circuits, and they didn't have to wait too long for that to happen.

Touring buses for country bands were unheard of in 1949, so the boys did the best they could in Hank's blue-black '49 Packard limo he'd brought from Shreveport. The Packard was almost state-of-the-art for touring cars at that time, with wide front and rear seats and two small folding jump seats in between. Hank also owned a big heavy trailer which was sometimes hitched to the car for towing equipment. "However," says Jerry Rivers, "the trailer did not have brakes and we soon discontinued using it on the road."

In his book *Hank Williams: From Life to Legend,* Rivers' description of the Road in those days is not particularly alluring:

> Although the Packard was luxurious traveling for that day, air conditioning, power brakes, or power steering were

unheard of—as were interstate highways. The first express-
way we traveled was the Kentucky Turnpike from Elizabeth-
town to Louisville, and later the Pennsylvania Turnpike.
After fighting the wheel over hundreds of miles of narrow
blacktop highway, it would often take several hours to snake
through large metropolitan cities like Cincinnati, Atlanta, or
Pittsburgh.

Bob McNett often drove on the long trips, and sometimes the
pressure would get to him. "One time we had a trip to make
straight through from Front Royal, Virginia, to a fair somewhere in Illinois," says McNett. "I drew the first shift as we
started out of Virginia, and it was raining—which slowed us
down quite a bit on the mountain roads."

McNett wanted to stop for breakfast as morning approached.
But Hank, who awakened and saw they were behind schedule,
would not hear of it. So the boys had a quart of milk and some
donuts while the car was gassed up at the next town.

"Not stopping for breakfast kind of got to me," says McNett,
"and so I started driving that old Packard too fast. I really
wailed into one particular curve, and at one point I didn't know
if we were going to come out of it. But we did, and after we
straightened out, I looked in the mirror. Hank was slumped in
the back seat, looking kinda pale."

McNett got over his anger and drove on. But shortly after
that he accidentally ran through a red light in the next town.
Bob relates that Hillous Butrum started to needle him about
the red light he missed.

"You shut up!" Williams ordered Butrum from the back seat.
"He might get mad again!"

Straight-through traveling was the rule, though, between
dates, otherwise Jim Denny couldn't fit enough one-nighters
into the week. So the boys made the best of it. They got as
comfortable as they could in the car, slept intermittently, and
horsed around. There wasn't much time left over between
dates, so the Drifting Cowboys were lucky if they could just
safely get into town, find a room, and get some rest before their
first show.

Then of course, the rooms were not in the local Holiday Inn, either.

"In 1949 it was always the town hotel," recalls Rivers, "and with the exception of the larger cities, we had a selection of one, maybe two." At least once, in Pennsylvania, the Drifting Cowboys and Hank Williams had to stay in a boardinghouse because everything else was full.

"The next morning found Hank Williams, Don Helms, Bob McNett, Hillous Butrum, a railroad engineer, a salesman, and me," says Rivers, "lined up at the bathroom door with our razors and shaving mugs."

Elsewhere around the country, it was crowds of country music fans who were doing the lining up—to hear Hank Williams sing "Lovesick Blues."

"Hank was drawing crowds above some of the old established artists who were playing the same places," Don Helms told Roger Williams. "The reason was that song." Hillous Butrum has compared this phenomenon of 1949 to "Presley later on," and the comparison is apt. Hank Williams was the biggest sensation country music had ever seen, yet many of his fans still barely knew who he was.

On these first great tours, Audrey often went along and performed with the band from time to time. One of the places in the show where Hank could always use her voice was during what he called "hymn time." Hank had more fun with these old shout tunes than any other part of his live show.

"I'd like to get the boys and Miss Audrey to join me now," he'd tell the audience, "and we're gonna do a couple of hymns for you folks. This is one I learned many years ago. I like it . . . hope you folks do too."

Often he'd add a more solemn admonition:

"I think this song says a lot," he'd say very seriously, "if you'd really listen, it might make you stop and think."

And then with a quick fiddle intro, it'd be off to Glory with "Where The Soul of Man Never Dies" or "I'll Have A New Body, I'll Have A New Life," as Audrey sang harmony and the Drifting Cowboys all joined in when the rousing old songs would shift gears into the choruses.

Having Audrey along as part of the troupe, though, was not the joy for Hank that it had been in the old days. Back in Alabama, they'd been young and in love and singing with her was fun, but now Hank was forced to think more seriously about his career; and about the effect that Audrey's spirited but unmusical singing was having on an otherwise polished stage show.

Hank Williams and the Drifting Cowboys were booked into Washington, D.C., in the fall of '49 when the issue first came to a head. The group was playing the Potomac River Cruise that was promoted by Connie B. Gay and featured young Jimmy Dean's staff orchestra. Audrey badly wanted to join the Drifting Cowboys and sing on the boat trip show, but Hank wouldn't let her. The fur flew.

Later, Hank stopped by the Drifting Cowboys' hotel rooms at the Ambassador Hotel. He seemed in a reflective mood as he talked with the boys.

Finally he let the guys in on what was bothering him.

"It's hell to have a wife that wants to sing," Hank Williams said as he stood looking out at Washington, D.C., with his cowboy boot on the windowsill. "It's even worse to have one that wants to sing and can't."

The early troubles, though, were overshadowed for Hank and Audrey by the revenue that was rolling in. "Lovesick Blues" alone made so much money that Hank commissioned a wrought-iron fence around his new home on Franklin Road with the notes to the old song cast into the metal. "That song built this place," he explained. At that time, $55 thousand bought a lot more real estate than it does today.

When Hank first joined he Opry, he and the Drifting Cowboys received $250 for a stage appearance. By late 1950, that figure rose to $1,000. At that time, this was an amount only commanded by a true star. Hank's highest one-show cash-ins of his career—about $1,500 apiece—were in the range then reserved for superstars in the musical world.

The Drifting Cowboys were always paid above union scale. Scale in 1949 was ten dollars a show; Hank paid Bob, Jerry, Don, and Hillous, fifteen dollars; that figure agreed upon when they joined together in June of that year. By the early fifties, the boys were drawing at least forty dollars a show per man, while the union rate was only up to twenty-five dollars.

During the good years Hank kept the Drifting Cowboys on a generous salary. This was not entirely kindheartedness on his part. By paying the band a weekly salary, he guaranteed himself a backup group whenever he needed them.

For his own part, Hank Williams was not hung up on money. He enjoyed the good things of life, yes, but he didn't crave them. Audrey seems to have been a different story.

"Audrey took Hank's success and began buyin' all the things she'd dreamed of when she was a little girl and didn't have nothin'," says Hillous Butrum. "She tried to 'go uptown,' and Hank didn't go for it."

But what about the long, low ranch on Franklin Road with its modern oriental-style formal living room and knotty-pine den?

"Hank would have been just as satisfied in an old house with mismatched furniture," says Butrum.

For Hank, the most enjoyable thing about having money was that he could indulge his fancy for good hunting dogs and collectors' pistols.

"Hank Williams' admiration for old guns, particularly pistols," Jerry Rivers relates, "was almost uncontrollable. He would usually become acquainted with local policemen, sheriffs and deputies wherever he worked, and they would help him locate and buy guns that he wanted."

Rivers also tells how Hank impulsively traded a wristwatch with "several diamonds on the face" for a fine squirrel dog named Skip, much to the shock of a Nashville-area farmer.

Hank made up his mind he had to have that dog regardless of the cost, and he asked the farmer what he would take for it. It seemed that Skip was actually a pet of the farmer's teen-age daughter and had just picked up his unusual hunting ability on his own time. But the next time we drove to White House the farmer told Hank that his daughter was no longer personally attached to Skip and would be glad for Hank to have the dog for anything he might want to give her toward a watch she was saving for.

Thereupon Hank "immediately pulled the wristwatch from his arm and gave it in exchange for the dog." This incident gives us a strong clue to Hank Williams' value system. Skip remained a close companion until Hank's back problems cut short his hunting days.

The boy from Alabama was getting rich. But he took it as casually as yesterday's newspaper. He walked around Nashville with wads of cash in his pockets and peeled off the bills as he needed them. He began to develop a reputation for big tips, but he didn't seem to be doing it for show. The money just didn't seem to mean that much to him.

Once, later in his career, he would give a hotel desk clerk in Beaumont, Texas, a hundred-dollar bill for a bottle of whiskey.

"Forget it," Hank told the man when he offered change. "You need it worse than I do."

He didn't even care to handle the money more than he had to. Back in Montgomery, either his sister or his mother or Audrey had handled all the money, and now that he was a star, Hank Williams would direct his band members to collect his fees from promoters.

Accordingly, there is an oft-told story of the time Hank walked into the Third National Bank in Nashville and plopped a heap of bills in front of the teller.

"How much is there?" the bank employee asked.

"How the hell do I know?" Hank reportedly answered. "My job is to make it. Your job is to count it."

During his first year as a Grand Ole Opry star, Hank Williams proved himself as a performer before all kinds of audiences. He took part in the historic first Grand Ole Opry–R. J. Reynolds Tobacco Company tour to Germany in 1949, along with Red Foley, Minnie Pearl, Little Jimmy Dickens, and others. Hank had no problem at all winning over the soldiers, but he had his troubles with the long flight. He never got up to look out the window of the specially-designed DC-4 MATS transport plane as it flew high above the Atlantic.

Canadian audiences were likewise charmed by Hank Williams that year, as he made the first of two sorties there. His second Canadian tour, two years later, would fall victim to the bottle and turn into an embarrassing failure.

The most significant early tour, though, was the 1949 California trip taken by Hank and some other Grand Ole Opry names. The Drifting Cowboys, as usual, made the long journey by car, but Hank flew out with one of the few pilots he trusted: Henry Cannon, Minnie Pearl's husband.

"There was a West Coast circuit for Nashville artists that existed at that time," remembers Hillous Butrum. "We'd always hit Sacramento, Fresno, San Jose, Long Beach, and certain other cities."

The West Coast then was the home turf of another whole world of country music in the forties and fifties. It was the lollapalooza realm of the big Western-swing dance bands. These ten-to-twenty-man aggregations musically punched the walls out of cavernous ballrooms like Tex Williams' Riverside Rancho in Hollywood, Spade Cooley's Santa Monica Ballroom, Will's Point, and Smokey Rogers' Bostonia Ballroom. Now Western Swing was about to get a jolt from Country Soul.

Hank's power was demonstrated as he'd step up on these stages, allowing the big bands to take a break while his four-piece string band took over. In Jerry Rivers' words, Hank then proceeded to "completely dominate the ballroom audiences of 1,500 to 2,000 people."

As Hank grew in poise with his travels, he began to lose his apprehension about playing for *any* audience. "The tougher the audience," he told friends, "the better."

Hank Williams was always up for a professional challenge, and in those days, one great challenge was having to follow Little Jimmy Dickens during an Opry package show. These were Jimmy's great years. The scrappy little guy from West Virginia was fast becoming one of the Opry's favorite performers with his songs like "Sleepin' At the Foot of the Bed" and "Old, Cold Tater."

"We did a lot of tours with Little Jimmy Dickens," remembers Hillous Butrum, "and he was a great showman."

On these tours Hank took the band aside before the show and told them, "Boys, we got to follow Tater tonight, so let's hit 'em hard!"

"So as soon as we hit the stage," says Butrum, "Hank would go to work. He'd get down into his stance and get those ol' long legs goin'—he'd even start pawin' with his feet like a horse. He'd really get into the music."

The combination was too much. The catchy songs, the shining dark eyes, the whipsaw voice, and Hank's lanky body hunched over and around the microphone, moving up and down with a rhythm that was in Jack Hurst's words, "arousing if not downright suggestive." If the audience had been bowled over by the snappy, boyish, hard-hitting Dickens, now they were being slapped into Silly Putty by Hank Williams and the Drifting Cowboys.

In June of 1950, the Packard breathed its last as a touring car for Hank and the boys. Some have cited the trading of the Packard as another sign of Hank's upward mobility, but the change was more practical than that. The Packard's engine had blown.

Hillous Butrum was driving the group out to an engagement in Beaumont, Texas, when it happened.

"I was goin' about eighty—as always," he says. "All of a sudden, a dog ran across the road in front of me and I had to slow down. When I hit the accelerator again, that ol' engine made a sound like a hundred mechanics had started poundin' on it." It seemed like an appropriate time for a trade-in.

Hank promptly bought a brand-new 1950 Cadillac limo. It was green and had the radical "fish-tail" taillights that would identify Cadillacs for the next six years. The car had all the toys you could order at that time: power steering and brakes, power windows, too. No air conditioning was available back then.

Still it was a welcome change. The Drifting Cowboys had put the Packard over a *lot* of road and had begun to doubt its reliability. Besides, the older car with its long wheelbase, wide turning radius, and lack of power assists had been more like a small bus to drive than a luxury automobile.

"Shortly after we got back to Nashville," remembers Bob McNett, "Hank said, 'We're picking up our Cadillac,' and Don Helms told Hank, 'If it wasn't you, I'd hug you.'"

A few weeks later, Helms took the new Caddy home with him after a tour, and got run into from behind by a careless Nashville driver. The next day, Hank looked over the damage to the rear of the Cadillac and asked Helms deadpan, "How'd you hit him?"

Don, always a man ready with a quip, replied, "Well, shoot, Hank . . . I was just backin' down the road. . . ."

How it was on the road then, those first great years: long ribbons of winding two-lane highway stretching through mountains and deep Appalachian valleys, past the Burma-Shave signs and the barns advertising King Edward Cigars across their roofs, past back-country shacks where whiskery old hill patriarchs watched down with quiet eyes from humble front porches, through the small towns—hundreds and thousands of small towns that couldn't be bypassed—with their porticoed gas stations, country stores, and feed-and-seed barns.

Then there were the plains, as the hills of Missouri or Arkansas would give way to the prairies of Oklahoma or Texas; out where the narrow black highway sizzled and the sun played mirror-tricks on its horizon, where the flatland only stopped for necessary interruptions like Whiting Bros. gas stations and oil rigs and occasional tiny taverns which never looked big enough to hold all the patrons who had parked outside in the gravel parking lots.

The crowds, always the crowds, coming to a county fair with their straightforward faces still red from a day on the tractor or an afternoon hanging clothes on the line; coming to the Opry, men with slicked-down hair wearing clean open collar shirts and neatly-pressed pleated pants, the young women beside them in long skirts (never slacks) under the blousy bulge where a third or fourth child was on the way.

Sometimes a shy girl's face could be seen smiling with her mouth suspiciously closed—until Hank's first song, and then the bigger smile would have to come, revealing the missing teeth. No matter now.

The crowds, too, of zoot-suits and wide-brimmed Dobbs hats like Harry Truman wore, of tighter, though not shorter, skirts and upswept Lana Turner hairdos—the smell and look and feel of post-war prosperity fairly oozing up from the big club audiences onto the stage. There it mingled with the sweet, fresh success and homespun magnetism of the young man who

wore the white Stetson and swayed in front of his band,
balancing his life on a Martin guitar and a roadhouse rhythm.

For the good years, the weekly pattern was always the same:
Friday and Saturday nights in Nashville for the Opry—with
exceptions when an Opry package show was out of Nashville
over the weekend—then hitting as many one-nighters as
possible through the week all over the country and up into
Canada. Hank began to fly more often back and forth to the
Opry as his success grew, leaving the Drifting Cowboys in the
Midwest while he flew to Nashville, then rejoining them again
by air after the weekend.

Minnie Pearl, the Opry's greatest comic star, remembers
those early years. She played many package shows with Hank.

"The first time I saw Hank work," she remembers, "was on a
package show in Great Bend, Kansas. Hank had not yet joined
the Opry, but 'Lovesick Blues' was already a tremendous hit, so
he came out and joined our troupe for a few dates."

It was a long show, and Minnie was slated to close it, with
Hank just before her.

"But they wouldn't let that man off the stage," she recalls.
"He had the same kind of impact as Presley did. Audiences
couldn't get enough of him."

Though Minnie and Hank would remain the best of friends
throughout their years of touring together, she told the
promoter that day in Kansas, "Never again will I follow Hank."
And she never did.

Back in Nashville, Hank and the Drifting Cowboys began
doing the early-morning "Health and Happiness" radio show on
WSM, sponsored by Hadacol tonic. (Two of these syndicated
shows, which were recorded onto large sixteen-inch discs and
sold around the South, can be heard on the M-G-M album,
Hank Williams On Stage.) There were several early morning
shows on WSM. They began at 5 A.M. and continued to about 7,
and appearances on them were a part of every Opry entertainer's obligation to the station. When the stars were in town,
they did the shows live. Often they would record several shows,
to be used for later transcription when they were out on the

road. Hank would also do the "Mother's Best Flour" show with the boys at 7:15 A.M. five days a week.

In August of 1949, Hank Williams and the Drifting Cowboys began doing the Duckhead Work Clothes program on Saturday afternoons at WSM. This show, called "Duckhead Saturday Night," was an Opry "warm-up" show, of which there have been legion over the years of Saturday nights.

Hank quickly won the respect of the WSM engineers. They remember him as a friendly, cooperative, radio performer who was thoroughly professional.

"He always dressed well," Aaron Shelton remembers, "but he looked almost emaciated. He was such a lean and lanky fella that his clothes flopped around on him when he moved with his music."

Hank's relaxed, offhand manner around WSM made him "one of the crew" rather than a distant star to the employees there.

"We all felt close to Hank," says Shelton. "He was good to work for doing radio shows or records." But Shelton qualifies the "closeness": "It was never really a buddy-buddy thing, because Hank was just not that buddy-buddy with anyone."

The shows, however, were done in a warm, friendly style that made radio audiences feel that Hank was a personal friend. He used the same kind of patter on the air as with his stage shows, things like: "Well, neighbors, now it's time to . . .," and "This next song's got a lot o' suffrin' in it. . . . We hope you don't have to go through too much of that. . . . We do it quite often." Hank seemed to open up as much or more with a radio audience as he did with most of the people he worked with and hung around with.

"Hank always had a woods-animal distrust of people," says Minnie Pearl. "He was afraid to let people know him. My husband Henry [Cannon] was one of the few people that Hank felt safe and secure with."

The shows were put together as casually as most other business was done in Nashville in those days. There was very little rehearsing, since the band would just be doing songs that Hank sang on the road, anyway. Jerry Rivers recalls the radio shows:

"Hank would just say somethin' like, 'We're gonna do a thirty-minute show. I'm gonna do 'Lovesick Blues' and 'Wedding Bells' . . . and he'd tell us a few more numbers."

"Then right in the middle, Jerry," Hank would say, "I'll probably want you to do a fiddle tune."

"We'd all get a chance to do somethin' special on those shows," says Hillous Butrum. "Jerry would do fiddle solos, Don would solo on steel, or Bob, Jerry, and I would sing a trio. Sometimes," Butrum adds proudly, "I'd even sing a solo myself."

The Drifting Cowboys, then, were an important part of Hank's radio shows on WSM. By the time Hank went with the Opry troupe to Germany in the fall of '49 the boys were so well-schooled that they kept Hank's early morning shows going without him while he was gone. Butrum would sing Hank's songs and the rest of the guys filled in with their various talents. Many of Don Helms' jokes, however, had to be saved for off-air telling only. (Some of them would still be bleeped in today's more permissive times.)

The Nashville Hank Williams radio shows developed at least one unbending tradition: Hank's signoff. First he'd intone real nice and peaceful-like, "Well folks, if the Good Lord's willin' and the creeks don't rise, we'll see you next time." Then he'd add excitedly, "I'm comin', Bocephus!"

Often the morning shows were performed with Hank and several of the boys in jeans and rubber boots, because as soon as they were off the air, it was a mad rush out to Rudy's boat dock on Kentucky Lake for a morning of crappie fishing.

Hank fished with characteristic enthusiasm and often wanted to stay all day. He'd buy two or three hundred minnows and sit on a good crappie hole, patiently checking the half-dozen lines he kept out at once.

Hank, Don, and Jerry also used the predawn shows to kick off hunting trips. "Hank would get the opening radio show at 5 A.M.," Jerry Rivers writes, "and we would play the program in our blue jeans, hunting jackets and boots with our shotguns propped against the studio wall. At the last note of the closing theme we would jump in the car and head for the woods just at the crack of dawn."

Vic McAlpin, a Nashville songwriter and contemporary of Hank's, has gained a certain amount of notoriety because he and Hank used fishing trips to combine relaxation with impromptu songwriting.

"When we went fishing," McAlpin once told an interviewer, "we used to shoot the breeze about songs. Matter of fact, we wrote four or five things."

The most famous of these "things" was Hank's followup to "Lovesick Blues," a song in the same vein called "Long Gone Lonesome Blues."

"He was laying in the back of the car on the way to the lake," McAlpin remembers, "and he couldn't sleep. So he sat up singing the line, 'long gone lonesome blues,' and he was kinda yodeling it. I said, 'What is that bit?' and he said, 'I've got to have a song kinda like the 'Lovesick Blues' with all the breaks in it.'"

So through the morning, as Hank and Vic drove out to Rudy's dock on the big Richland River, as they put the boat out under a Tennessee sunrise and rigged up their rods and bait, Hank was still singing that same yodeling line. McAlpin slowly got exasperated with the repetition.

"Hank, are you gonna fish or just watch the fish swim by?" he finally said.

"Hey, that's it! The first line!" Hank replied.

Hank added the next line about getting to the river and being "so lonesome I could cry." Whereupon McAlpin suggested they borrow a line from "Worried Mind" and say "the doggone river was dry." In a matter of weeks, "Long Gone Lonesome Blues" was the number one country song in the nation. Hank Williams was listed as the composer; he'd paid McAlpin a flat sum for his efforts. On other songs written similarly, McAlpin would share the credit. Unfortunately for Vic, none of their other collaborations did as well as "Long Gone Lonesome Blues."

Hank wrote songs wherever and whenever he got the chance. "He'd start a song backstage, riding in a car, anywhere," McAlpin told Roger Williams, "and once he got an idea, he wrote fast."

The Drifting Cowboys all remember the night on a rainswept

road in Arkansas or Louisiana when Hank wrote five songs in one inspired spurt.

"The brakes were out on the Packard," Hillous Butrum recalls, "and we were just inching along the highway while this storm was goin' on. Don had gotten a guitar out of the trunk. I was playin' it while Hank made up songs and Don wrote down the words."

The boys got a chuckle out of some of the lyrics composed that night, but Hank swore he'd get all five songs published and recorded. One of the songs was "Sing, Sing, Sing," a rousing gospel number about singing in heaven. Butrum remembers it as "too vanilla" and he told Hank it'd never go; nevertheless, the Drifting Cowboys were asked to record it with Charlie Monroe a few weeks after the night it was written.

"And Hank came in to watch the session," remembers Butrum. "He just grinned at me all through it." The song became a hit.

"He wrote another song that night that I thought was the best one," says Butrum. "It was called 'The Night Is Dark and Stormy' or somethin' like that—but evidently he never got it down."

Though Hank composed lyrics with an artist's insight, he always treated songwriting as a craft, not a holy calling. He wasn't defensive about the words he wrote; in fact, he'd bug his fellow performers with on-the-spot demos and requests for suggestions. He'd debut new songs in hotel rooms, backstage at the Opry, or wherever else he ran into someone whose opinion meant something to him. Sometimes his openness backfired on him with the practical-joking Drifting Cowboys.

"What's a good line to follow 'One day I passed you on the street?'" Jerry Rivers recalls Hank asking once from the back seat.

"And I smelled your rotten feet," shot back Don Helms. This kind of foolishness didn't keep the song Hank was working on, "I Can't Help It (If I'm Still In Love With You)," from becoming one of his all-time hits.

Hank Williams wooed thousands of fans through his in-person performances, but it was in the recording studio that he reached his largest audience. Between June of 1949 and the time of Hank's death, M-G-M released twenty-two Hank Williams singles on their yellow label with the lion on it. Of these, at least five were million-sellers before Hank's death, and another dozen or so were well-received hits. Hank was singing to people in numbers literally too high for him to imagine.

Just as important, it is his recordings that Hank Williams left as a permanent reminder to posterity of his performing artistry. Like all singers and musicians lucky enough to have been popular in the twentieth century, Hank Williams owes a debt of gratitude to the recording industry, which can preserve the musician's art and put him into the timeless category of painters, sculptors, and poets.

During his ascending years of stardom, from June, 1949, through the end of 1950, Hank had four big hit records. The first, already mentioned, was the follow-up song, "Long Gone Lonesome Blues." It was on the "Long Gone" session that the Drifting Cowboys of Rivers, Butrum, Helms, and McNett first worked with Hank in the studio. Throughout the Montgomery and Shreveport years, Fred Rose had put together Hank's Sterling and M-G-M releases with musicians hired on a session-by-session basis. Now at last Hank had a studio band.

The other big songs of this period were "Why Don't You Love Me Like You Used To Do?," "Moanin' The Blues" (another "Lovesick Blues" sound-alike), and "Cold, Cold Heart." The latter was destined to open up a whole new audience for Hank's songs.

It was also right at the time of Hank's entry into the Opry circuit that he began to record his first recitations, which were marketed under the name of "Luke the Drifter." Some of these were humorous, others as serious as Hank could make them, but all of the "Luke the Drifter" recordings reflect a simple down-home philosophy of faith in God, compassion, perseverance and morality. Hank loved the recitations, because he believed them and also because they required a special kind of showmanship to put across.

The "Luke the Drifter" moniker was used so that these

special spoken numbers wouldn't be mistaken for normal Hank Williams fare and promptly ordered for every honky-tonk juke box in the South. Neither Fred Rose nor Williams himself felt that these selections, some of which were almost like sermons, should be playing out in the land of dim lights, thick smoke, and loud, loud music. Nobody was supposed to know who this "Luke the Drifter" really was, but as Wesley Rose has noted, it was the worst-kept secret in Nashville.

During the great years from '49 to '52, M-G-M released only one Hank Williams gospel single. It was recorded in 1950 and featured "I Heard My Mother Praying For Me" on one side and "Jesus Died For Me" on the other. Although many people remember Hank for his many gospel songs, most of them were recorded either during the early, lean years— like "I Saw The Light"—or else released after his death. Gospel songs were not a mainstay of Hank Williams' recording success while he was alive to enjoy it.

Hank's earliest recordings were done in WSM's studio D, but by 1949 the sessions had moved to Castle Recording Studios, also run by Aaron Shelton, Carl Jenkins, and George Reynolds. The Castle Studio had been set up in the now-defunct Tulane Hotel at Eighth Avenue and Church Street in Nashville.

The Tulane, to put it nicely, was not a luxury establishment.

"It was an old hotel where the rooms were cheap," Bob McNett remembers. "You walked down to the end of a hall and there was the Castle Studio." The studio was the size of a large hotel room, with a control room adjoining it.

"Doing a recording session at Castle was like sitting down for a jam session," says McNett. "We arrived as a group and sat down to play, working over whatever was going to be recorded that day. The engineers miked each instrument, and as soon as the song was ready, we'd all try to get a take. Of course we were recording right onto wax . . . one mistake meant going back and starting the cutting lathe all over again."

"Most of the songs we recorded," adds Jerry Rivers, "were songs that Hank had written recently. We had heard them being written. By the time we got to the studio, Hank had already tried the songs out on us and a hundred other people."

This was Hank's way of polishing a song. He'd sing a new song to a friend and say, "How'd you like that one? . . . oh you didn't . . . well, here. Listen to it with this line instead." Some songs were also put into the final form in Fred Rose's attic studio over on Rainbow Trail. It was Fred Rose who often made the final decision as to whether a particular Hank Williams song was ready to record. He and Hank got together with a bunch of Hank's recent stuff before a recording session. They'd go over the material together and make an acetate disc of each song that seemed complete. Other songs would be left for further polishing or simply passed over. Then Rose would bring the acetates with him to the studio to help acquaint the musicians with the song in its final form.

"We'd often not have any idea what we were going to do until we got to the studio," says Jerry Rivers, "and this still holds true today in Nashville." But the Drifting Cowboys were with Hank so much of the time that when Rose spun the acetate, they were seldom completely surprised.

"Oh yeah!" they'd say. "That's the one you were playing backstage in Little Rock," or something to that effect.

"Yeah, that's the one," Hank would reply, and he would note any final changes.

On other occasions, Hank would simply start playing the song he wanted to record. He'd play it through, then start again and the boys would begin to play along. After a few times through, they were usually ready to put it down.

"A record session is and always was three hours in Nashville," says Rivers. "Back then we could easily do four sides in those three hours. 'Course now that sessions are more complicated, you're lucky to get two sides in three hours."

While the group was learning the song, Fred Rose would be thinking about how to arrange it. He and Hank would discuss how the song would progress: "Well, this sounds like a good one for a fiddle intro . . . Jerry, you work one up. Then I'll sing two verses and Don'll play through a verse, . . ." and so on.

"We had a lot of instrumental playing back then," recalls Rivers. "They felt in those days that the *sound* sold as much as the performer—that if they got a good country sound on a record, they *had* somethin'." Rivers and other veterans believe that Nashville lost a lot of its personality when the singing artists began to dominate most records completely.

"Now the only thing that's instrumental is the intro and maybe a little turnaround in the middle of the song," says Rivers, "and we've all gotten used to it that way. When I go back and listen to 'Jambalaya' I can't believe that I played that much on one song."

So these sessions that would make musical history went along casually and easily. When Hank and the Drifting Cowboys and Fred Rose were all ready, the engineers would start the wax disc turning and make ready the cutting lathe while the musicians watched from the other side of a glass window. The cutting needle would drop, the engineer would signal, and the entire band would play and sing right through the song just as if it were a live performance. If it went all right, they had a record. If not, they'd have to do it all again. There was no remixing and no overdubbing. The only difference between Hank's records and his personal appearances was Fred Rose's piano playing, which gave an added body to the sound. An organ was often added to the "Luke the Drifter" recordings. Otherwise, there was no studio embellishment of the straight, sharp, hillbilly string-band music.

"The things that Fred Rose did with Hank's sound," says Jerry Rivers, "were mostly what ordinary people would call 'little things,' but what record industry people would call 'big things.'"

There was Rose's insistence that Don Helms play his steel on the highest-register strings, thereby creating the unique Drifting Cowboys sound. This is one reason that "Cold, Cold Heart" and "Your Cheatin' Heart" are both so quickly recognized. Those high, twanging steel guitar intros have now become quite familiar, but back then they were almost revolutionary.

Rose also suggested, along with Williams, that Jerry Rivers do most of his session work using the "double stop" fiddle technique, which meant playing a melody and harmony on two strings at the same time. This style wasn't new; in fact it was traditional. It was the rage at that time, however, to play the kind of one-string "scat-fiddle" solos that had made the Bob Wills Texas Swing sound famous. "Mind Your Own Business," one of Hank's pre-'49 recordings, featured such a fiddle break. But evidently Williams and Rose now agreed that Hank's records should not be imitative of anyone else's style, and should develop their own sound to match the simple, country-boy sincerity of the songs Hank wrote.

The sessions were jived up, however, by the addition of a "dead-string" electric guitar, playing at low amplification and adding a funky thump in the place of a drumbeat, which was taboo.

"Fred Rose was nuts about tempo," Jerry Rivers stresses. "In fact that's how he wound up doing the first piano session work in Nashville—he'd play the piano to demonstrate the tempo he thought the song should have."

Most of Hank's songs are *movers*, even those considered to be "slow" numbers. There's not a lot of tempo difference between the light songs like "Move It On Over" and the ballads. The reason for this was that Hank Williams had been primarily a *dance* musician throughout his young, hurly-burly career. The tempos he played were the dance tempos of his time, waltzes and fox trots.

"This was back when it seemed like all the records said 'Fox Trot,'" recalls Rivers. "Personally I never knew what the fox trot was, but I knew that tempo."

The fox trot tempo was of course a holdover from the big band era and was basically a two-four or four-four beat in moderately fast time. Unlike the jitterbug or the boogie-woogie, it was meant to be danced in traditional ballroom style, but it kept your feet moving right along. So Hank's songs like "Cold, Cold Heart" and "There'll Be No Teardrops Tonight" joined the ranks of similar-tempo records by Frank Sinatra and the McGuire Sisters.

By late 1950, Hank Williams, through his M-G-M records and his charismatic personal appearances, had become the biggest sensation the country music world had ever seen. It wasn't that he took fans away from Acuff, Arnold, and Foley; it was just that he created a more intense excitement than they ever had. Country music was far too well-established and its older stars too well-loved for Hank Williams to become the center ring of the whole industry. The Opry went on as always with its long list of regulars, great and small, and Hank Williams was one of the great ones.

Still, everybody knew he was in a class by himself. He could do it all. He could do the funny numbers right along with Little Jimmy Dickens, he could out-cry Acuff, and he turned the women on, too—all without losing the simple unguarded style that was the linchpin of his success.

But Fred and Wesley Rose weren't satisfied. They felt that Hank's material had pop potential, even if his voice didn't, and they were determined to do something about it. So Wesley took Hank's country hit, "Cold, Cold Heart" to New York in early 1951.

Polly Bergen had already had a pop success with Hank's "Honky-Tonkin'," but it was regarded by the industry as just another one-time fluke country hit, much like "Tennessee Waltz," by Redd Stewart and Pee Wee King or Jimmie Davis' "You Are My Sunshine."

It was a good thing that Wesley Rose believed in what he was doing, because the initial reception in New York wasn't encouraging. He made the rounds of the record company A and R [Artists and Repertory] men he knew, but each one had the same reaction to "Cold, Cold Heart."

"That's a hillbilly song," they told him. The implication was that more sophisticated listeners wouldn't be touched by it.

Finally Rose found someone who could listen past Hank's twangy delivery into the strong poetry of the song itself: Columbia Records' pop music chieftain at the time, Mitch Miller.

"Who else has heard this song?" Miller asked Rose after hearing it for the first time.

Rose explained that he'd taken the song to everyone, and that they'd all disdained it.

"Well, we'll show 'em," was Miller's reply.

Miller looked around for the best singer to put across "Cold,

Cold Heart" to the pop audience and came up with a fresh young Italian-American named Anthony Benedetto, who had recently adopted the stage name of Tony Bennett. The young singer was talented, enthusiastic, and hungry for a hit.

So it came to pass that Columbia Records issued a single that year on the pop market by Tony Bennett called "Cold, Cold Heart," and it didn't sound like a country song anymore. It was just plain good words and music. In Miller's words, the song was "the complaint of every lover:" how to free his partner's "doubtful mind" and melt her "cold, cold heart." And of course it applied to women too. "No matter who you were, a country person or a sophisticate," Miller said years later, "the language hit home."

The language hit home so well that "Cold, Cold Heart" went to the number one position on the pop charts. It sold over a million copies and became one of the biggest songs of 1951. Thus began an entirely new phenomenon—a country songwriter's songs actually being sought out by pop singers.

In the months that followed, Joni James, Frankie Laine, Jo Stafford, Rosemary Clooney, and Tommy Edwards all recorded Hank's tunes with great success. Stafford and Laine actually competed for the chance to record "Jambalaya." Bennett, whom "Cold, Cold Heart" had made a star, followed it up with his version of "There'll Be No Teardrops Tonight."

The instincts of Fred and Wesley Rose and Mitch Miller proved overwhelmingly right. Pop singers, and now soul and rock singers, too, have never stopped recording Hank Williams' material. The list extends right up to Linda Ronstadt's version of "I Can't Help It" and Jesse Winchester's funky "Jambalaya."

"Hank earned two major distinctions as a songwriter," says Wesley Rose. "He was the first writer on a regular basis to make country music national music. And he was the first country songwriter accepted by pop artists and pop A and R men."

So now in early 1951, Hank and the Drifting Cowboys had a new thrill. Taking a break from a long cross-country pull in the Cadillac, they could stop for coffee at a roadside restaurant and play Bennett's version of "Cold, Cold Heart" on the juke box.

There would be Hank's simple, timeless melody hanging above the lush strings of a full orchestra. It was like a signal of acceptance by the larger world, the world Hank had so much trouble trusting. The savoring of that acceptance was sweet.

Almost sweet enough to make a difference.

The grove of trees at the top of the hill in this photo shaded the back yard of Hank Williams's birthplace, a tiny cabin near Mt. Olive, Alabama. The fenceposts mark the edge of an old road, now grown over with pasture grass.

This building housed the Mt. Olive Baptist church in the days when Hank sang hymns in a four-year-old's soprano while his mother pumped the organ. Next door in the present church structure is enshrined the bench that young Hank stood on when singing.

This is one of the houses that Hank Williams lived in as a boy growing up in Georgiana, Alabama. His mother operated a WPA cannery in the side yard.

Downtown Georgiana, which flanks the Louisville & Nashville railroad tracks on their way from Montgomery to Mobile.

Hank Williams poses with his mother, Lillian Skipper Williams, at the age of seven. (Courtesy Thurston Moore Country)

Hank at age twelve with his sister Irene. Though his vision was far from 20/20, he soon abandoned his glasses. (Courtesy Thurston Moore Country)

Thigpen's Log Cabin was a popular Georgiana roadhouse and dance hall in the years when Hank played out of Montgomery. The dance hall, now removed, extended to the left of the building as shown in the photo.

Hank Williams with bride Audrey Sheppard Williams shortly after their marriage in December of 1944. (Courtesy Thurston Moore Country)

Hank and his first group of Drifting Cowboys gather around the microphone at WSFA in Montgomery for their first broadcast together. The year is 1937 and Hank is fourteen. The group is (l. to r.) Shorty Seals, Indian Joe Hatcher, Mexican Charlie Mays, Hank, and Boots Harris.
(Courtesy Thurston Moore Country)

Hank with the Drifting Cowboys and Miss Audrey in 1944. Band members are (l. to r.): Lum York, Louis Brown, Hank, Redd Todd and Jimmie Webster. (Courtesy Thurston Moore Country)

Hank Williams introducing a new song to his friends backstage at the Grand Ole Opry. From left to right, announcer Grant Turner, Little Jimmie Dickens, Red Foley, and Hank. (Courtesy Country Music Foundation Library and Media Center)

Fred Rose late in his career as a composer and publishing executive. (Courtesy Country Music Foundation Library and Media Center)

Hank and Audrey pose with the final assemblage of Drifting Cowboys. From left are shown Howard Watts (Cedric Rainwater), Jerry Rivers, Audrey, Hank, Sammy Pruitt, and Don Helms. (Author's collection)

Hank Williams signing M-G-M movie contract as Frank Walker, President of M-G-M records, looks on. (Courtesy of Country Music Foundation Library and Media Center)

Hank at home on Franklin Road with Hank Williams, Jr. Little "Bocephus" was his father's foremost object of affection. (Courtesy Country Music Foundation Library and Media Center)

A publicity photo of Hank which has often been reproduced in oil. (Courtesy
Country Music Foundation Library and Media Center)

Hank married Billie Jean Jones in October of 1952. They are shown here during the "mock wedding" paid-audience festivities which drew 30,000 fans to the New Orleans Municipal Auditorium. (Courtesy Taft and Erleen Skipper)

The car which carried Hank Williams to his death on January 1, 1953. It is a 1952 Cadillac convertible with black pleated-leather seats, spotlight, and continental kit. The Cadillac is owned by Hank Williams, Jr., and is shown here at Hank's former home near Cullman, Alabama. The car has since been moved to the Hank Williams Museum in Nashville.

Hank's mother and sister Irene looking over the thousands of sympathy expressions they received in the aftermath of Hank's death. (Courtesy Thurston Moore Country)

Audrey Williams at the zenith of her career as Hank Williams' widow. This photo was snapped at the Montgomery premiere of the 1964 M-G-M film, "Your Cheatin' Heart." Audrey had served as chief consultant for the project. (Courtesy Country Music Foundation Library and Media Center)

Hank Williams's grave in Montgomery's Oak Hill Cemetery Annex.

Ryman Auditorium, home of the Grand Ole Opry from 1943 to 1974.

The new Opry House on the grounds of Opryland U.S.A. in suburban Nashville.

Nashville, circa 1940–45. This photo is taken from the southwest, with the Ryman Auditorium appearing in the center of the background. It is the building with the peaked roof. (Courtesy Nashville Area Chamber of Commerce)

Nashville today, shown from the north of the downtown area. The Ryman is lost in the midbackground amid the tall office buildings. (Photo by Robert Johnson, courtesy Nashville Area Chamber of Commerce)

Hank Williams makes a special guest appearance on the Prince Albert Tobacco NBC radio network segment of the Grand Old Opry. (Courtesy Thurston Moore Country)

10

Ridin' High/Draggin' a Chain

In the fall of 1950, Hank Williams and the Drifting Cowboys were playing a week-long stint at Baltimore's Hippodrome Theatre. At one of the afternoon shows, the audience was somewhat taken aback by the unusual manner in which Hank was announcing 'his show. It was his custom, many people knew, to introduce his band members one at a time between numbers. But something was different today.

"Like ya'll to meet Don Helms, an ol' Alabama boy I been knowin' for a long time," Hank drawled after his second number. "We call him 'Shag' . . . why don't you make him feel welcome!"

After the applause, the band went into the next song and played it through. Then it was time for the star to introduce another band member.

"Right here on the steel guitar," Hank offered, "is ol' Don Helms . . . ol' Shag. Let's have a big hand for him."

The audience came up with a smattering of applause and the Drifting Cowboys went back to work. But Hank wasn't through introducing Don Helms. He did it two more times.

"The fourth time Hank introduced Don," Hillous Butrum remembers, "Don turned around and started tuning his instrument."

Hank Williams—as most of the audience could perceive and as the band members knew full well—was looped. The Hippodrome engagement was the first time since his rise to stardom that Hank did a show drunk. If there had been sprees in 1949 or

137

earlier in 1950, they had been off the road and out of the public
eye.

With this series of shows came a new era, the era of
Watching Out for Hank. It would be a while before his career
was adversely affected by alcohol, but from now on the Drifting
Cowboys took on new responsibilities.

"We'd often have to carry him from place to place," Hillous
Butrum remembers.

"It made me sad," says Don Helms. "I'd think, 'Come on,
Hoss. We've come a long way. Let's don't blow it now.'" Helms
and the rest of the band were proud of what they'd helped Hank
to accomplish, and they'd hoped perhaps the drinking problem
would be beaten. Now it seemed to loom bigger than ever.

"We were doing four shows a day that week at the Hippodrome," Butrum recalls, "so we posted a guard at Hank's
dressing room door between shows—we'd have somebody there
all day to keep Hank away from the booze."

Butrum was left one afternoon to watch the door.

"I was sittin' out there for a while, and then I heard the door
squeak," he says. "Hank was peepin' out. At first he thought he
was safe, but when he started into the hall, he saw me."

"Oh. They left you here, huh?" Hank mumbled.

"Yep."

"Well, Hillous, let's you and me go over to the hotel for a
sandwich," Williams suggested.

He looked like he needed it, so Butrum reluctantly agreed.
The pair left the theater and started across the street toward
the hotel. Naturally to get where they were going, they had to
go past a bar.

"Hillous, you got any money?" Hank asked. "Buy me one
drink, will ya?"

"I can't, Hank," Butrum answered. "Oscar would shoot me."
(Oscar Davis was promoting the Hippodrome show.)

"Come on."

"Nope."

"But I need one *bad*," Hank pleaded. "Jus' buy me one . . . to
get me through the next show. . . ."

An embarrassed Butrum finally said he'd buy one drink, and

they walked into the dimly-lit bar. As the flustered bass player looked on, his boss buddied up to the bartender.

"Gimme a double shot," Hank told him. And he downed the drink in one gulp. "Gimme another one," he said. Before Butrum could protest, the bartender had put the second drink in front of Williams. Hank swilled it as quickly as the first.

"OK, that's all," Butrum told Williams.

Hank didn't argue. He went peaceably back to the dressing room with his employee holding his arm. Later, at their hotel room, Williams asked Hillous Butrum a surprise question:

"Hillous, you want me to get you a recordin' contract?"

"You can't do that, Hank," the younger man scoffed. "I can't sing." (Actually he could in a pinch.)

"You don't think I can get you a contract."

"No."

"The hell I can't," Hank snorted. "I got Audrey one." Then he added, as if to nail down an iron-clad argument: "If I can get her one, I can get one for anybody."

The Hippodrome engagement went from bad to worse, and toward the end of the week, Jerry Rivers reports that Hank missed at least one show completely. He was holed up in his hotel room "extremely depressed."

In truth, Hank's drinking had never really stopped for any great length of time. Perhaps he'd been at his best in Shreveport, but he couldn't resist the beer at that Easter Sunday party down there. Though he may have been on the wagon during his first months as a Nashville Opry star, Don Helms remembers that he had to cart Hank out to a hospital in suburban Madison to dry out as early as the fall of '49.

"He was pretty much the same the whole time I knew him," Helms concludes. "He'd stay off for awhile, then one day he'd turn up too drunk to walk."

It always seemed that the sprees coincided with disagreements between Hank and Audrey, but it's impossible to lay the blame for them entirely upon her. To begin with, Hank already had a drinking problem when he met Audrey, but the lifestyle in which Hank and Audrey found themselves by 1950 offered several conflicting elements that also strongly affected Hank.

First there was the affluence.

"In the early years, Hank enjoyed his success," claims Minnie Pearl. To all appearances that was true. Hank liked having plenty of money. He was generous, and enjoyed buying gifts for friends and for Audrey. Furs, jewels, dresses, all were lavished upon her by a husband who vividly remembered their lean years.

Hank soon bought a 500-acre farm outside Nashville which he stocked with horses and hunting dogs. He hoped that someday he'd remodel its large, run-down main house into a family home. Aside from some roof repair, though, the plans were never carried out. The place served mostly as a retreat for hunting, or for riding "HiLife," Hank's favorite horse.

Then Audrey decided they should open a store in downtown Nashville. After all, other stars had record shops and amusement parks, why shouldn't Hank Williams' name make some money for a family business? So "Hank and Audrey's Corral" was established on Commerce Street in Nashville, offering the tourists a full line of men's and ladies' western apparel. Hank and Audrey also did a remote broadcast from the Corral. They sponsored themselves out of the store's advertising budget.

Hank had bought Audrey a yellow '49 Cadillac convertible when they moved to Nashville, and he continued to buy her a new car every year. At any given time, the Williamses owned at least two of GM's finest in addition to Hank's current touring car. Hank was literally making money faster than he could spend it. There were spurts where a hundred thousand a month would pour in.

Along with the money came business pressure, and that didn't jive with ol' Harm's outlook. He had no time for meetings or conferences or sometimes even contract-signings.

"Hank's philosophy was 'Let me do my shows, and when I'm done, I want to go fishin' or huntin' and I don't want to be bothered,'" says Jerry Rivers. Of course it couldn't be that way. Rivers illustrates:

"One day me and June [Jerry's wife] had gone out on the lake with Hank for a day of fishing, and along in the afternoon, here came a big seaplane right down and landed on the water."

Soon a motorboat came out to Hank's boat from the dock, with Audrey aboard waving to him. She'd chartered the plane to come and get Hank because he was about to miss an important business meeting back in town.

"I honestly believe he was *tryin'* to miss that meeting," says Rivers.

Other complications in Hank's life as a star included women. What was he supposed to do with all the females who came by his dressing room after a show or even followed him to his hotel?

"All he had to do was open the door to be with a woman," says Don Helms. Occasionally a "come in" was also necessary.

Helms testifies that other women were never a problem for Audrey and Hank. "She never knew about 'em, so it wasn't a problem." Even so, Hank Williams was not a person who took infidelity lightly. He'd take it, all right, but later it would haunt him.

"An unfeeling man would have drank and caroused and savored the memory," Ed Linn wrote in his article, "The Short Life of Hank Williams." "Hank cursed himself." If Hank had the "morals of an alley cat," as one acquaintance asserted, then he would have been better off with the alley cat's shamelessness, too.

Still he could have come up with enough shame to force himself into staying true to Audrey, but the emerging impression is that he felt his out-of-town dalliances were not really affronts to her person. By contrast, when the time inevitably came that Hank first heard rumors about Audrey, it tore him up emotionally and sent him reeling into deep depression.

Finally, Hank Williams' psyche was threatened by the "woods-animal distrust" that Minnie Pearl speaks of, a deeply-imbedded bitterness that was hatched on the Georgiana sidewalks and grew thick and stubborn on his soul in the years of scuttling from one tough honky-tonk to the next.

"Hank always figured somebody had an angle on him," one colleague explained. Wesley Rose hypothesizes that Hank had suffered his share of raw deals in his early show-business years.

It wasn't really shady business tactics that planted this bitter seed, it was the social coolness of the upper classes that had chilled Hank's dreams back when he was Montgomery's resident wild man.

Much later, Hank went through Montgomery on a tour with an Opry package show and shared a hotel room with Ernest Tubb. Tubb remembered later how Hank got a call in their room from a banker in town. Hank was not particularly hospitable.

"What's wrong?" Tubb asked Williams after he'd hung up the phone.

"He invited me up to his house for dinner," Hank answered with a strange voice.

"Well, what's the matter with that?"

"Look," Williams exploded. "I've known that guy all my life. When I was starving in this town, the sonofabitch wouldn't buy me a hamburger. Now there's nothing too good for me. What's the matter, ain't I the same guy?"

Neither Ernest Tubb nor anybody else could convince Hank that society's respect and recognition had to be earned. By the time he became a star, Hank's ambition to earn recognition was all twisted up inside him with the twin convictions that he *was somebody* and that the somebody he was was ultimately a failure.

"I'm nothing but a drunkard," he cried out once to a friend. "Why do people expect me to be anything else?"

Failure returns itself and answers itself across great gulfs and small circumstances. It comes back to whisper in the ears of the superachievers as well as the louts. Hank Williams had enough guts to work for many years at becoming a great musician, but along the way the helpless despair of those early, hungry experiences crept into some ragged corner of his mind and hid itself permanently.

Perhaps the absence of a father had something to do with this eventual despair, or it could have been something else that caused it. All of us have felt at least a glimmer of the conviction that life with its challenges and hopes and pratfalls is nothing in the end but a cruel joke. With the alcohol gorilla on Hank's back who could have blamed him for such a conclusion?

An ambitious, hard-willed wife, a career running out of control, a nagging faceless insecurity, and a body that couldn't begin to handle the Southern culture's main ingredient—these were just some of the smirking demons Hank's mind could call up at will.

Accordingly, he developed a motto. "Don't worry 'bout nothin'," Hank Williams would tell a friend or an audience with a wry smile, "'Cause nothin' ain't gonna work out all right, nohow."

Still Hank's sensational tours, through 1950 and 1951, continued to work surprisingly well. Opry Artists Services Manager Jim Denny initiated a bodyguard system to keep Hank straight for important engagements, while promoters Oscar Davis and A. B. Bamford put together sellout shows all across the hinterlands.

By this time Hank's live-audience poise was so well-perfected that he loved to get heckled, because he always knew how to handle a bothersome loudmouth.

"Hey, buddy," Hank would yell. "Wait right there! Yore mommy and daddy are comin' by in a minute and we're gonna get 'em married!"

When more disgusted he'd use a terser line while pointing straight at his antagonist: "Would somebody get a shovel and clean that up?"

The Drifting Cowboys went through a couple of personnel changes. Bob McNett left the band in May of 1950 to return to his native Pennsylvania, where he and his brother had a dream of opening a country music park.

"Hank had always done right by me," McNett recalls. "That wasn't the problem." One night shortly after Hank joined the Opry, McNett had gotten mixed up and played the wrong song introduction in the middle of a Saturday night show at the Ryman. The entire group had to stop and begin the song over again.

After the show, McNett caught up with Hank and Audrey as they were pulling away from the back door of the auditorium in their car.

"I'm really sorry I blew that intro, Hank," McNett told his boss. "Maybe I oughta leave the group. I've been thinking maybe I'm not ready for the big-time."

Hank smiled at the young guitarist and said, "You've been off for a week or so. You were nervous and tight. We'll be going out on the road again next week. . . ."

Hank put the Cadillac in gear. "You'll be all right," he assured McNett as he drove off down the alley.

"I left the group," says McNett today, "mostly because I wanted to do something on my own. I had the feeling I was traveling all over the country lookin' at someone else's back and that's as far as I could see."

When Bob McNett told Hank of his decision, he was surprised at Hank's reaction. "I don't want to see you go," Hank told him.

"It was as if he took it personally," says McNett. "I didn't think he'd care one way or the other, but it seemed like he was kinda hurt . . . like he needed all of us around him and didn't want to lose any of us."

A night or two later, Williams tried to get Bob to reconsider. "Me and the boys figured out how you're gonna stay," he said. "Besides, there's no money up there in those Pennsylvania mountains." But McNett's mind was made up.

"We lost a lot of money the first year with our park," he says, "and Hank heard about it." When the two saw each other in 1951, Hank asked McNett how he was doing financially. He pressed and pried, trying to get the truth, but Bob maintained everything was fine.

"He was either going to give me some money, or come up there and play for free," McNett speculates today. "Hank was that kind of guy. One time a letter came in to WSM from a lady who said she was in bad shape and really needed some money. Everyone advised him against it, but I'm pretty sure Hank sent that woman a check."

Sammy Pruitt, another Alabama boy who had first become a Drifting Cowboy with Don Helms in 1943, was Hank's choice to replace Bob McNett on electric guitar. Pruitt had gone into the Navy, then rejoined Hank in Montgomery from 1946 to 1948, until Hank went to Shreveport.

"I was playin' with Happy Wilson's Golden River Boys and Joe Rumore on WAPI in Birmingham," says Pruitt, "when Jerry Rivers called me from Sioux City, Iowa, in the spring of 1950." Pruitt met and joined the Drifting Cowboys in Nashville shortly thereafter. He stayed with Hank until August, 1952, when Hank was fired from the Opry.

The change from McNett to Pruitt was the final refinement in the Hank Williams road and recording sound. McNett with his "commercial feel" had added some electric leads to the basic fiddle/steel sound featured on most of Hank's instrumental breaks, but Pruitt says of himself that he "hardly played any lead at all." Instead he concentrated on "electric crack rhythm" as they called it back then. This technique was what gave the Drifting Cowboys their rhythmic, bluesy sound, forerunner to the Memphis rockabilly revolution a couple of years after Hank's death.

"We were the first band to take that kind of sound out to the nation," says Pruitt. "I picked the thing up from Zeke Turner and played the crack rhythm with Hank before most people had ever heard it." A little later, Luther Perkins would use the electric crack rhythm as the primary stylistic "innovation" of a young Arkansas boy named Johnny Cash when he went to the top of the country and pop charts in 1956 with "I Walk The Line."

In January of 1951, Hillous Butrum left the Drifting Cowboys to join Hank Snow, the "Singing Ranger" from Nova Scotia who'd become the Opry's first Canadian star. Perhaps Butrum was looking for more chances to sing (not very likely), maybe he was just looking for a change, but most likely the reason for his leaving was tied to Hank's drinking problem. The job of taking care of Hank most often went to Don Helms, who had known Hank longer and played with him more years than anybody else in the group; but often Butrum, too, would get the honors. Helms had been putting up with Hank's alcoholism since 1943. Butrum had not. Perhaps with a more objective eye he could see the handwriting on the wall.

Butrum's replacement as bassist/comedian was a tall, amiable young showman named Howard Watts. Watts was already building a following under his stage name of Cedric Rainwater,

and brought to the Drifting Cowboys more comedic talent than
any of Hank's groups had ever known.

"Ced" is the only member of the post-1949 Drifting Cowboys
fraternity who is not still living, but he contributed his share of
memories to the group. The boys still talk about the time Jim
Denny came along with them on a fishing trip, got his business
suit wet, and wound up walking around the camp in Ced's
baggy pants and red-striped shirt.

Then there was the time Don Helms and the rest of the
Cowboys decided to break Hank of his annoying habit of
running his fingers into someone else's pocket when he wanted
a cigarette and was out. (Jerry Rivers maintains Hank was
"constantly" out.) Helms loaded up a packful of smokes with
small exploding loads in a hotel room one day and waited.
"Within an hour," Jerry Rivers writes in *Hank Williams: From
Life to Legend,*

> Hank dug into Don's pocket, put a cigarette in his mouth
> and picked up the hotel telephone to call a business associate.
> Just as he said, "Operator . . ." the cigarette exploded with a
> loud bang, leaving a short stub in Hank's mouth and tobacco
> scattered over his face.
>
> We all died laughing, but none like Cedric, who laughed
> and rolled on the floor until he cried. Five minutes later, Ced
> lit a cigarette that blew his glasses off, and he got so mad he
> wouldn't ride to the auditorium with us, and took a taxi.

The Road stories go on and on: the afternoon Jerry Rivers
was driving Hank's Cadillac into Tampa and a buzzard flew
through the windshield, filling the car with blood, guts, glass,
and feathers; the morning in Amarillo, after an all-night drive,
when Don Helms poured a pitcher of ice water from a hotel
window into the bass horn of a high-school marching band
assembling below for a parade at 9 A.M.; and the night in Illinois
when Hank and the boys were playing a show from the roof of a
drive-in theater projection booth. The floodlights, according to
Jerry Rivers, were drawing "bugs by the thousands" to the
platform area, "and just as Hank opened his mouth wide
yodeling 'Lovesick Blues,' a huge candle-moth flew right in."

Hank coughed heartily and managed to spit out the moth, which drew him a "five-minute ovation of car-horn blowing."

An interesting kink in the Road experiences of Hank and the boys concerned Hank's frequent campaigns against any of the Drifting Cowboys using the Lord's name in vain.

"He took a cigar box," remembers Don Helms, "and put a slot in it. Then he'd make anybody who used the Lord's name in vain put a quarter in the box for every time they did it.

"Then one time we were late for a show and got off the highway in a little town in Illinois," Helms continues. "The more we tried to get out of that town, the more lost we got. Hank must have used up a couple of dollars worth of quarters that day."

The Drifting Cowboys always looked forward to a date anywhere near Biloxi, Mississippi. A local club owner named Si Simon—owner (naturally) of Si's Place—became a loyal fan and host to Hank and the boys. Whenever they'd play in the area, they'd also do a late-night show at Si's club, which he would follow up with a boiled shrimp dinner and a wee-hours yacht ride out into the Gulf for a couple of hours of fishing from a barge anchored above a mackerel or lemonfish paradise.

Hank Williams must have liked Si Simon, as evidenced by the fact that he once took a cab from Nashville to Biloxi to avoid missing a show at Si's, and on another similar occasion chartered a DC-3. "The plane landed in Biloxi," writes Jerry Rivers, "with Hank, the pilot, and co-pilot aboard."

Hank's recording success in 1950–51 went from hot to torrid. No sooner did "Cold, Cold Heart" begin to cool on the country racks, than "I Can't Help It (If I'm Still In Love With You)" was released and Hank was hot again. Then "Hey Good Lookin'," one of his greatest up-tempo jump numbers, became an even bigger hit than "I Can't Help It." It came along in the summer of 1951.

By the time "Lonesome Whistle" was released in September of '51, Hank was so hot that the record sold 100,000 copies in its first week of release. That didn't happen very often in 1951—there were no promotion blitzes or Ed Sullivan debuts for Hank—just an adoring public who learned from their local country disc-jockeys that Hank had a new record out. That was all it took. By the time of his death, Hank's fans were estimated to be fifteen million strong; in those days, that figure was one-tenth of the population of the United States.

This kind of popularity was not lost on the Hollywood community. Obviously Hank's looks had something to do with his success. Why not put that straight jaw and those haunting eyes up on the silver screen? Producer Joe Pasternak saw Hank's act in California and sent a script back to Nashville with him. He was offering Hank a small but significant part in "Small Town Girl," a picture he was doing with Jane Powell and Farley Granger. Unfortunately when Pasternak was ready to set up a shooting schedule, Hank was not in shape for working. The deal fell through.

Then on September 24, 1951, the *Nashville Banner* made the following proud announcement:

> Nashville's Hank Williams—the Grand Ole Opry's long, lean, lonesome singer of the blues—last night signed a long-term contract for a series of motion pictures to be made in Hollywood. . . .

There had been rumors around town, but now it must be true! Frank Walker from M-G-M records was quoted in the story as saying the movies would be "top-quality, regular feature-length pictures, with Hank Williams starring with some of the top names of Hollywood."

So ol' Hank was going to be a movie star! Well why not? There had been lots of singing cowboys—Ritter, Autry, and others—and some of them had considerably less singing talent than Hank, not to mention potbellies that contrasted sharply with Hank's trim, angular frame.

But the thing was not to be. Though M-G-M had been talking excitedly about Hank starring in his own life story, nothing but an uncharacteristic silence leaked from M-G-M's publicity department in the months following the September 24 announcement. When questioned much later about the matter, M-G-M officials declared there "never was a contract."

This last assertion seems doubtful. For one thing, a seasoned show business veteran like Frank Walker knew better than to announce an event that could not be verified. For another thing, neither Hank nor his business associates *needed* the movie contract. He was a star already. There was no need for Hank Williams to exploit Hollywood—the opposite was more the case—so a phony contract-signing dreamed up as a publicity stunt is highly unlikely.

Finally, there are the several photos taken of Hank purportedly signing an M-G-M movie contract. Among those also photographed at that time were the Drifting Cowboys, Frank Walker, Wesley Rose, and Jim Denny. It's impossible to believe that such an august group would have gathered for the signing of a bogus contract.

There was a contract, all right, and in Nashville the rumor mill went mad. "Hank's gonna be a movie star!" "The contract calls for five thousand dollars a week!" "It's a million-dollar package extending for four years!"

The terms were never made public. Before any production wheels could begin to turn, the entire venture was dropped by M-G-M. No explanation. No press releases. Nothing. Why?

Wesley Rose is sure he knows why. He accompanied Hank to the office of Dore Schary in Hollywood. Schary at the time was M-G-M's production chief. Hank was on the coast to do some shows and also to enter a series of meetings with M-G-M's movie production people about his film career. According to some sources, Hank was depressed and upset about his marital woes about this time and was in the middle of a long bout with the bottle. In any case, he was not on his best behavior when he and Wesley Rose walked into Dore Schary's plush office. Roger Williams feels that the meeting meant so much that Hank rebounded from anxiety into the old bitter pride, he wasn't going to suck up to anybody.

"When we came into the office, Hank didn't take his hat off," Rose recalls. Perhaps ol' Harm didn't want the movie people to know how bald he was, but that was just a start.

"As the gentleman began to talk with us," Rose continues, "Hank leaned back in his chair, pulled his hat down over his eyes, and stuck his boots right up on the man's desk."

Schary was not immediately sure he was being insulted. Perhaps all hillbillies behaved this way. But as he tried to question Hank and make small talk, he was answered by a succession of curt one-word hyperboles sprinkled with a few smirks from underneath Hank's white ten-gallon headpiece. Schary got the message and adjourned the meeting without discussing any business at all.

Outside on the M-G-M lot, Wesley Rose asked Hank why he had chosen to jeopardize his movie chances by acting so disrespectfully. Williams had stopped to get his boots polished by a studio-lot shoeshine boy.

"You see this kid here?" Williams asked Rose, gesturing down at the small black figure hurriedly shining Hank's tooled-leather stage boots. "This kid here is more of a man than that guy in the office will ever be." And before Hank Williams left the M-G-M studios behind him, he gave the shoeshine boy a large-denomination bill.

This kind of behavior might have grieved Fred and Wesley Rose—after all, they were working beyond the call of duty to make Hank Williams as big a star as possible. Fred Rose, for example, was never paid by M-G-M for his virtual management of Hank's recording career. Wesley Rose, while his father chose and timed Hank's record releases, was in charge of getting Hank's songs into the hands of pop A and R men in New York and Hollywood. Wesley had been instrumental also in getting the entire movie contract thing off the ground in the first place.

Yet the Roses seem to have regarded his fluffed chance at a motion picture career as just the result of a quirk in Hank's nature. "He had a negative concept of most business people," Wesley recalls. "You could see it because he didn't want to meet with many of them, outside of Frank Walker at M-G-M and possibly Mitch Miller. He didn't actually respect businessmen too much. I guess it was a flashback to his being turned down as he was coming up."

Hank kept all his business dealings to a minimum. Earlier in his Nashville years, he had been befriended by Sam Hunt, then an officer of the Third National Bank and later Vice-Chairman of the Board there. Hunt remembers Hank Williams as a man who was strictly looking for a place to cache his cash; Hank was not interested in investments or real estate like some of the other Opry clients with whom Hunt worked.

Hank, after all, was earning plenty of cash. Through his songwriting royalties, record sales, and personal appearances Hank Williams averaged over a hundred thousand dollars a year in 1950, 1951, and 1952. In today's economy, his earnings might have topped a million per year.

Though the movies were denied them, the Drifting Cowboys did manage to get on the two biggest network television shows of the early fifties. Hank and the boys flew with an Opry show unit on a chartered DC-3 to New York for an appearance on the Kate Smith Show, and Hank Williams was also a guest on Perry Como's program. Whether or not Hank was thrilled with these appearances, the Drifting Cowboys were pinching themselves with pride and exhilaration.

As Roger Williams has noted, there's no telling how much money Hank would have made if he'd been working in the heyday of television instead of its infancy, and if he'd kept himself together for a movie career. As it was, he was still the biggest moneymaker of his time in Nashville.

Hank's attitude about his success was decidedly ambivalent. Minnie Pearl remembers one side of his reaction:

"We used to gather in what they called the musicians' lounge at WSM," she says. "It was just kind of a recreation room with pop machines and comfortable chairs. This was back before we were all so busy.

"Hank would come in after a recording session," Minnie continues, "and say, 'Fellers, I just recorded a song that's gonna sell 65,000 copies the first day!' and we'd all take it like the gospel truth." Hank clearly enjoyed being a success.

Still, much of the significance of his stardom eluded him. The fact that he was selling millions of records and becoming rich because people loved and respected him and his music never quite sank in, at least, not in any way that brought satisfaction.

"Hank was the kind of guy," says Don Helms, "that if you ran up to him and told him another one of his records had just hit Number One on the charts, he'd say, 'Yeah, well . . . let's go fishin'.'"

The Drifting Cowboys came to a point where nothing Hank might have pulled could have surprised them. In Dallas in July of 1950, they drove the tour car in for a series of shows and were supposed to meet Hank at the Adolphus Hotel. When the group arrived, however, Hank had not checked in. They parked the car and spent some time walking around downtown, then came back to the hotel desk. Still no Hank. Getting a bit edgy, the four musicians sat down in the lobby to wait for their boss.

It wasn't long until Jerry Rivers spotted a familiar-looking tall, slender figure slipping onto the elevator, wearing dark glasses. "I jumped up and asked the Bell Captain if that man getting on the elevator wasn't Hank Williams," Rivers writes in his biography of Hank. "He said, 'No, sir. That was Mr. Herman P. Willis in number 504.'"

Herman P. Willis was a "mythical name" used by the Drifting Cowboys for "any dummy who never does anything right." The musicians went to room 504 where they found Hank sitting in a chair having a good laugh.

One biographer believes Hank used this disguise to get away from the band so as to get to the booze, but Rivers asserts it was for an opposite motive. According to his account, Hank was doing it to elude a certain Dallas clubowner who was trying to get Hank out on the town. Finally, Williams had a notarized letter drawn up by the public stenographer at the hotel authorizing Jerry Rivers as his manager "during my stay in the State of Texas." Thus sanctioned, Jerry went back to the hotel room and intercepted all telephone calls for Hank.

"That evening," writes Rivers, "I began to receive persistent, repeated calls, and as soon as Mr. Williams could be located, I was to have him immediately call his local contractor, Mr. Jack Ruby."

After that incident, Rivers never heard of Jack Ruby again until late November of 1963.

Hank did make attempts to stay away from alcohol. He had to, because he couldn't stop once he started. It was either nothing or Rip City. When he was on the wagon, he'd even order booze for friends and decline it himself.

"I saw him do this for the first time in Memphis," Hillous Butrum recalls. "Eddie Hill, a Memphis deejay, was coming to Hank's room with some friends. So Hank ordered a tableful of booze."

When the revelers arrived, Butrum remembers, Hank

pointed to the table and said, "There it is. I wish I could drink with you, but you know what'd happen. You'd be carryin' me around the rest of this tour."

On the other hand, there were the tours where the Drifting Cowboys *did* carry him around. Sometimes the band members wouldn't know which kind of tour they were on until they were onstage.

"We'd go to a show and start our opening at the appointed time," says Hillous Butrum, "sometimes that would be before Hank arrived at the theater or club. We'd be on the stage and looking over in the wings to see when he'd arrive."

The group learned to tell from the stage whether or not their leader, when he arrived in the wings, was drunk or sober.

"If he was standin' there kinda natural, you knew he was sober," continues Butrum, "but if you saw him make this peculiar motion with his arm—if he brought it straight up and then down by his side—watch out. He'd always do that when he was drunk. Don't ask me why. He'd throw his arm up in the air, and bring it down and make a sound like a horse blowin' air through his lips—phhppppplllph—and then he'd flash this crazy grin. . . ."

And the Drifting Cowboys knew they'd better be ready for anything.

"One time we were playin' Saint Joe, Missouri," says Butrum, "and Hank walked on—we knew he was loaded—and greeted the people with 'Move It On Over.' When he was done he said, 'Thank ya'll . . . Glad you enjoyed that . . . got another song like to do for you. . . .'

"Well, the people hadn't really enjoyed it *that* much," Butrum continues, "because Hank had only sung one verse of the song over and over again."

Next Hank introduced "I'm A Long, Gone Daddy" and according to Butrum, sang the same repeated verse from "Move It On Over" (a similar song) instead of the words to "Daddy." Somehow they made it through the show.

Hank's humor as well as his music suffered when he was drinking. He always introduced the band members with a little joke of some kind. For instance, here's how a funny introduction of Butrum once got grounded at its conclusion:

"Now I'd like to interduce our bass player," Hank told the audience. "I want ya'll to take a good look at him. He's particular about his appearance . . . You see he's got his pants pressed real nice (gesture to pants) . . . he's got his shirt pressed (gesture to shirt) . . . Look at his hair. It's all pushed down and that big wave looks just right. . . . He even went next door and borrowed Jerry's toothbrush. . . ." By this time, Hillous had blushed on cue several times.

Next Hank went for the punchline: "He run into some trouble, though. He was tryin' to put some toilet water on his hair and the lid fell on his head. . . ." As the laughter roared up onto the stage, Hank turned, pointed right at Hillous, and said, "Here he is . . . *Jerry Rivers!*"

Hank never realized his mistake that night, partly because most of the audience didn't know Rivers from Butrum. But most of the time, if Hank was drunk, the audience knew it.

"He didn't do many shows drunk," recalls Rivers, "because he went too quickly into a condition where he couldn't even find his way out of his hotel room."

"If Hank was scheduled to do a show at eight o'clock," says Rivers, "and he started drinking at seven—you could just kiss that show goodbye."

One show Hank did manage to get to was in Richmond, Virginia, on January 30, 1952, but perhaps he should have stayed home. A reviewer for the Richmond *Times Dispatch* named Edith Lindeman caught his stumbling, swaying, first show that night and gave the Grand Ole Opry star a scathing account in the morning paper. Hank managed to recover in time for the next night's performance and dedicated his first song to Miz Lindeman: "Mind Your Own Business."

By the time of the Richmond debacle, Hank was under constant watch by one of several appointees whose job it was to keep him from drinking. But it was never easy. Many times Hank would arrive at the auditorium sober, only to run into some friends who'd slip him a few slugs backstage (such was the case in Richmond). Hank also had several tricks he could pull solo: He'd buy up quantities of miniature airlines-size bottles and hide them in his boots or in the auditorium men's room stalls. His connections for these purchases were often bellhops or radio station porters, because the boys wouldn't let him near a liquor store.

Jim Denny of the Opry Artists Services Bureau seemed to have a soft spot for Hank. He put up with the headaches of booking Hank Williams longer than he had to, partly because he empathized with him. Denny's childhood had been no picnic, either. Jim Denny's relationship with Hank was as close as anyone's in the business, yet he always maintained before his own death that "nobody really was close to Hank."

Since Jim Denny's summation is essentially true, it's difficult to pinpoint the reasons for Hank Williams' personal breakdown amid such towering professional success. Most of his songs, contrary to popular belief, don't give much of a clue. The great hits of the high-riding years are nearly all in one of two veins. Either they are songs of pining love— "Cold, Cold Heart," "I Can't Help It," "You Win Again"—or else they fall into the pop-novelty category of "Hey, Good Lookin'," "Honky-Tonk Blues," "Jambalaya," and "Settin' the Woods on Fire."

Not that these songs are not illuminating: The heartbreak songs tell us graphically of Hank Williams' love for Audrey and of the pain it brought him, while the jump tunes give us an idea of how Hank shook off the blues by shouting the blues.

But why did Hank's heartbreak have to end in self-destruction? Why was he so *trapped* in the "honky-tonk blues"? What incredible chemistry of psychological pressure points caused a gutsy young man like Hank Williams—alcoholic or not, broken love or no, bad back aside—to burn out in such a very, very short time?

There are, after all, many alcoholics who float along for decades and live to tell about it. There are show business personalities whose marriages break up and who manage to capitalize financially on the pathos and the publicity. And if Hank's back problem was serious (it was), still not every person with a couple of ruptured discs winds up a death-slave to his prescribed pain medication.

No, Hank Williams' tragic fall into oblivion was, like the rest of his life, greater than the sum of its ingredients. But there is one song, one of the Luke the Drifter recitations that was recorded in the closing days of 1950, that puts down in the best words since "I'm So Lonesome I Could Cry" the essential Hank Williams self-revelatory statement. The song, the poem, is "Men With Broken Hearts."

The song opens as Luke the narrator makes it clear that, unlike most of the other stories he's told, here he is going to use himself as an illustration. He tells us that we'll meet many men just like him along life's "busy street." Men with stooped weary shoulders, bowed heads, and eyes that reflect defeat.

"Men With Broken Hearts" is primarily a treatise about people who have given up. The thrust of the song asks—really tells—the listener not to judge too quickly that kind of individual. Hank reminds us that we've never really known what these men have had to go through.

Our temptation is to analyze the song word by word, line by line, but it really must be *heard* for its impact to be fully felt. Just a few phrases are all we need to glimpse the interior of Hank Williams' tortured world.

What are the characteristics of the broken-hearted? First Luke tells us they live "within the past" where sorrow reigns, it "plays all parts." Here it is late in 1950—Hank is on the threshold of his biggest year—and Luke (Hank) is talking about his own life as having *no future*. Professional success is not even an issue here—that's all external, unable to touch the place inside where a "livin' death" is all that remains for these "Men With Broken Hearts."

Just as the storyteller in "Lost Highway" points to a time in the past when the tragedy began, so Luke says that just one misstep or merciless deed is all it takes to start the misery. From that point on, hope is gone. The Drifter's fate is sealed.

Luke cites a loss of faith in "love and life" as a further step toward despair. He doesn't mention loss of faith in God; in fact the song assumes both God's creation and God's grace. In the fourth verse, the verse where Hank tells us we've never walked in his shoes, he cites one experience we may not have encountered: the feeling of helplessness when watching one's own heart die spiritually. He follows this up, almost before this has had time to make its full impact on the listener, with a footnote that this type of experience can happen to people from all classes and all walks of life. There are no social distinctions where true cosmic despair is concerned.

The fifth verse is the capper. Here Luke describes how the pain and cruelty of life can become so intense that some men begin to wish for death in order to escape. He then asks God why this must be so. Why should some people seem to be singled out to suffer inside?

Finally, Luke turns back to his audience to suggest that we always be ready to help these men, or any men, along their way, no matter what the circumstances might be. In closing, he reminds us that the same God has made us all: we the more fortunate and the "Men With Broken Hearts."

It's apparent that this song-poem is slightly out of place in the general category of good ol' country songs in there with "Rollin' In My Sweet Baby's Arms" and "The Battle of New Orleans." The words, especially as Hank speaks them on record, have a dignity and poignancy that belong to great literature.

But what is he saying?

Hank lived and worked and thought in a Christian culture. Many of its presuppositions were his: right and wrong exist, bad deeds bring bad consequences. Hank's supposition underlying "Men With Broken Hearts," and also underlying his entire self-destructive slide, was that God—if He existed—had given up on Hank Williams. Therefore Hank Williams gave up on himself. He didn't have the moral strength to change the way he was—to kick alcohol, for example—and he really felt too much shame, mixed with an amount of pride known only to himself, to call out to God for help. If indeed God helped people, which was doubtful, He surely wouldn't want to deal with such a drunken adulterous bum as ol' Hank.

There were probably a number of people in Montgomery's fundamentalist churches who would have stuck up their eyebrows and agreed that God wouldn't want to deal with that drunk Hank Williams, that guy who cussed and drank and talked about snot comin' out of people's noses. God didn't mess with no-goods like *Hank Williams*. It's all too probable that Hank picked up and believed this line of reasoning from the "Christians" of his own background.

That it wasn't really a biblical proposition never got through to Hank. He never read the Bible . . . he'd have had to pick one up off Grandma's or Aunt Somebody's tissue-table where it sat gathering dust between the doilies and the Last Supper fans from Jackson's Funeral Home. Hank went for monster comics instead. You could pick one of *those* up at any newsstand along with your *Billboard* and *Cash Box*.

You had your people whose paths were kept from the Lost Highway by the Grace of God. (If not for that grace, Luke reminds us, it could be those people instead of him who ended up broken-hearted.) So those people went home and sat in stuffed chairs and fanned themselves with the Jackson Home fans and listened to the preachers sellin' baby chicks on the radio. The other folk, outside God's grace, got to have fun and drink and go to honky-tonks and read monster comics and *be* on the radio. But there was a price involved—your soul.

Dr. Crawford "Corky" Adams doesn't have any doilies in his library. His library is two stories high with a vaulted ceiling. Within it are a walnut desk, a fireplace, several comfortable sofas and chairs, and a baby grand piano. The long brick house which contains this impressive hideaway sits atop three acres or so of a shady hill on Nashville's fashionable Overton Lea Road. It's only minutes from the old Hank Williams home on Franklin Road.

Long years ago, before Doctor Adams had a swimming pool, before he became a President of the American College of Chest Physicians, before he'd collected two stories of books and memorabilia to relax with, Corky Adams was just a young Nashville heart specialist who dabbled in songwriting as a hobby. He had friends over to his house and they'd sit around the piano, drink a few drinks, and compose music and lyrics. Not all of Corky Adams' friends were amateurs like himself. One of them—a man named Beasley Smith—had written several popular songs including one called "That Lucky Ol' Sun."

Another young man who joined Corky's little fraternity was a newcomer to Nashville—a guy who sang on the radio and wrote songs himself—a real likable fellow named Hank Williams.

"Hank came to me first as a patient," says Corky Adams, "but it wasn't long before we became friends as well."

Wasn't this a bit odd? This was the same guy who wasn't good enough for the folks in Montgomery—how could he be hobnobbing around with one of the finest young families in Nashville? Well, it seemed that as far as Corky Adams was concerned, despair wasn't the only thing Hank possessed that transcended social boundaries.

"It didn't take long," he says, "to recognize that this fellow was a genius."

Adams and his wife Barbara couldn't get over the way this young Alabaman could write words and music so easily, but they also noticed very soon that Hank "drank rather heavily." Slowly, through the music and the fellowship, a unique relationship was built between the physician and the country singer.

It *was* unusual for Hank Williams to be holding forth in the company of the degreed and pedigreed. He would nearly always have felt more comfortable with some other social group. But two factors seem to have won him over—and won the group over to Hank—first the shared interest in songwriting, and second, genuine, ungrasping friendship.

"Hank needed a lot of understanding," says Doctor Adams in retrospect. "He was a very unhappy man, and this was his stimulus for writing."

"We'd gather around a piano—Hank and Beasley Smith and Del Wood and I—and talk and write together," Corky remembers, "and Hank always had something to contribute that was entertaining."

"This was when he was the happiest," the Doctor continues, "when he was around people who were not trying to take anything from him or ask for anything . . . but just liked him as a person. I think he could understand who really cared for him and who didn't."

It always seemed to Adams that Hank had an entourage of ten or twelve people around who appeared to be sponging off him. These may have been other legitimate musicians, they may have been genuine friends, or maybe the Doctor was right. In any case they didn't do much for Hank's needs, Adams felt. Hank needed to find some direction, some goals for his life other than his next party. Corky tried not to push too hard when Hank came to visit.

"He'd come over when he was in town," says Corky, "to talk about his travels and his occupation and his difficulties . . . and I'd give him advice. . . ."

Though Hank wasn't in the habit of taking advice from anyone but Fred Rose or Frank Walker, he did have within him the capacity to respect another man and listen to him if that person commanded his respect. Obviously, Hank wouldn't have taken much advice from Dore Schary, or anyone he felt was using him, patronizing him. Williams was actually capable of calling up two completely polar attitudes with people in positions of importance: He could be totally obtuse, as with Schary, or else he could be as meek and pliant as a child.

Corky Adams became one of those rare people, like Fred Rose, or Frank Walker, whom Hank Williams deeply respected. Hank was no doubt flattered that an up-and-coming young Nashville physician would befriend him. After all, aside from his music, who was Hank Williams? Just a drunk from south Alabama. Yet this Adams guy really seemed to like Hank, and what's more, when they got together, Hank found himself for the first time in his life enjoying the camaraderie of a group of people who weren't basically just ol' hill people like he was—and by God, they were *comfortable* with him! If Hank could have had this kind of experience some years earlier in life, before his body was quite so addicted to alcohol and his self-respect quite so buried, the support of a fraternity like this might have made a real difference in his life.

As it was, the good times with Doc Adams and his friends became just an occasional oasis in the desert. They were, like his beautiful innocent son Bocephus, just a reminder to Hank of what life could be when it was right. But that kind of life—the good life, the straight life—was beyond some invisible, impenetrable curtain that Hank had sensed for a long, long time.

"Hank would often call me when he was coming off a drunk," says Adams, "and I found that these times were sometimes his most productive times as a songwriter. I'd lay the law down to him. I'd tell him he shouldn't throw his life away . . . and I'd try to encourage him to write."

Hank expressed his affection to Corky Adams in the same way he showed consideration to many of his friends, through personalized gifts. For Corky, a fellow gun freak, Hank came up with a Colt Frontier model pistol and a two-gun black and white tooled-leather holster set made by H. H. Heiser in Denver. (The second Colt was promised, but Hank apparently never found one.) He also brought by a similar tan one-holster belt after another tour, this one to hold Corky's .357 magnum. On both holsters of the two-gun set are carved the words, "Doc Adams."

"I didn't hear much from Hank after he really got in bad shape," Corky Adams says. "I'd taken the role of a disciplinarian with him, and I guess after a point he didn't want to hear from me."

The public may have known by 1951 that Hank Williams did some drinking—though WSM allowed precious little publicity about it—but very, very few people knew that Hank Williams was in any kind of emotional trouble. How could he be? Nineteen fifty-one should have been the happiest year of Hank's life. It certainly had its happy moments.

Like the time Hank and Moon Mullican sat in the back seat of Henry Cannon's Beechcraft Bonanza and wrote down a series of nonsense lyrics in a Cajun dialect that only Mullican could really understand. By the end of the flight the song turned out to be "Jambalaya," Hank's tribute to the Louisiana Delta folks who loved him crazily in spite of the fact that they didn't understand most of the words to his songs. It became one of the most-performed country songs of all time.

Like the Hadacol Caravan. The Hadacol Caravan was the last and biggest medicine show ever staged on the North American Continent. Dudley LeBlanc, a colorful Louisiana inventor, businessman, and sometime state senator, had developed and patented his Hadacol tonic back in the 1930s, and by 1950 his various forms of advertising had made Hadacol a household word in many parts of America, especially the South.

LeBlanc was a visionary. He dreamed up medicines, then he dreamed up ways to promote them. Inevitably he came up with his biggest idea of all: Why not use the railroads to transport carloads of performers from town to town across the South to promote Hadacol and bring a big dose of joy, laughter, and entertainment to the great folks out there? He tried the idea in 1950, then in 1951 he put together an even bigger Caravan. He mapped out a long circle, from Louisiana east through the gulf states and the Southeast, then up to the Midwest, out to Kansas and Oklahoma, and finally through Texas and back to the starting point at Lafayette, Louisiana, site of the Hadacol factory.

LeBlanc spared no expense. His spectacle would cover eighteen states in forty-plus consecutive one-night stands, yet nothing was going to detract from the quality of the show. LeBlanc produced a two-and-a-half-hour extravaganza showcasing all styles of music, with comedians, dancers, and acrobats also gracing the stage. Tony Martin's orchestra was secured to back up the stage presentations, and a string of stars was hired that reads like a cast of an Ed Sullivan afternoon-nap dream: ten beautiful "Hadacol Queens," picked from local contests staged to promote the show; five of Barnum's off-season clowns; juggler Lee Marx; singer Dick Haymes; Caesar Romero; Carmen Miranda; Jack Dempsey; Candy "The Man of a Thousand Voices" Candido; Sharkey Bonano's Dixieland Band; Rudy Vallee; the Dorothy Darlen Adorables from the Chez Paree in Chicago; the Acrocats; and a Grand Ole Opry troupe, last but not least, which included Minnie Pearl and Hank Williams and the Drifting Cowboys.

Whew. These acts were supplemented by several sideshow-type performers including the "World's Tallest Man" and Emile Parra, "the Man Who Skates on His Head." As if this wasn't enough, LeBlanc also signed some superstars to headline the show in the large metropolitan areas like Cincinnati, Kansas City, and St. Louis. These headliners included Bob Hope, Jack Benny, Jimmy Durante, and Milton Berle.

"For transportation," Jerry Rivers writes, in *Hank Williams: From Life to Legend,*

LeBlanc secured nineteen Pullman cars which housed the approximately one hundred and fifty entertainers and crew, the company office and staff, photographic lab and personal equipment. The large portable stage, lighting equipment, tremendous sound equipment, stage sets and related gear were assigned to ten tractor-trailer trucks painted with the familiar blue and white Hadacol trademark.

The entertainers were to be treated like royal guests: They would have open privileges in the dining car and lounge car, and a daily free laundry service was instituted. The operating expense of all this, of course, was tremendous. Jerry Rivers reports the figure he heard at the time was ten thousand a day, but total costs for the Caravan had to have been at least a million 1951 dollars. And all LeBlanc asked for admission to the shows was a Hadacol box-top.

The Caravan, in terms of attendance, was a tremendous success. In the larger cities, the troupe was pulling crowds of fifteen to twenty thousand. And why not? Who had ever heard of such a show at such a price?

Meanwhile the performers enjoyed themselves. Living as they were in a Pullman dream-world together, a great feeling of togetherness soon spread through the Caravan. It was a great time, and Hank enjoyed it as well as anybody. For his contributions, he was paid $1,000 a week plus berth and all the free extras. LeBlanc also picked up the tab for plane fare when Hank and Minnie had Opry Saturday night obligations to fulfill.

LeBlanc knew Hank Williams was a crowd-pleaser; that's why he hired him. But he had underestimated Hank's appeal. At first Hank had a medium-high spot on the show, in the far vicinity of the closing act. But before they were on the road two weeks, the crowd reactions to "Cold, Cold Heart" and "Lovesick Blues" caused Hank to be moved into the closing spot in the small towns and the next-to-closing spot when the superstars joined the troupe.

It's a fairly well-told story how this arrangement backfired in Louisville. There the Caravan had filled the old Louisville Colonels' Parkway Field, and Hank was going to be followed by Bob Hope, who had been flown in for the performance.

Hank Williams closed his act that night with "Lovesick Blues," and Jerry Rivers relates that when he'd hit the last note of the song, "the packed stadium seemed to explode, the ovation was so great." It was the same old thing, only bigger. This crowd was so huge that their roars made it impossible for the M.C. to make himself heard as he tried for several minutes to calm the crowd. After all, *Bob Hope* was waiting to go on.

But the crowd wasn't worried about Bob Hope. They just kept stomping and whistling and clapping and cheering for Hank Williams. Finally, since the show was already running overtime, the announcer brought Hope out and he stood for "several minutes" while the applause gradually weakened. Always the opportunist, Hope waited until the roar had partially subsided, then he pulled an enormous cowboy hat out from behind his back and down over his head and said to the audience:

"Hello folks, this is Hank Hope. . . ."

The stadium went wild again and, as Jerry Rivers puts it, "Bob Hope shared in some of Hank Williams' glory."

In the midst of this supertour, when Hank Williams was at the absolute zenith of his popularity and his abilities, Jerry Rivers first noticed that something must be wrong with Hank's marriage. Hank would return from his weekend flights to Nashville clearly upset, and no one could get out of him exactly what was the matter, only that it had something to do with Audrey.

Before the Hadacol Caravan could complete its vast circle through the South and Midwest, Dudley LeBlanc took an obscure medical research company up on their offer to buy the Hadacol operation lock, stock, and barrel. Of course, the lock, stock, and barrel included the Caravan, whose expense the new owners could not justify. The show played its last date in Dallas in mid-September of 1951, after being out almost forty days. There was a mad scramble for everyone to get their pay, retrieve equipment and costumes from the Pullman cars, and make arrangements to get home from Dallas. It was over. Dudley LeBlanc accepted an offer of something like $8.2 million for the Hadacol empire. He later confessed that of that amount, all he ever received was a half-million-dollar down payment.

Coming on the heels of the Hadacol romp was another great Hank Williams experience. The Montgomery city fathers, having forgiven a now-rich superstar for his poor-boy mistakes, pulled off a gala Hank Williams Homecoming Celebration in the "Lovesick Blues Boy's" old home town.

The Montgomery Jaycees were the prime organizers of this late-September spectacular. They staged the show at the Alabama Agricultural Coliseum in Montgomery, which seated "more people than Madison Square Garden over an area as large as a football field."

For the show, Hank headlined a cast made up of Opry regulars and home-town hopefuls. There were speeches, tributes, and appearances by Audrey, Hank Junior, Lycrecia, and Lilly, who by that time had married again and was Mrs. Lillian S. Stone.

For the occasion, Hank was not decked out in his normal coat-and-pants stage uniform but in a full-blown, fringed, San Fernando Valley-variety white cowboy shirt with matching rhinestone-studded trousers.

In fact, Hank and Audrey's white outfits that day were a matched pair tailored especially for them by Nudie. Match that, Roy 'n Dale!

It was, according to Hank's mother, "the happiest day of his life." Well, it had to feel good, going back home to the cheers and adoration of the people he'd grown up with, the people he'd been tryin' to please since the "WPA Blues" days. In photographs taken that day, you can almost see the lump in Hank's throat.

A turning point in Hank's life occurred during an early morning squirrel hunting hike that same autumn of 1951. By this time, his relationship with Audrey was on shaky ground for several reasons, and ol' Hank could have done without any more troubles. On that fateful dawn, he was trying to forget his blues in the calm dewy woods outside Nashville.

Hank and Jerry Rivers had taken the dog Skip out for Skip's favorite pastime of treeing squirrels. Skip, however, wasn't particular on this occasion and soon "treed" a large groundhog in a hollow tree stump.

The groundhog, for his part, wasn't intimidated and decided he'd take on this uppity hound. At this point, Hank and Jerry came upon the scene, with fifty yards still separating them from the two animals. Both men began to run toward the tree stump, fearing that the larger, heavier groundhog would make mincemeat of the small, gutsy, hunting dog.

"Carrying a heavy double-barrelled shotgun, I jumped across a deep gully," Rivers writes in *Hank Williams: From Life to Legend*, "without slowing down." Jerry reached the scene of the fight and killed the groundhog with a large stick before it could do any more damage to Skip, who was already bleeding but "still pushing the fight."

"Discovering Hank was not still with me," Rivers continues, "I walked back to the deep gully and was surprised to find him lying there on his back, his face pale, and experiencing severe pain." Hank had tried to jump the small gully, lost his balance, and fallen four or five feet backward and down onto a rocky creekbed. Rivers allowed his friend to rest for a few minutes then "half-carried" Hank home where a doctor was summoned.

Hank was never the same again. "Maybe the time had come," Rivers writes, "when Hank's career had become so gigantic, so complicated and demanding that he would have been forced to give up spending time in the woods or on the lakes anyway, but from that day on he never had or took the opportunity to devote time to these pastimes he had enjoyed so much."

That wasn't all that was changed. The pain of the reinjured back was added to the depression of his marital problems and the pressures of his career, and Hank never bounced back. His relationship with the boys in the band became distant—not unfriendly really, but still a world away from the shared excitement they had known together in days past.

Throughout that late fall of 1951, the doctors treated Hank for his back, and it was at this time that he first began to get pain medication prescribed for his "comfort and well-being." Almost immediately he began to abuse the privilege, and Jerry Rivers remembers Hank soon over-medicating himself on a plane trip and going to sleep with a lighted cigarette burning down in his mouth. His lips were beginning to turn brown with a second-degree scorch before somebody shook Hank and woke him up.

Finally, an operation was called for. Hank entered a Nashville hospital and a spine fusion operation was performed on two ruptured discs by orthopedic surgeon Dr. Ben Fowler. (Doctor Fowler, besides being the best orthopedic surgeon money could buy, was and is a professional friend of Corky Adams.) Hank's surgery was pronounced successful, and he was brought home to his Franklin Road home to rest on Christmas Eve.

One week later, after drinking in the New Year with some friends, persistent Nashville rumor states that Hank Williams got into an argument at home with Audrey and took a couple of shots in her direction with one of his pistols. That story may or may not be true, but it is a fact that in early January of 1952, Audrey Mae Williams filed a separate maintenance suit against the man whose career she'd worked so hard to bolster. The marriage was over.

11

Audrey II

Hank Williams' favorite movie stars were John Wayne and Jane Wyman. His favorite entertainers were Moon Mullican and Johnnie Ray. Boxing, wrestling, and baseball were his favorite sports, while fried chicken was his favorite food. Then, of course Audrey was his favorite woman.

When she was in the right kind of mood, that is. When the times were flowing and the friends were smiling and Audrey sat at Hank's side, tossing her hair and laughing with him, there was no one else who could compare. But when ol' Harm fell off the wagon on the road and Audrey heard about it before he got home, Hank Williams would have rather faced the Devil himself than that fiery-eyed, sharp-tongued she-hawk who swooped down on him the minute he crossed the front door threshold—if she let him in at all.

They were both strong-willed people. Both of them felt that they had earned the money and fame and glamor, but Audrey believed she had paid for her right to a share of the limelight for herself. This would be a central issue from the time they arrived in Nashville. Hank was, by God, not gonna let any woman tell him he *had* to let her perform with him, while by the same token Audrey was damned if the career she believed she deserved as a coentertainer was going to flicker out just when Hank was burning his brightest.

Both partners were "guilty"; there was no strict delineation of Wronger and Wrongee in this marriage, just a long string of offenses and counter-offenses conducted over a period nearly as long as the marriage itself.

By far the biggest and most nerve-wracking problem in the

Williams household was Hank's drinking. It had been a problem since the beginning, when Audrey came to pick Hank up for their first date and found him standing outside the trailer where he was staying, a bottle in his hand, hair uncombed, cheeks unshaved, and his shirttail hanging out over his loose, baggy pants.

She always swore he'd have to quit drinking, but she loved him too much to leave him when he turned up drunk with that silly, half-sad, half-laughing, hangdog look on his face. But if she wouldn't leave him, neither would she leave him alone.

As Johnny Wright attests, Audrey was always "concerned about Hank's drinking problem" but her way of dealing with it was to browbeat Hank, to deliver ultimatums they both knew wouldn't be carried out, to yell warnings at him not to drink, and to yell accusations at him after he'd done it.

By 1950, the fights didn't blow over as quickly as they had back in Alabama. Sammy Pruitt remembers the extra responsibilities he took on shortly after joining the Drifting Cowboys in Nashville:

"I was the only one of the boys who wasn't married, so Hank could always get hold of me at the YMCA where I lived," Sammy remembers. "Hank would get in a fight with Audrey and call me up to drive him down to his Momma's in Montgomery."

This response of Hank's to their battles must have been particularly maddening to Audrey, yet Hank did it regularly. "He'd not talk much," Pruitt says. "Sometimes he'd be on the bottle, so he'd just get in the car and go to sleep."

So as Hank moved up from his 1950 green Cadillac limousine to his 1951 two-tone green model with the lighter-green top, this was one of the standard chores reserved for the touring car: the customary midnight hump to Montgomery when the connubial sparks flew too hot, with Sammy at the wheel feeling, he says, "skinnier than ever in that big ol' wide seat."

It was not what you'd call a satisfactory arrangement for settling Hank and Audrey's problems. Not only was Lilly unable to offer any useful advice or encouragement to her son when he'd drop in, but she had a way of getting herself paid back for the trouble she took with Hank.

"She was always callin' Hank up and saying, 'Son I just got to have five hundred dollars,' and then the next week she'd call back and want money again," Sammy Pruitt recalls. With Audrey's eye for Hank's expenses, you can bet his donations to Momma's cause were no joy to his wife's heart, either.

Sometimes, it seemed though, Hank couldn't win for losing. On one tour, he fell off the wagon, then stubbornly climbed back on again. As he was going through the painful "straightening up" process, the boys were talking to him.

"You oughta leave that bottle alone, Hank," they were saying. "You've got everything going for you."

Hank thought a minute, then he turned to Don Helms.

"Don," he began, "when you get home, Miss Hazel's gonna have you a good supper fixed. She's gonna be tryin' to make you as comfortable as she can." He then looked at Butrum.

"Buel," Hank said as he looked into Hillous' eyes, "you'll call Betty and the two of you will go out to a movie or go bowlin' to have some fun."

"Bob and Jerry, you'll both go home to wives that love you and want to take care of you, won't you?" Hank asked. Both young men nodded.

"Well boys," Hank said of his own plans, "I've got to go by Acuff-Rose on the way home and pick up a check for two thousand dollars. I'll go home and give Audrey half of it and then I'll have to fight the rest of the night because she'll want *all* of it."

This was Hank's way of telling the boys why it was hard for him not to drink.

"When we got to Nashville that day," Hillous Butrum remembers, "we took Hank by Acuff-Rose and then we took him home. But when Hank tried to get in, he found he was locked out."

Audrey had heard the bad news by phone (that Hank had tanked up) but not the good (that he'd straightened out). So she'd quietly barricaded ol' Hank out. She was *tired* o' that messin' around on the road.

"Boys, take me back uptown," Hank said as he dejectedly got back in the limo. Things had turned out even worse than he'd predicted.

"So we took him up to the Tulane Hotel," says Butrum, "and that was the night he got drunk and fell asleep with a lit cigarette and set the bed on fire."

Hank's problems with Audrey didn't change his strong feelings about his children, especially Hank Junior. Former WSM engineer Jimmy Lockert remembers one afternoon when a recording session ran late and Hank hurriedly left town for Memphis to begin a tour.

"They'd gotten half-way to Jackson," Lockert recalls, "when Hank suddenly remembered he hadn't told little Bocephus good-bye. So he turned around and came all the way back to Nashville to do that before going any farther."

It would be unfair to leave the impression that the entire Williams home life was devoted to fighting. Lycrecia Morris is one who was there who swears it just wasn't so.

"All couples fight," she says. "Hank and Audrey didn't do anything more than anybody else." Perhaps it was just that they had more to do it with. Not every wife for instance, has thousands of dollars worth of clothes to throw out on the front lawn when she gets mad.

"Daddy and Momma were both moody, high-strung people," Lycrecia says in their defense. "They were ambitious, talented people who clashed a lot."

Of course it was the clashes that people always heard about and talked about, rather than the calm, happy times in between.

"We had our good times," says Lycrecia, "plenty of them. Hank was a true father to me in every sense of the word, and I always loved him. He never laid a hand on me."

Unfortunately he did lay a hand now and then on Audrey. This sometimes happened in public, because of Hank and Audrey's other chronic problems besides Hank's drinking: Audrey's desire to sing.

There had been a time when Hank could always put up with his wife's off-key warbling and harmony-shouting as part of his act, but everybody knew he'd become a hit without her. Not one of Hank's hot singles was a duet. Yet Audrey believed in herself and always fought for the right to perform with Hank. She sang with him on many of his WSM programs, but sometimes she wanted to sing when Hank had other ideas. These were the times, according to WSM employees, when Hank would sometimes use physical persuasion as a last resort.

Still Audrey was determined to have a career. She landed—rather, Hank landed for her—a contract with Decca records, and she cut a few sides and sold a few discs. She also had a couple of her own compositions published, but nothing much came of them. Sometimes it seemed Hank was under tremendous pressure from Audrey to allow her to perform on the radio.

One WSM official told Roger Williams that Hank would often come to him and say apologetically, "I have to use Audrey tonight."

The WSM staff people weren't particularly wild about Audrey's talent, but they'd let her on the air for the sake of family stability. Nobody wanted Hank's marriage to break up; he was wild enough as a married man, let alone what he might be if he were set loose on his own.

Hank, for his part, responded to the situation with a growing resentment that expressed itself in the way he'd make jokes at Audrey's expense.

"We used to send down to Johnny's Pie Wagon by the old YMCA for breakfast when we were recording radio shows," says former WSM engineer Jimmy Lockert. "One morning we were taking a break and somebody asked Audrey if she'd had breakfast yet. 'Yeah, she had eggs,' Hank answered back. 'She's wearin' 'em.'" That was his way of saying that Audrey was no Jane Russell.

"First off, let me say this about Audrey," says the genial, middle-aged man across the table, "she was never anything but nice to me." The speaker is Don Helms, a Nashville veteran who's played with several Opry greats, but who is now back on the road with the original Drifting Cowboys. Helms is aging gracefully. His eyes crinkle comfortably at the corners when he smiles, and his voice has a honey-like smoothness to it. We're talking over coffee at a Shoney's Big Boy restaurant, near a Hendersonville studio where Don has just finished a recording session. I want to hear what he's got to say, because nobody spent as many total years in professional contact with Hank and Audrey Williams as this man did.

"Audrey could be nice or she could be not so nice," says Helms. "I saw her do things to Hank that I was offended by— like spendin' all his money, naggin' him, stuff like that—which is not unusual, by the way.

"But other times," he adds, "she was very nice to Hank."

To hear Helms tell it, Hank and Audrey had a habit of communicating through the things they slammed, kicked, banged, locked, and mutilated.

"I went out to Hank's house one day," Helms says, "and Audrey was gone. They had had an argument.

"What had happened was Hank had come home and he was probably drinkin' . . . and she wouldn't let him in," Helms explains. "So he took his guitar and broke the storm door out, just tore his guitar all to hell. . . ."

By the time Helms arrived, Hank had thrown a lot of Audrey's clothes out in the yard.

"But I missed out on most of the physical stuff," Don says with no particular regret.

"Hank never harmed her physically or anything," Helms continues. "There were times when they'd get along fine, and times when they wouldn't. Most of the time when they were on one of these spats, they'd just pout like two little kids. . . ."

Helms had said that some of Audrey's actions "offended" him. What did he really think of her?

"I liked Audrey OK . . . I really did," he says. "She was no more demanding than a lot of other wives . . . but Hank had millions of fans who resented anything that anybody did to Hank Williams. Some of them disliked her very much."

This of course, because Hank wouldn't hide it when they were fighting. He brought his digging comments right onto the air at WSM, along with lines about how he had to suffer. What else were people to think but that Audrey was some kind of torturous witch? Why else would a man be driven to complain right on the radio? Actually, it was more a case of the childishness Helms alluded to. Hank knew he could get away with laying his personal blues before the public, so he did it. It was a way of getting back at Audrey.

What about Hank's vices? Did he instigate problems?

"Drinkin' was the main thing," says Helms. "She'd harp on him for drinking, and that just made him drink more.

"Hank loved to fish and hunt," Don continues, "and sometimes he'd go out three or four days a week. Audrey didn't like that after he'd been out of town . . . That might have had something to do with it. . . ."

What else?

"Not gambling."

"Not women."

Wait a minute. Hank *did* have affairs with other women from time to time throughout his Nashville years.

"I don't say that he was pure," Helms says. "Hank saw some other people *after* their problems were already started, but Hank runnin' around [with other women] was not part of their problem."

However, all the band members have pointed to times when Hank made after-show dates on the road—sometimes motel dates—through cordial local policemen who'd help him find women. At least one of these instances is rather well-known, and it happened *before* Audrey and Hank separated.

"I saw Hank with other women, but Audrey didn't know about it, so it couldn't have been a problem," says Helms. "That motel incident was not a problem because she didn't know."

Perhaps. But it's a recurring theme of country music that a man or woman can always tell when his or her mate is cheating. "For a guy like Hank to never be seen with another woman was almost impossible," says Helms. Didn't Audrey know this as well as anyone else? Perhaps this is one reason she would have liked to always sing with the group, so she could travel with Hank, rather than sitting in Nashville wondering how her weak-willed sweetheart was standing up to the twin Road temptations of whiskey and whoopee.

"At least," says Don Helms, "Hank didn't get into trouble like another country singer did lettin' women into his room. The fellow got in a lot of trouble with a seventeen-year-old. That cost him a great part of his reputation."

To blame Audrey because she couldn't become a competent alcoholic therapist with Hank is to be unaware of the severity of

Hank's alcoholic illness. Don Helms, probably more than any other person except Audrey herself, was painfully aware of how hopelessly addicted Hank Williams was to alcohol.

"I often assumed the job of taking him to the sanitarium," Helms recalls. "Not because I cared more, but because I'd been with him the longest. It was not always a pleasant role to take him . . . to go to the 'hut' as he called it."

The "hut" was a small square building on the grounds at the Madison sanitarium. It had barred windows and a door. Helms' job would be to take Hank out there and turn him over to the hospital staff. They'd put Williams in the building and feed him and take care of him.

"And the next day or so, I'd go out and take him some candy and cigarettes and comic books," Helms remembers. "He loved comic books."

Little Jimmy Dickens would also go out to the hut frequently to visit Hank, at Hank's own request. For some reason, ol' Tater was someone whom Hank liked to talk to when he was low. Presumably Jimmy had a gift for cheering up his fellow show-stopper. Hank's manner when he was confined was subdued, almost resigned, even relieved.

"When do you think I can get out of here?" he'd ask Helms when Don came by with goodies. "We'll have to wait and see," his friend would reply.

How often did Hank require this kind of drastic treatment?

"He went to be dried out at the sanitarium," says Helms, "at least two or three times a year, beginning back in '49."

Hearing Don Helms describe his feelings about Hank's repeated self-destructive rampages, it's possible to understand how Audrey must have felt after so many years of living with this madness.

"After two or three years of that," Helms explains, "you get to where it's not that you don't feel regret at seein' him do this to himself, but you get to where you kinda wash your hands of it. It tore me up to see my friend destroy himself, but after awhile. . . ."

The emotional investment required to go through it with him wasn't worth the return.

"The only way to help Hank was to take all his problems on

yourself for about two weeks," says Helms. "There's only so many times you can do that."

And there were only so many times Audrey could do that, too.

"The first time I saw Audrey," says radio/recording engineer Aaron Shelton, "was also the first time Hank recorded at the Castle Studio." Hank had brought Audrey up to Nashville with him from Shreveport in March, 1949.

"Audrey was pregnant with Hank Junior," Shelton remembers. "She came and sat in the control room at the studio. I can see her now, sitting on a radiator there . . . smilin'. . . ."

In the excitement of Hank's ascendancy, Shelton didn't perceive that Hank and Audrey were anything but a happy young couple. Later, though, he began to notice things.

"I got the impression after awhile," he says, "that Audrey was jealous of Hank, that she somehow resented his success." Shelton says he thinks Audrey "had the feeling that she should be up there with him."

Shelton remembers that at first this didn't seem to be a large problem, but later on in Hank's career, he says, "entrepreneurs were tryin' to take Audrey in order to get to Hank." The implication is that as Audrey grew more frustrated with her own small struggling career, she became more vulnerable to business deals in which she was duped into getting Hank involved as well as herself, thinking all along that the "entrepreneurs" were only interested in Audrey Williams.

Gradually in the Nashville years, Hank and Audrey went their separate ways, long before their actual physical separation in January of '52. A lot of the explanation for this was the incredible amount of traveling Hank did . . . how were they supposed to map out any plans together? And what was she supposed to do while he was out in Los Angeles or Seattle or up in Indianapolis or Baltimore?

The first, flushed, shared excitement of success gave way to a pattern where two people took the fruits of success and each built a separate life—not all that unusual in our society.

Hank took the Road, the applause, the willing women, and the lion's share of the glory . . . Audrey was left in Nashville with her cars, her furs, the kids, and her checkbook. All of a sudden, she wasn't needed anymore. In the struggling years, she'd booked shows, counted money, made clothes, carried Hank home . . . now there were other people to do all of those things. Yet she possessed as much energy as ever. Sure she loved her kids, but she was just not the kind of woman who could settle into some mousy Nashville housewife mold. Audrey had ambitions. She had drive. And she had time on her hands. They had hired a governess, Mrs. Ragland, who was a big help with Lycrecia and Hank Junior. Now what to do?

Her checkbook.

Hank Williams was making at least an average of ten thousand dollars a month during the good years, often twice that or more. Yet Don Helms remembers plenty of times when Audrey would get the Williamses overdrawn at the bank. Clearly Audrey knew how to spend money. The gifts from Hank were nice—her fifteen-hundred-dollar platinum and diamond wristwatch, her Cadillacs, her three-thousand-dollar diamong ring—but accepting gifts was too passive. Audrey longed to create. She took over the decorating of the home on Franklin Road, making it a showplace. She widened the driveway, bought new furniture.

But there was more to do than spend money. Audrey had business ambitions too. She kept tabs on Hank's career, trying to stay as involved as possible. She'd keep track of his appointments, make sure he didn't miss them; she'd converse with his associates.

Then there was the store. Most Nashvillians agree that "Hank and Audrey's Corral" was Audrey's idea. At least it was Audrey who took the initiative in actually getting the thing off the ground. One writer gives Audrey sole credit for starting up the store, and that's probably not far wrong. What did *Hank Williams* care about the *clothing business?* But Audrey . . . ah . . . that was her element. *Business.* Buying, ordering, designing—important decisions, people asking *her* questions (what did Hank know?)—here was some excitement, after all.

So at last she found plenty to do. But then, just as things would start to pop along nicely, here would come Hank home from God-knows-where wondering who's spending all the

money. Why, honey, she'd tell him, you've spent some money
too, haven't you? I'm spending money as an *investment!* What
are you spending it for? Rather *who* are you spending it for?
You think I don't hear things?

Then he'd be gone and the next thing she'd hear would be a
call from somebody down at the Tulane Hotel (one time they
called and said he'd shot some holes in the ceiling of a room
down there.) Or else he would run off to Momma.

There wasn't any use letting Hank in the house when he was
drinking. There was bound to be a fight. Then he'd get violent
and start cussing and throwing things around and breaking
things . . . but Lord, she hated to think of him cooped up out
there in that place he called the hut. What was she supposed to
do?

Actually it was a marvel that they made it two years in
Nashville before things really began to crumble. According to
Johnny Wright, it was Audrey's squelched singing career that
lit the final fuse.

"Audrey wanted to sing on the Grand Ole Opry," says
Wright. "But the Opry finally told Hank, 'You've got to keep
her off or you'll both get off!'"

When Hank passed this message on to Audrey, says Wright,
something broke inside her. "She got to where she didn't care"
is his way of expressing it.

According to Wright, this don't-care attitude led to a new
chemical in an already-explosive marital brew: "She got to
triflin' on him." If Hank had been depressed before, it was
nothing to what he felt when "the news was out all over town."

"That's what really started his drinking," says Wright. Hank
had been drinking since 1934. So we assume that what Johnny
means is that this is when Hank went completely out of control.
Now there were two of them who didn't care.

"It got so bad then," says Johnny Wright, "that Hank started
missing shows. . . ." Well, he'd missed them before, but now
the batting average slipped from .850 or so down into the .500
range. By the time of Hank and Audrey's separation in
January, 1952, Hank Williams was a booking nightmare for the
WSM organization. Always before, the drinking bouts would
last a week or two and then Hank could be counted on for the

next several months, but now the sprees and parties and botched shows came piling one up behind the other with scarcely a break for Hank to regain the strength he was wasting.

The best information available indicates that this was the scenario for the final months of Hank and Audrey's life together: Sometime in the summer of 1951, WSM officials tell Hank that Audrey is no longer welcome on their airwaves. Then while Hank is on the Hadacol Caravan in August and September, the news first breaks that Audrey is "trifling" back in Nashville (this is when Jerry and the band members first notice Hank's depression about his marriage; everything else up until now he could take pretty well). The result of this is an escalation of offenses on both sides. It is at this time that Hank reinjures his back. The closing months of 1951 find Hank and Audrey beyond the point of caring about the consequences of their actions, lashing out at each other verbally and sexually, while Hank adds a drug habit (fighting off the back pain) to his already-smothering alcohol habit, and his career begins its long downward slope. (It's worth noting at this point, that according to M-G-M's notes, Hank Williams did not go into a recording studio between August, 1951, and June, 1952.)

Was it merely coincidental that during the Hadacol Caravan, the time when Hank may have first heard the shattering rumors of Audrey's infidelity, he wrote a song (since lost) called "Heart of a Devil, Face of a Saint" in the back of Henry Cannon's Beechcraft Bonanza?

So December brought the back operation and in the first week of January came the separation. At the end of the month, Hank was back on the road but under constant supervision of one of his several "bodyguards." That was the backdrop of his January 30 show in Richmond that was seen and reviewed by Mrs. Lindeman.

Through early '52 Hank wouldn't believe that Audrey would really divorce him, even after she changed her suit from separate maintenance to outright divorce. He moved out and rented the house on Natchez Trace and sent her the monthly amount decided by the court, but still he hoped that they'd get back together.

Along the way, though, he did little to prove himself any more able to change his ways. He went back to Canada where he had been such a hit in '49 and managed to erase the good impression he'd left there. He performed so miserably that it's said some areas of Canada have never brought in a country music act since. During one of these drunken Canadian performances, probably in Toronto, Hank fell off a stage in the middle of his act. With that fall, he not only ended that evening's show, but he tore loose the reconstructive work that Ben Fowler had so carefully performed on his back. The dull pain of the previous few weeks was replaced by the presurgical agony of the preceding fall.

Now Hank's receptions by his audiences were varying widely. Hank was once more than three hours late for a show at the Dallas Sportatorium, Hillous Butrum reported to Roger Williams, but the people waited faithfully. No one left.

"It was 12:30 A.M.," says Butrum, "Hank walked on stage with a grin and said, 'Mornin' friends, nice to see y'all.' They gave him a terrific cheer. One of the big names in country music, I think it was Hank Snow, was standin' next to me, and he shook his head, saying, 'I don't understand it.'"

Other audiences were not so forgiving. Hank could handle hecklers, but when the chuckles turned to derisive laughter at his drunken attempts to perform, Hank would lose his temper with his audience. Sometimes he'd yell at them. Other times he'd infuriate them by refusing to sing a song they wanted.

Audrey went through with the divorce. She got an attachment on $133,000 worth of real and personal property, estimating Hank's 1951 income at $90,000 (in this, she probably aimed low). Hank couldn't believe she was going through with it. "Stunned and deeply hurt," in Roger Williams' words, he didn't contest the suit. Audrey was charging "cruel and inhuman treatment," and Hank, though he might have, did not bring any countercharges.

A chancery court granted Audrey her divorce from Hank Williams on May 29, 1952. The terms granted that day gave her:

• the house on Franklin Road, then valued at $55,000, with $13,599 yet owed;

• a Cadillac convertible "with outstanding notes amounting to $706;"

• $1,000 in cash;

• $4,000 for lawyers' fees;

• finally—and most important—one-half of all royalties owed to Hank (at the time the divorce action was filed) by Acuff-Rose Music and M-G-M Records *and* one-half of all future publishing and record royalties. (Though the action was never needed, a provision guaranteed Audrey at least $10,000 per year from other sources should the royalties ever fail to net that much.)

Audrey was going to become a very well-to-do woman. Every year, for the rest of her life, she was going to get half of a six-figure income, over and above her own earnings from other enterprises.

She also got Hank Junior. Randall Hank Williams was to remain in her custody, with Hank given a "reasonable number" of visits and also summers with his son, to begin in the summer of 1953.

Hank, for his part, got Audrey's interest in the Corral (how little it must have meant to him!) and freedom from the responsibility to support and educate his son, except when Hank Junior was in his custody.

The divorce removed the last restraining element from Hank Williams' life, the hope of reconciliation with his family.

"He was doing real fine when he thought she wasn't actually going to divorce him," said singer Ray Price, who shared Hank's Natchez Trace house with him. "But when the divorce came it got real bad."

Price, who at that time had just come to Nashville, and the veteran Williams became very close during the few months they lived together. Hank rented the upstairs of the house to Price, and the two of them more or less batched it together, with Ray doing most of the housekeeping.

"Hank was a lonely person," Price told Roger Williams. "I think he drank because he wanted people to pay attention to him."

Price also maintains that he accompanied Hank on one of his trips to the lawyer before the divorce, and that Hank's lawyer told him he didn't have to give Audrey his future royalties;

whereupon Hank replied, "I want to." It was a gesture, Price said later, to try to show Audrey he still loved her. The gesture failed to win her back.

With the divorce proceeding, a long painful spring slipped into Hank's last summer in Nashville. Hank was still making some shows sober, but others were complete bombs. He began to surround himself with more and more people. The partying momentum picked up.

"He called at five A.M. one morning about that time," says Corky Adams, "and wanted to talk." (By this time sleep was one of life's most elusive commodities for Hank.) "So I went over to his place there on Natchez Trace and cleared out some of the people hanging around . . . he was just coming off of a long drunk."

Adams applied the only therapy he knew how.

"I want you to write the words and music to six songs today, Hank," he said.

"What'll I write about?" Hank replied.

Corky Adams says he then told Hank, "You've told me about Louisiana. Write something about Louisiana."

"I went back that evening and he had written almost exactly what I had outlined for him," says Doc Adams. "He had five new songs, including 'Jambalaya,' 'Window Shopping,' and 'You Win Again.'" (Naturally at this point you remember that certain reliable sources have placed the writing of "Jambalaya" elsewhere . . . in the back of Henry Cannon's plane, to be exact. But it's not out of the realm of possibility that Hank polished up the song as part of his performance for Doc Adams, or that perhaps the melody hadn't been written yet.)

"That night Hank invited us over to his house on Natchez Trace," says Barbara Adams, who looks for all the world like June Allyson about the time of "The High And The Mighty."

"He called the Doctor and told him he had some songs for him to hear," she continues. "It was a lovely summer night and I just went along for the ride . . . and also to glimpse this man I'd heard about.

"As we entered the door," says Barbara, "there was all this noise. . . ." It was one of Hank's rather loud and confusing parties, filling the downstairs of the small house. People everywhere, record players going, guitars thumping from time to time, and the windows thrown open to let in the sultry suburban Nashville summer night.

"It was just a very informal-type party," Barbara says. "It seemed to me like the people really didn't know Hank all that well. It was just a gathering . . . it was the place to be."

Hank ran over to Adams when he and Barbara came in.

"Guess what, Doc!" he exclaimed. "I've written five songs today." And he immediately led Corky and Barbara over to the piano and started playing "Jambalaya," according to their account.

Hank sat down in that summer evening at his piano and banged out the now-familiar tune with its collection of Cajun expressions and Louisiana recipes set in the context of a love song about a mythical love-object named "Yvonne." The party stopped momentarily while the sloe-eyed girls and the hillbilly musicians gathered with the young doctor and his wife to listen.

"I knew nothing about music," says Mrs. Adams, "but I thought, 'Oh, boy. That's catchy! I wonder if that'll be a hit,' because I thought it could easily become one."

According to Corky and Barbara, Hank was "very friendly" that night. "He wasn't drinking," Barbara recalls. "He was just in a good mood because he'd written all these songs in one day."

Barbara adds one more comment: "You know, it impressed me that I was in the presence of a genius. Hank had something special. I knew nothing about music or songwriting, but you just had that feeling when you were around him."

That was the last time that Corky and Barbara would see Hank Williams. Corky likes to remember him that way, but he knows that Hank was only experiencing a temporary reprieve.

"He'd try *everything* to forget Audrey," the doctor concludes, "women, parties, everything. He'd apparently get to thinking about losing Audrey . . . and he wouldn't give a damn. He'd just drink like it was water. . . ."

On June 13, Hank went into the Castle Studio and recorded "Jambalaya" and "Window Shopping." It was his first recording session since "Half As Much" late in the previous summer. ("Half As Much," written by Curly Williams, had been recorded by Hank because Fred Rose liked the song. Hank himself couldn't stand it. But the song became a hit, and ironically many people believe Hank wrote it.)

It is difficult to ascertain what other songs were recorded on June 13. "Settin' the Woods On Fire" was one of them, and Hank may have put down one of his last two Luke the Drifter performances: "Why Don't You Make Up Your Mind?" or "Be Careful Of Stones That You Throw." Though no one knew it, Hank's active recording career was now rapidly drawing to a close.

"It took me awhile to notice how Hank was declining," says Minnie Pearl. "For one thing, Hank was always such a sweet guy around Henry and me. I never saw him take a drink. His drinking was something that built up on the road."

When she and Henry would see Hank in Nashville, he always seemed to be sober and possessed "great dignity." "But when I was in town," she admits, "I just did my nine o'clock (Opry network) show and went home, so I didn't notice what was happening to Hank for awhile."

However, in the late spring of '52, Minnie and Ernest Tubb played a southern California package tour, and Minnie's eyes were opened to how serious the situation had become. It was on this same tour that Hank accepted an "Outstanding Achievements Award" from a group of California publicists, but Hank was really past the point of achieving much of anything in his road appearances.

"We played Bakersfield on a Saturday night," she remembers. "Then Hank joined us for a Sunday afternoon show in San Diego. He was in the worst shape I'd ever seen him."

Hank was in no condition to fulfill his obligations, but the Opry people and the promoters were determined that he would. A lot of money was riding on ol' Harm. A companion was with him acting as a male nurse, but apparently Hank was slicker than the bodyguard was watchful.

"We played the first show that evening, and he sang a couple of songs," Minnie recalled later. "They were pretty bad, but the audience didn't care. They'd take it from him, where they wouldn't from one of us."

After the first show, the troupe drove Hank around, trying to sober him up. Hank, though, could think of nothing but another drink.

"Finally he said, 'Let's sing something,'" Minnie recalls. "And we all said, 'What'll we sing?' We woulda done anything right then to keep him from thinkin' about whiskey."

Hank wanted to sing "I Saw The Light," so that it was. The troupe began singing Hank's great gospel song as the car wound around the San Diego back streets. Suddenly, Minnie remembers, Hank stopped singing and burst out anxiously, "That's the trouble. It's all dark! There ain't no light!"

By the time Minnie saw Hank again, it was late summer and they were scheduled together on a package show in Oklahoma City. Hank was even worse. Minnie told him he shouldn't go on, but he assured her he'd be all right, then proceeded to stumble and forget his way through his act. His voice, Minnie later said, sounded like that of a "wounded animal."

"Y'know," she says today, "the old show-business adage is, 'The show must go on,' but sometimes I question that. If a man is sick, he's sick."

Hank *was* sick. Now his drunks began to wear severely into his health, because he wouldn't eat once he got on a bender. Ray Price, though Hank had practically forced the Opry to hire him, couldn't balance his gratitude to Hank against the hassle of living under the same roof with him. He moved out of the upstairs of the Natchez Trace house.

"I just can't take it any more," he told Hank. And suddenly Williams' old loneliness came rushing to the surface. "Don't leave me," Hank pleaded. "I'm gonna be all right."

But Ray's mind was made up.

So was Jim Denny's. By late July, it became apparent to him that it would not do for Hank to be excused any longer from the discipline imposed on other Opry artists. The pressure from the WSM brass was getting heavy, and perhaps, like Don Helms, the Opry's Artists Services Manager was simply ready—after a long vigil—to wash his hands of the problem.

Hank was scheduled to do a Friday night radio show on WSM in early August, the "Friday Night Frolics." The Tuesday before that Friday night, Denny took Carl Smith with him to Hank's house. He warned Hank that if he didn't make the

"Frolics" program, Hank would be suspended from all WSM broadcasts, including the Opry itself. There was a party going on at the time, but Hank took time out from the hell-raising to assure Denny he'd be there.

He wasn't.

The next morning was the day that Hank, bewhiskered and bruised, got that fateful, painful call from Mr. James Denny. They talked for forty-five minutes. Denny told Hank he was going to have to stand by his word. Hank was promising that he'd get straightened out. According to some accounts, by the time Johnny Wright took over the telephone, both Williams and Denny were crying.

It was over for Hank in Nashville, but then it had been coming for a while. Once it was over with Audrey, it had been just a matter of time.

Jimmy Lockert could almost chart the course of Hank's decline by the way his behavior changed during his frequent early morning trips to WSM.

"I used to open the doors at four-fifteen in the mornin'," Lockert recalls, "and many's the time Hank'd be waiting there for me—hung over most times."

In the earlier days, Hank had not gone home because Audrey would probably have had the door locked anyway. During those easier times, he'd talk freely with Lockert, about songs, fishing, guns.

"Sometimes he'd pull loaded guns out of his boots—as many as four of 'em," says Lockert. "He'd say he'd bought the guns or found 'em. . . . He was gonna take 'em home. 'Aw, they won't go off,' he'd tell me."

Lockert had begun to see, in these early morning sessions, how Hank's pain and his songwriting were tied together. Hank would sings songs for the engineer, and press him for reasons if Lockert was not impressed by a particular number. Toward the end, though, toward that summer of 1952, the mood of Hank's sleepless early mornings changed. There was no one on Natchez Trace locking him out, but still he didn't go home.

"He'd come in and sit on a draftsman's stool in the control room," Lockert remembers. "Just sit there bug-eyed for a

couple of hours, not saying a word, 'til seven or seven-fifteen
. . . then finally he'd say, 'Well, see you later,' and he'd go out
for some coffee."

Hank sat out his last dark summer mornings in Nashville
quietly, blankly staring into the future. And there was nothing
there.

12

Sadly the Troubadour

"When I heard that Hank was definitely leavin' town," says Don Helms, "I had to go see him." Hank probably wouldn't have remembered it, but Helms had some of Williams' belongings in his car: "a couple of shotguns, some clothes, and a watch of his I'd been wearing while mine was broken. . . ." It was the watch that had been given to Hank at the Hank Williams Homecoming in Montgomery.

"So I went over to his house and caught him just as he was leaving," recalls Helms. "He was out of it. I gave him his stuff, and it was kinda sad." The two didn't say good-bye, since they were fairly certain they'd still record together, if nothing else. The Drifting Cowboys would continue to play with Ray Price, who had filled in with them on many of Hank's missed dates. Sammy Pruitt would go with Carl Smith.

There goes my job, my friend . . . fired, Helms thought as he drove home. "I went home that day and told my wife 'Hank won't live six months,'" says Helms. "And he didn't."

When Jim Denny fired Hank Williams from the Grand Ole Opry, he was hoping Hank would change. "It was the toughest thing I ever had to do in my life," he said a few years later. "But I had to do it. I figured, too, that maybe it would shock him into changing his way of living."

As far as the WSM management was concerned, by August of 1952 it wasn't any longer just a matter of Hank's drinking versus the clean Grand Ole Opry image; it was a matter of Hank Williams' health. He was obviously becoming a physical wreck, and as such was simply a detriment to himself and the Opry.

But if Hank was going to change, he obviously didn't think he needed to get started right away. He rode out of Nashville in

188

Johnny Wright's Chrysler with as much alcohol inside him as his low tolerance would permit. The next day, while Hank was sleeping it off in his mother's Montgomery boardinghouse, a short article ran in the Nashville paper, explaining that Hank Williams had been released from WSM "for failing to appear on scheduled radio programs and missing personal appearance performances."

When Hank woke up in his old room, he knew he still had two things to keep him going: the Louisiana Hayride and a girl named Billie Jean.

The Hayride thing was put together with the help of Fred Rose and Jim Denny, both of whom were interested in softening the blow of the dismissal from WSM. The Shreveport-based radio enterprise was willing to welcome back ol' Hank, for their part. He was hot enough still to be worth the risk. So at least Hank Williams wasn't out of work.

He wasn't out of love, either.

Hank had stumbled onto a delicately-featured nineteen-year-old Louisiana beauty backstage at the Opry a few weeks earlier. Her name was Billie Jean Jones Eshlimar. The "Eshlimar" was the result of a brief previous marriage to a U.S.A.F. airman who'd left Billie and disappeared into the wild blue yonder. Jones was her family name, a poor but honest Bossier City clan who'd lived down the street from Hank and Audrey during their earlier Hayride days.

How a beautiful but pitifully naive young Southern Bell telephone operator named Billie Jean Jones from Shreveport, Louisiana, came to meet and marry Hank Williams, the King of Country Music, in the last, sputtering, star-crossed days of his meteoric earthly reign will never replace Cinderella in the storybooks, but it is still quite a tale.

"I drove up to Nashville with Faron Young, a Shreveport boy who was just then breaking into country music," Billie told Shreveport writer Wesley Pruden, Jr., a few years ago. "I wasn't going with Faron seriously or anything like that," she maintained, but simply thought it was worth getting some time off at the telephone company to go up to Nashville and see the Grand Ole Opry, especially with someone who was supposed to perform on that legendary show.

"I was sitting backstage at the Ryman, waiting for Faron to go on, and ol' Hank came up to me and asked me if I was married," Billie recalled. "I told him no, and he said, 'Well, girl, if you ain't married, I'm gonna marry you. You're about the purtiest thing I ever saw.'"

Williams took the initiative and arranged an after-Opry party at a now-defunct Nashville club called the Nocturne. Don Helms, who was along that night, remembers how Hank and Faron traded dates.

"Some girl was there who'd come to see Hank," Helms remembers. She'd driven all the way from Pennsylvania, but all Hank wanted to do was look into Billie Jean's eyes, so once the group sat down at a big table, he began talking to the beauty who'd come backstage with Faron. Faron, not acutely alarmed, began dancing every dance with the girl from Pennsylvania. According to Helms, Young was happy because she was tall and he was short and he liked where his head rested when they danced. "Faron was that kind of guy," chuckles Helms.

Billie Jean didn't drink and Hank didn't dance, so the two of them sat at the table for a few hours talking and drinking coffee. "Hank thought she was knocked out," says Helms. Ol' Harm was grinning with delight at the voice and mannerisms of the innocent, doll-faced, lucky charm he'd found.

"Pretty soon," says Helms, "they just traded and Hank left with Billie." So began what can only be called a whirlwind romance. What else do you call a courtship that *begins* with a proposal? A few days later, Billie Jean went back to Shreveport, but Hank kept after her by telephone. At the time, he had not yet been fired from the Opry, but he told Billie he was coming to Shreveport to get her. He said he wasn't going to stop bugging her until she married him.

So in a sense, Hank's demotion to the minor leagues of country music worked out fine for him when it came. After the initial shock wore off, he got himself somewhat together and arrived in Shreveport toward the end of August with two Cadillacs and two small trailers full of show uniforms, guitars, and his other personal items. He'd promised Billie Jean he'd come down, and now, thanks partly to his WSM dismissal, here he was.

It might have been better if Billie hadn't been there to sweeten the pain of Hank's being kicked off the Opry. Her presence was a distraction that kept Hank from realizing how far down he'd come. The shock value that Jim Denny had hoped his banishment would have was lost in the excitement of Hank's new love.

But it didn't matter anymore. Billie Jean would do her best to hold back the inevitable, but in the end she served merely as a final sweet dose of devoted feminine affection, unable to cure this terminal patient, but still a welcome comfort while she could be—like the young women brought to King David in his old age to sleep in his arms and warm the death-chill from his bones.

So Hank came back to Shreveport, down but not out. He hired a new manager, Clyde Perdue, to help him get some bookings. He also retained his ties with promoter Oscar Davis, as well as making himself available, ostensibly at least, to KWKH for the Hayride and its related personal appearances.

Fred and Wesley Rose had told Hank that he could make it back to the Opry, and Hank held onto that hope like the last strand of the last rope between him and limbo. Hank's dreams for his personal life were dashed; all that was left was his professional pride to keep one foot moving in front of the other. The Opry became, like his son Bocephus had been, a symbol of What Life Should Be, and ol' Hank just had to grasp it once more. Hank Williams *belonged* on the Grand Ole Opry. He'd get back.

Actually, because of his still-overwhelming popularity across the country, his hopes were not entirely empty. Don Helms, along with Wesley Rose, maintains that the Opry was planning to take Hank back when the time was right. "Jim Denny wouldn't let me and the boys take a steady job with anybody else the whole time Hank was in Shreveport," says Helms. "We just assumed at the time, and I still believe it, that Denny thought Hank was coming back and he wanted us to be ready." Pruitt's job with Carl Smith was an exception within Denny's plan; he probably was most concerned about losing Helms and Rivers.

While Hank's Hayride appearances kept up his pattern of hit

a few-miss a few, his recording career continued to flourish. "Jambalaya" was becoming one of Hank's monster tracks, both in terms of country sales and pop "cover" recordings of it. Except in the South, where the folks could see Hank's decline being acted out in person before their eyes, Hank Williams was still as bright a star as ever, still, in fact, a relatively new star in the hillbilly firmament.

There were several reasons for this. First, M-G-M records was playing out its hand as if nothing was wrong. (An official M-G-M bio sheet of Hank published in March of 1955 lists his death as due to an "automobile accident.") Second, Fred and Wesley Rose were sending Hank Williams masters to New York with the same clockwork regularity as always. Third, and most important, the quality of Hank's recordings never deteriorated. If anything, the records got better. Williams never showed up drunk for a recording session.

"Jambalaya" and "Settin' the Woods on Fire" were both recorded in June of 1952, and along with "I'll Never Get Out Of This World Alive" (probably recorded on July 11) these tunes blanketed the country music world and the nation's country stations with Hank Williams material through the rest of that year. At the close of 1952, "Jambalaya" was the number one country song in the nation, "Settin' the Woods On Fire" was number two, and "I'll Never Get Out of This World Alive" was also in the top ten. ("Alive," though it expresses a strangely prophetic sentiment, was not a case of Hank playing the Grim Oracle, but rather a whimsical, up-tempo, moaning blues.)

Obviously, though Hank was moving into the latter stages of alcoholism, his creative powers remained strong. He had a new song he wanted to record called "Your Cheating Heart"—a message to Audrey, Billie Jean later said. And he had another one that was unlike anything he'd ever done before. It had started out by Hank's pen as a sort of sad story of two ill-fated Indian lovers, but Fred Rose had reworked the lyrics into a classic bit of nonsense about the unhappy love life of a wooden Indian with a heart of "knotty pine." The song, of course, was "Kaw-Liga," the single best example of Hank's inspiration and Fred's craftsmanship brought together on a songwriting project.

Fred Rose set up a recording session at Castle Studios for September 23. Hank come up from Shreveport by car and arrived sober, bringing the ever-lovely Billie Jean, now his fiancée, into the studio with him for the evening session.

"She was the prettiest thing I ever saw," says engineer Glenn Snoddy who worked the session that night. So struck was Snoddy by Billie's beauty that he hardly remembers anything else about those three hours.

Rose had contacted Helms, Rivers, and Watts to work on the session, and Fred himself would play some piano, of course. A couple of other studio professionals were brought in, including one hollow-cheeked young guitarist who was awestruck about recording with Hank Williams. Chet Atkins would nevertheless play a quite acceptable electric rhythm guitar on "Kaw-Liga" during this historic session.

Hank recorded "Your Cheating Heart" and "Kaw-Liga" that night, as well as a Fred Rose–Hy Heath number called "Take These Chains From My Heart." If in fact he recorded a fourth track in this session it remains uncertain what that song was. It may have been "Weary Blues From Waitin,'" a tune Hank had just put together for his friend Ray Price while the two traveled together between show dates.

Though no one knew it, Hank Williams had now completed his last professional recording session. Less than six years had passed since his first. He would not live to watch these tunes climb the *Billboard* and *Cash Box* charts the following year. He would never know that "Your Cheating Heart," his simple new song of love and guilt, would surpass even "Lovesick Blues" as the song most identified with Hank Williams in the years and decades to come.

By now Hank and Billie had worked out an interim arrangement so that she could tour with him though they were not yet married. Billie's family wanted everything on the up-and-up, so a compromise was reached whereby Billie could travel with Hank, but Hank had to hire her brother as his lead guitarist. The brother's wife would then accompany the band and Billie and Hank on tour as chaperone to the couple.

"Lord, I was young and dumb," Billie has said of those months. She'd never been "anywhere, or done anything." She'd never stayed in a hotel and owned no luggage, not even an overnight bag. "We stayed in the good hotels," she recalled later, "but I still carried my shoes in one hand and all my things in a big Kotex box. I didn't even know enough to get another kind of box."

Too naive herself to be embarrassed as they walked through hotel lobbies in Dallas or Oklahoma City, she thinks Hank just thought her habits were "kind of cute."

That's assuming he noticed such details at all by that time. In Billie's words, the skinny singer—who had never been a robust specimen—was "already awful burned out and used up" by the time she met him. Billie noticed that a lot of people hung around Hank and, like Corky Adams, felt that they were "using him."

One of these camp followers was a self-proclaimed physician known as Doctor Toby Marshall. Horace R. Marshall attached himself to the Williams entourage when Hank was doing some shows in Oklahoma City. He soon became a fixture of that last shadowy fall season of Williams' career, spending hours in "counseling sessions," and prescribing various drugs for Hank's alcoholism and his ever-present severe back pain: amphetamines, Seconal, and a strong sedative called chloral hydrate, which Hank dissolved in water glasses and drank quite frequently as the weeks wore on.

Marshall, as one might suspect, turned out to be an outright fake, one of this century's more notable flim-flam men. Though he admitted to an Oklahoma City legislative investigating committee after Williams' death that he "never went beyond high school," Marshall posed as a medical doctor with a B.S., an M.A., and a "DSC" (this last supposed to make him a "doctor of science and psychology"). The "degree" Marshall showed to prove he was a doctor had been purchased in an Oklahoma City filling station from a traveling magazine sales crew. They had a machine that printed diplomas to order, and Marshall's "DSC" had cost him thirty-five dollars.

Toby was on parole that fall and had a previous record of forgery and armed robbery convictions, yet apparently he had little problem convincing ol' Hank he was indeed a medical doctor who specialized in the treatment of alcoholism. After all, how else did he get those prescriptions all the time? (Marshall did it through an alarmingly simple system: He would first call a physician's office posing as a pharmacist and ask for the doctor's registry number, then with the registry number to verify his authenticity, he would call the drugstore of his choice and order a prescription for Hank Williams.) Marshall thus became a $300 a week employee of the ailing singer.

In addition to the drugs being administered by his "personal physician," Hank had a card given to him (presumably back in Nashville; perhaps by Marshall) that cleared him to receive morphine injections whenever the pain in his back became more than he could handle—which was often. And of course Hank never stopped drinking for more than a day or two; now the alcoholism had gone so far that sometimes he wouldn't get drunk, but merely sick. Either way, he couldn't perform worth a boo when he was drinking. In the words of an associate, he "flatted out all over the place" when he sang, and he became rude to his crowds as well.

It was in this atmosphere that Oscar Davis and Clyde Perdue were trying to get dates for Hank Williams. "I had to apologize for him to a lot of our audiences," the Hayride's Frank Page said years later. "I'd say, 'Hank is sick tonight and can't make it,' I never said he was drunk, though sometimes it was evident that's what he was."

Though Hank's talent still shone through the bleary haze of his booze and drug habits, and though most audiences still loved him and forgave him, he was becoming hard to book. And the money was coming in now in much smaller chunks. "His top had been about fifteen hundred dollars a day in his prime," Oscar Davis told Roger Williams, "but now, in towns around Louisiana, we just got whatever we could. No local promoter would handle him. It was too risky. We'd have to buy the radio time, hire the auditorium, do it all—and then take our chances."

Meanwhile Billie Jean was trying to get used to the shock of Hank's alcoholism as seen close up. She quickly noticed that when Hank drank, he didn't eat. So she took up the job that others had tried before her; she tried to keep booze and Hank apart. And if he did drink she'd force-feed him protein foods to make sure he was getting some nourishment.

One day while they were still traveling with Billie's brother and sister-in-law she caught Hank stashing two cases of beer under the bed: "God damn, baby, I was just lookin' for my shoes." She opened every can and poured the beer down the sink. As the pills became more plentiful, she'd flush bottles full of them down the hotel toilets.

Billie was unwilling to tolerate Hank's drinking. She wanted him to "walk like a man" or not at all—with her, at least. In that, she was like Audrey; but unlike Audrey, she had no interest in show business nor in the High Life. She was content with Hank himself and wild about him.

The pair were waiting until mid-October to be married, because that was when Billie believed her divorce would be final. In the meantime, Hank and Oscar Davis came up with a plan to kill two rubes with one pitch. Why not make the most of Hank's wedding by selling tickets? That'd be one show they'd all want to see!

Oscar Davis took on the project with gusto. He began contacting halls, talking to associates, and decided that the wedding "show" would be staged in the Municipal Auditorium in New Orleans. There would be a 3 P.M. "rehearsal" and a 7 P.M. "wedding." Again, no one was forgetting the sales technique of giving the people plenty of whatever it was they wanted.

Before the planned extravaganza could come off, though, Hank heard unsettling news from Nashville. Audrey was furious about his forthcoming remarriage. So he decided to get the legal stuff over with quickly one night after a Hayride show at Shreveport's Municipal Auditorium.

"The day before we got married in New Orleans," Billie explained later, "Hank said he thought we ought to get married up here in Shreveport, just in case something went wrong. We borrowed my brother's '50 Ford and drove over to Minden to get married." Hank was so excited he forgot to put gas in the Ford, and on the way home from the J. P.'s, they ran out. Finally Hank flagged down a farmer on the little-used country road and he helped the couple get some fuel. "Hank was so grateful he asked the man to spend the night with us," Billie said later, "but I convinced him that it wasn't necessary."

For the second time in his life, Hank Williams was married as an afterthought to a show date, with a quick mouthful of words mumbled by a sleepy, small-town magistrate. And though he didn't know it, for the second time Hank was marrying a girl who was still days away from being legally divorced.

The next day in New Orleans made up for any lack of spectacle that might have accompanied the short Minden betrothal rites.

Oscar Davis had had no problem getting some excitement stirred up in New Orleans. The big delta city was nuts over "Jambalaya" about that time, and Hank Williams was becoming the town's most popular adopted hero since Andrew Jackson. Knowing that the happy couple needed a few things to help them set up housekeeping, the promoter arranged with local merchants for a cornucopia of "wedding gifts" to be presented to Hank and Billie Jean. Flowers, champagne, a rack of clothes for Billie, furniture—all were made possible through the efforts of the indefatigable Davis.

He had promised Hank he could sell out the 14,000 seat auditorium and he did—twice. At 75¢ to $1.50 a ticket. That meant that Hank and Billie would have a nest egg of $30,000 or so, minus rent for the hall and Oscar's cut. No one mentioned that Hank and Billie were already married as the scalpers worked the front of the auditorium that day.

Red Sovine and a Hayride troupe plus some Opry performers were there to liven up the program during the ceremonies, but none of the Nashville crowd Hank had invited showed up. Fred and Wesley Rose were absent, along with Jim Denny. Wesley Rose later said his father felt he'd be a part of a "carnival" if he went to New Orleans. Hank had also sent an invitation to Audrey, who understandably declined. "There's nothing I wouldn't do to spite her," Hank said of his ex-wife.

At three and again at seven, the spectators got what they paid for: a breathlessly lovely bride whose dark red tresses were set off by an ankle-length white wedding gown, and an in-the-flesh appearance by the groom, that rascally old Hank Williams, looking pretty good for himself (in spite of the rumors) in a dark cowboy outfit with contrasting fringe and customary white hat. The folks were a little shocked when ol' Hank swept off his Stetson to kiss Billie, finding that the entire top of his head was nearly bald, but it was still a thrill to watch the services as performed by Reverend L. R. Shelton from the First Baptist Church of Algiers, Louisiana, and to follow the happy pair as they left the auditorium in a blaze of glory, off to a new adventure.

The new adventure was supposed to be a honeymoon in Cuba, but Hank partook too heavily from an iced tub of champagne at the reception and crawled into the arms of Somnis in their hotel room without leaving the city. Billie said later she got rid of bothersome reporters by coming to the door and telling them Hank was "resting." Seeing the wide-eyed Billie Jean in her flimsy negligee and bare feet, the press believed her.

So Hank returned, a married man, to the Hayride circuit. Billie's devoted efforts to keep him nourished could be seen on his bony frame, and the October 18 issue of *Billboard* that year stated that "Hank Williams has gained 30 pounds and reports that he is in the best of health." He may have gained that much weight, but Billie said later that Hank by this time was in need of daily nursing-type care to keep him going. "He tried," Billie told Wesley Pruden. "He really tried. And so did I." Billie began to ration to Hank two beers a day, in sympathy for her husband who had developed a peculiar fondness for beer again and would literally beg for anything alcoholic.

"I'd always get my brothers to help me when we had to take him to the hospital," she said later. "It got so that when he'd see my brothers come up the walk, he'd grab his hat and say, 'Well, it's time for Ol' Hank to go again.'" They'd take him to the hospital in Shreveport and up the freight elevator, to avoid embarrassment. Hank would normally be singing "Jambalaya" in his unmusical inebriated style. The elevator attendants would laugh, and Hank—seeing at the time no reason not to—would laugh along with them.

According to Hank Junior, the trips to the hospital with Billie's brothers gave birth to rumors that Hank had become a virtual captive, told what to do by Billie Jean's father and brothers and beat up when he refused to cooperate. One piece of fuel that seemed to add to this story was Hank's appearance late in the year at the Big D Jamboree in Dallas. Ray Price reported that Hank sang pretty well, but his head was "skinned up a little."

It's hard to believe that Hank was a captive of the Jones family. Billie's father, a sometime police officer, and her brothers were neither of the moral nor opportunist stripe necessary to carry off such a prolonged abduction. Hank was perfectly capable of skinning himself up with no help at all, as he had proved back in his Natchez Trace house shortly before leaving Nashville. He had simply leaned on a screen door, thinking it was locked, and pushed it open as he crashed down onto his back steps. However, this is not to say that Hank Williams was in control of his life. Toby Marshall was still hanging in the near background with his black bag of pills and his prescriptory pen always at the ready, and Hank had begun to slide from booze to pills to morphine shots in such a casual manner that Billie feared for him. Hank's only landmarks by now were the shows he made; the ones he missed he scarcely knew about.

Still he managed to come through like his old, happy, generous self fom time to time. Whenever he and Billie Jean went to see her grandparents, who lived on welfare, Hank would deliver huge bags of groceries to them. He also got in the habit, these last few months of his life, of giving away his stage uniforms and pistols to anyone who professed to admire them.

"I walked into a liquor store with him in Shreveport," says Red Sovine, veteran country star who was then on the Hayride, "and he bought a fifth of whiskey and left a hundred-dollar bill on the counter." When they got outside, Sovine asked Williams why he'd give away money like that and yet argue over how much Sovine and his band would receive for backing ol' Hank on a tour.

"Aw, I'll pay you," was Hank's reply. Dickering over paying musicians was an ingrained habit; so was big tipping. "That's just the way he was," says Sovine. "He'd buy a beer and a sandwich at a restaurant and leave a twenty-dollar bill and think nothing of it."

Sovine, whom Hank had helped to land a job on WSFA back in '48, had come to the Hayride when Hank went to the Opry and played many dates with him in that last autumn. According to Sovine, most of Hank's Hayride dates were played before the wedding, and only one tour was completed in connection with KWKH after Hank's New Orleans mock-wedding extravaganza in October.

"We were gettin' ready to leave on that tour—a five-day swing through southern Louisiana—and it was a Sunday," Sovine recalls. Suddenly Hank grimaced and put his hands up on his breastbone.

"You know, Red," he said, "my chest feels like it's about to bust."

"Why do this tour, anyway?" Sovine asked Williams. "You don't need the money."

"Well, I promised Dupree," said Hank. According to Sovine, Mr. Dupree was the man who had set up the short, percentage-basis tour for Williams.

The first date, at Houma, Louisiana, came off well.

"Hank did a beautiful job," says Sovine. "And he'd really packed 'em in, too. They had to put seats in the aisles."

But on the rest of that five-day westward swing, "Hank made it rough on everybody all the way," says Red. He even made it rough on Billie Jean. "I talked to Billie one day and they'd gotten into a fight," recalls Sovine. "She'd hit Hank in the head with one of her spike-heeled shoes and some of his blood was in her hair."

On that same tour, Hank was supplied by an admiring disc jockey with a bottle (against the will of the Hayride troupe members) and got sick right before going on to perform in front of a small-town Louisiana audience. Though most crowds by this time put up with Hank any way they found him, he enraged this group by weakly yet stubbornly refusing to sing "Lovesick Blues" for them. They wound up almost overturning Hank's car before he could be driven away from the place.

Hank was booked next into Jennings, Louisiana. Before arriving, the troupe got word from Jennings that Hank Williams had better show up sober, or else he might as well not show up at all.

When they got back to Shreveport, Hank asked for and received some time off, and he and Billie went to Montgomery and stayed at Lilly's boardinghouse for awhile. But soon Hank was back at work doing the only thing he knew to do, singing his songs for the folks out there. He and Billie then moved back to Shreveport and rented a small house. They bought some furniture and settled in somewhat, though Hank was still in touch with people back in Nashville. Sometime in November or early December, the date of February 1, 1953, began to take on a special significance.

"We saw Hank a couple of weeks before the first of the year," says Wesley Rose. "He was getting ready to come back on the Grand Ole Opry February 1 as a surprise. . . . We told him to be sure and play all his dates, so there wouldn't be any mess-up, then to come on up."

Rose also maintains that as of that meeting it was Hank's intention to leave Billie Jean in Shreveport and try to make up with Audrey. "That's exactly what he planned," says Rose.

There may have been some differences between Hank and Billie Jean, probably about drinking, as anyone would expect. M. C. Jarrett remembers running into Hank at a downtown Montgomery coffee shop late that fall:

"I talked to him awhile," says Jarrett, "then I asked him if he had a band. 'All I got is a wife and a git-tar,' he said, and I wish I only had the git-tar.'" Complications in Montgomery may have included a girlfriend who had hoped to tie the knot with Hank before Billie stepped in.

Hank Williams remained incredibly mobile for a man in the physical shape he was in. Aside from whatever chest pains he may have experienced, there were the near-constant drunks, lapses of consciousness, hangovers, climb-ups on bennies, and come-downs on Seconal. There was also the chronic and sometimes excruciating pain of living that relentless nomadic backseat or hotel life with two ruptured discs in his back. But for that, of course, there was the chloral hydrate, and morphine was always an available ace in the hole. So he moved . . . from town to town through November and early December, from Shreveport to Montgomery for a week or so, then back out to the Shreveport area to try the temporary housekeeping arrangement with Billie Jean, but few nights were spent in either the furnished apartment or later the little house in Shreveport.

Instead Hank, with his eye on next year, was instinctively playing out as many dates as he could to close out this year with a decent batting average.

Hank turned up in Oklahoma City for a show date on December 12, and after the show he got a prescription from Toby Marshall for twenty-four capsules of chloral hydrate. By the time Hank filled the prescription he was back in Montgomery again. It seemed the entire South was Hank's staked-out territory now, where like some wounded wolf he was given the freedom to roam at will until he would play out his solitary hunt.

Still none of these jumps—from southern town to town, from the plains to the piney woods and back, and back again—was made on turnpikes, but on the same winding two-lane roads Hank had ridden over with two generations of Drifting Cowboys in his fifteen restless Road years.

Like a punchdrunk fighter still gamely throwing sluggish jabs and awkward roundhouse hooks, Hank was not giving up. He was gonna get back to the Opry. *Jus' hold on to me, girl, jus' help me through a few more o' these no-good, stale-beer honkytonk dates and we'll be back in business.* Ol' Hank wasn't through; at least he never thought so. He'd get back to Nashville, and someday . . . yeah, someday he'd get himself back together. He knew it'd have to happen sometime—well, maybe they'd throw him in the hospital to dry out after the holidays. There'd be time for that. There'd be time. After all, he was still young.

Hank had temporarily gotten off the bottle almost completely when he and Billie started for Georgiana a few days before Christmas 1952. There were a couple of reasons for it: He didn't want to make a scene around the old folks at home, and he was actually looking forward to being with them. Besides, he'd heard some good news from his old friend and promoter A. B. Bamford. Bamford had booked Hank for a large auditorium show in Canton, Ohio, on January 1. Hank saw this show as a step back up from the cheap southern honky-tonks to the bigtime. Maybe, who knows, if he could stay straight he could play some more big dates in January before going back to the Opry.

Hank and Billie Jean drove up into the yard of Taft Skipper's house just east of Georgiana after causing a minor stir coming through town. After all, it wasn't every day the townfolk saw a robin's-egg-blue '52 Cadillac convertible with a continental kit on the back. It could only be one person. It was Friday afternoon, December 19. Hank had come home.

Taft and Erleen Skipper were now in their early thirties and had built up two solid businesses in the years since Hank had left south Alabama. They ran a small general store together while Taft bred and raised pure-bred hogs. The Skippers told Hank that they'd be proud to host him and his new wife while they were visiting in the area. It'd be kinda like old times, when Hank had played Evergreen with a carload of boys and Taft and Erleen had put 'em all up.

Compared to their memories of Audrey, Billie Jean was a breath of fresh air for the Skippers. They remember Billie as friendly and likable. "When Hank used to come with Audrey, she'd wait in the car or sit out on the front porch," Taft remembers, "but Billie Jean just fit herself right in here."

Taft and Erleen, with characteristic hospitality, gave Hank and Billie their bedroom that Friday night. The next day, Saturday, December 20, Hank and Billie, Taft and Erleen drove up Highway 31 to Montgomery for the Blue-Gray game, staged annually in that city. "Hank and Billie sat 'way up high," Taft remembers, "while Erleen and I had our seats down lower where the wind wasn't so cold." At half-time, Hank decided to leave. He hadn't worn an overcoat. Taft offered his coat and then offered to trade seats, but Hank and Billie didn't stay for the rest of that day's gridiron battle under the steel-gray Alabama clouds.

Hank and Billie Jean went back to Georgiana. He was planning to spend Christmas Day with his father Lon, and then get back to Montgomery until it was time to go to Canton.

The next day, Sunday, the Skippers and the Williamses attended services at the East Chapman Baptist Church a few miles north of Georgiana. Hank was clearly enjoying himself singing the old hymns. "They wanted Hank to get up and sing right there in church that mornin'," Taft Skipper recalls. "But Hank said he couldn't sing his songs in church." It was mixing two different worlds to Hank, like carrying a Last Supper fan into a honky-tonk. So when church let out, Taft opened up his store down in Georgiana and a group of Butler County natives trooped over to hear their boy sing some of those famous songs. Hank sang "Kaw-liga" for them. They all knew it was named for Lake Kowaliga, up there beyond Montgomery. Some of 'em knew the lake wasn't far from Hank's grandma's place. And he sang that "Jambalaya." They'd sure heard that one.

"He had a new one, too," Taft Skipper recalls. "It was about the loggin' trains that ran through Chapman. Hank said he'd just wrote it . . . real purty tune." Hank's creative juices were still flowing, but he apparently never wrote this song down and it was never found.

Everyone in Georgiana was struck by Billie Jean's charms; the kinfolk had come to see "Yvonne" and they *liked* her. "Some of those people said she was the purtiest girl they ever saw," Taft remembers.

That Sunday afternoon Taft and Hank spent some time together. Hank had gone out to his car to have a beer. "He said he really loved Billie," Taft recalls. "I believe they'd 'a' made it. They talked like they wanted to settle down and live a good life together."

Early in the week, Hank and Taft took a walk across a large field one evening while they talked, and Taft remembers that as they came back and neared the house, Hank got a pain in his chest and felt that he couldn't breathe. "He said he thought he had a touch of the asthma," Hank's cousin remembers.

Between Sunday and Wednesday night, the Skippers learned quite a bit about Hank and Billie. They learned that Hank was no longer wealthy, since Audrey had gotten nearly all the property he'd ever owned. He had with him a four-thousand-dollar certified check from KWKH, and told the Skippers it was "the only money he had in Alabama that Audrey didn't have tied up."

They also learned that Billie Jean had some admirable character traits—like helpfulness. "When we finished eatin' a meal," says Erleen, "she'd get right up and clear off the table."

On Christmas morning, Hank and Billie said good-bye to Taft and Erleen and drove twenty-odd miles westward to Mc-

Williams, one of Hank's childhood homes, where Lon Williams lived. But Lon wasn't there to spend Christmas Day with, because Hank hadn't told him he was coming. They had seen each other only occasionally over the years, in the manner of distant friends.

So the day was spent with Hank's aunt, Lon's sister, in Pine Apple, Alabama, where Hank left some presents for his father. Then it was up to Montgomery. He'd paid his last visit to the piney woods.

Things were less than festive at the boardinghouse, seeing's how Audrey's shadow still hung around there from all the years she'd spent in or near the premises. She and Lilly had learned to live with each other, too, which now made it harder for Lilly to learn to live with Billie Jean. But the visit went along peaceably.

On Sunday night, December 28, Hank played an unusual gig. It's unclear how he happened to be asked to play for the American Federation of Musicians' local union holiday party, but Hank rose to the occasion. Though he didn't read music and most of his audience didn't get near country material, Hank managed to win over this tough audience. Local union president Tom Hewlett later wrote, "We forgot our talent, technical skill, and musical training; we truly enjoyed every note. . . ." It was of course another unconscious good-bye, this one to the musical establishment of the town where Hank had long worked one side of the tracks while these guys worked the other. Some of them still had never heard of him.

The party was held at the Casino Lounge, and Hank brought along Billie Jean and sat at a table with Leo Hudson, who'd been with Hank in Portland eight long years before.

"I remember that night well, at least the early part," says Hudson. "Hank introduced Billie Jean to me as his wife . . . later on I don't remember much. The party broke up. Every-body was drunk."

Meanwhile Hank had gotten in contact with Don Helms up in Nashville to try to get the Drifting Cowboys back together for the Canton date. Hank had left the two-tone green '51 limo in a garage in Nashville, looking to the day it would be needed there again. He thought Helms might be able to take it and the

Cowboys to Canton. But they couldn't. They were already supposed to play that night of January 1 in Cleveland with Ray Price. However, Helms thought he could come to Canton himself and put together a pick-up group to help Hank out. So it would be: Don would bring guitarist Autry Inman and some other musicians with him from Nashville and meet Hank in Canton.

Now it was the afternoon of December 30. Hank had heard that a winter storm was coming in, so it didn't look like he'd be able to fly to Ohio. He'd have to get a driver. He'd been using a clean-cut young guy named Charles Carr for several long overland pulls in the past couple of months, but maybe there was someone better. Hank drove his blue convertible with the black top over to the Hollywood Drive-In. When he pulled up in the parking lot, he saw Leo Hudson sitting there in his old Cadillac sedan. Maybe Leo would do it.

Hank walked over and said hello and got into the back seat of Leo's car. He began ordering bottles of beer as he talked.

"I got a show 'way up the other side of West Virginia," he told Hudson. "I wisht you'd drive me up there. I'll pay you well."

Hudson couldn't go. He had another date with a band to play saxophone on New Year's eve. He wasn't going to throw away his membership in this other band to take Hank Williams to Ohio.

"He offered me two hundred and fifty dollars," Hudson remembers, "but I couldn't do it. He must have drunk five or six beers in my back seat trying to talk me into it."

"Charles is a good boy, but I don't trust his driving," Hank told Hudson. But Hudson wasn't going to change his mind.

"After a while he ordered two six-packs and left," says Hudson. They were probably the last two six-packs Hank Williams ever bought.

That night back at the boardinghouse, Hank couldn't sleep. Billie Jean woke in the middle of the night and found him up. "What the devil is the matter with you?" she asked him.

"Billie, I think I see God comin' down the road," he answered.

Tears came to Billie's eyes. "Oh, Hank, don't say that," she told him. Somehow, both of them got some sleep before dawn.

When Wednesday morning came, the storm Hank had heard about had begun. Hank packed his show uniforms and guitar into the trunk of the Cadillac. He dressed and made sure he had an overcoat.

"When Hank was ready to leave," Billie Jean said later, "he came in and sat down on the edge of the bed. He just looked at me, not saying a word. 'What're you lookin' at, Hank?' I asked him. 'I just wanted to look at you one more time,' he said. I stood in front of the mirror, my back to him, and he came over and kissed me on the cheek. Then he said good-bye and left."

Hank drove over to Charles Carr's house and crawled into his black pleated-leather rear seat as the younger man took over the wheel of the car. They rolled out of Montgomery in the mid-morning, heading northward toward Birmingham on Route 31. The highway was covered with a thin layer of snow and more was falling.

They had something like twenty driving hours ahead of them to make it to Canton. Hank was going to be hurting, he knew, but he'd refilled his prescription for chloral hydrate capsules, and he could drink beer all the way, if need be. Charles Carr quietly and dutifully maneuvered the big convertible up Highway 31 to Birmingham, then turned its robin's-egg-blue nose northeast for Chattanooga on Highway 11, which would carry them all the way into Virginia.

Meanwhile, Jerry Rivers and bassist Howard Watts were getting ready to leave Nashville in Ray Price's tour car. Jerry and Ced were bound for their Thursday night date in Cleveland. Price himself managed to book himself on one of only a couple of flights that left Nashville for Cleveland that December 31. Cold freezing rain, sleet, and snow were moving eastward, tying up airlines and highways all over the South.

Nevertheless Don Helms also made ready for a ten-hour drive northward from Nashville, snaking Hank's Cadillac limo down the out-ramp of a downtown Nashville garage. Helms left Nashville with his Canton-bound group before Rivers, thereby scooting out of Dixie that afternoon before the worst of the storm hit Kentucky and Tennessee. Rivers, Watts, and the Cleveland group left Nashville in the late afternoon, still allowing themselves more than twenty-four hours to get to Lake Erie.

At 7:08 P.M. that evening, a well-groomed, neatly dressed young man of medium height and build walked into the lobby of the Andrew Johnson Hotel, the best hotel in Knoxville, Tennessee. The desk clerk noticed as the young man registered that he was wearing a diamond ring. It was Charles Carr.

Carr told the bell captain that he was going to need some special assistance. He had a sick man out in the car who needed to be helped up to his room. The bell captain dispatched two black porters to go with Carr out to the Cadillac and get Hank Williams, who had drunk several beers on the drive up from Montgomery and had probably taken a chloral hydrate capsule or two. Carr also told the desk clerk that they'd been out to the airport to try to get a flight out of Knoxville, but that none was available. Now they were going to rest for awhile, before continuing northward to Canton, Ohio.

The porters carried the long-legged, well-dressed, barely-conscious white man up to his room and with Carr they undressed him and put him to bed. Carr gave them a liberal tip and told them to take care of the car and luggage and stay where he could reach them—he might need them again soon. Then he called room service and ordered two T-bone steak dinners. By the time the porters had parked the car and brought Williams' clothes up to the room, the steaks had arrived. Carr told the men where to put the luggage and calmly sat down to his meal. He found that his employer was too sick to eat, so one of the porters ate the other T-bone.

While Hank Williams rested in bed, Charles Carr carried out the next step of his orders. He sent for the house doctor. In a short time, Dr. P. H. Cardwell, a middle-aged Knoxville physician, arrived at the room. He noticed some capsules on the dresser when he came in, but he didn't get nosey. Carr explained that Mr. Williams had had back surgery and was in need of a shot of something to ease his pain while traveling by car. He may have shown Cardwell the authorization card Hank carried.

Doctor Cardwell stayed only a few minutes, just long enough to administer one hypodermic and then another. Each shot contained one-quarter grain of morphine with a small amount of Vitamin B-12. After the doctor left, Hank Williams dozed comfortably in bed for an hour or more.

Then Carr received a long-distance phone call. The message was that he and Williams were to proceed to Canton so that Hank would be ready for sure to do the show Wednesday night. Presumably A. B. Bamford figured that it would be better if Hank rested in Canton, where he could be watched and taken care of properly in preparation for his show.

Around ten-thirty, Carr began to get ready to get back on the road. He summoned the two porters again, and they dressed Williams in his suit and boots. They draped his overcoat across his torso and carried him back downstairs, one man holding Hank Williams under his arms and the other clutching his bony legs. Whether or not they put a hat on his head—for warmth if not for style—or left him bareheaded is not certain. They did remember later that he felt limber, and that he didn't move. It was difficult for all four men to fit into the elevator, and the porters found it necessary to bend Williams' body at the waist. While in this position and traveling downward in the elevator, according to the porters' later testimony, the man they were carrying made a "gurgling sound." Otherwise the trip out to the waiting Cadillac was uneventful. Charles Carr checked out of the Andrew Johnson Hotel at 10:54 P.M. and started out of Knoxville on the Rutledge Pike.

By this time Jerry Rivers, Ced, and company had made it as far as Louisville, but the weather was rapidly growing worse. The streets were glazed with ice as they drove through town, and now heavy snow began to come in blizzard force. They made it in an hour or so up Highway 42 toward Cincinnati, but by then there were two-foot drifts on each side of the road and they ran into backed-up traffic. The Highway Patrol was in the process of closing down Kentucky's highways for the night, so Rivers was forced to turn around and head back for Nashville. The blizzard was not so blinding to the south. Ray Price would not have a band in Cleveland. Don Helms, Autry Inman, and their group in the meantime had cleared the storm front and were purring northward to Canton.

Shortly after eleven-thirty, Tennessee Highway Patrolman Corporal Swann Kitts was driving west on Highway 11W outside of Rutledge. Suddenly he noticed that two cars were speeding toward him side by side on the highway ahead, and one of them was in his lane. He had to slow his patrol car down to narrowly avoid colliding with a robin's-egg-blue Cadillac convertible that was whooshing past another eastbound car. Kitts immediately turned his car around and chased down the Cadillac, whose driver pulled over obediently when he saw the flashing light on Kitt's patrol car.

It was clear and cold in Grainger County that night. The storm front had not moved that far eastward yet. Corporal Kitts got out of his car and approached the big Cadillac with the continental kit on its extended rear bumper. Just as he began to question the young driver, the driver of the other car, the one the Cadillac had passed, came back to the scene. He was incensed about the dangerous attempt to pass him and he was cursing.

"You go on," Patrolman Kitts told the irate citizen. "I'll handle this." He was already planning to give Charles Carr of Montgomery, Alabama, a ticket for reckless driving.

As he questioned Carr, he noticed that someone was lying across the rear seat of the convertible. It was a slender man dressed in a suit and covered with an overcoat. His uncovered head was on the other side of the car from the driver's side, propped up on something. His mouth was open and he was unconscious.

"He looks like he might be dead," Patrolman Kitts told Charles Carr.

Carr told the police officer that the man was Hank Williams and that Williams had had six or seven beers as well as some pain medication for his back. He was just sleeping, Carr assured the lawman. He seemed unconcerned, as if it were an everyday situation.

Patrolman Kitts was impressed by Carr's politeness and

clean appearance. He soon concluded that this young man was neither a drunk nor particularly dangerous driver, but was just in a big hurry. Still, in cases like this, it was normal procedure to take an offender back to Knoxville to pay his fine. He told Carr of his intentions.

"How 'bout lettin' me pay my fine here in Grainger County?" Charles Carr asked, conscious of time. "It all goes to the state, anyway."

Kitts relented and led the Cadillac into Rutledge, where Charles Carr went before magistrate Olin Marshall. Kitts told Marshall and the Grainger County Sheriff, who was also present, that he thought they should investigate the situation of the man who was passed out in the car outside.

Carr explained again that the man was Hank Williams, that ol' Hank had had a few beers and some pain medication for a back operation. He was a sick man. He went into some detail, describing the stop in Knoxville at the Andrew Johnson Hotel, the injections, and so on.

Magistrate Marshall decided not to press the matter. "Don't bother him," he told Kitts. "We might get a boisterous drunk on our hands. He's not bothering anybody. I don't think you should disturb him. It might be invading his privacy."

Thus Charles Carr drove out of Rutledge, Tennessee, after paying his fine for reckless driving. But Patrolman Swann Kitts was still reasonably sure that Carr's passenger was either dead or dying.

So the big flagship of a car rolled northeast for Virginia. Charles Carr drove through Kingsport and Bristol, Tennessee, and on into the big Rich Valley of Western Virginia, still following Highway 11 northeast, parallel with the folds of the Appalachian Mountains they were entering.

In all probability Carr drove to Abingdon on 11, then bucked northward across the lower end of the Clinch Mountain Range on Highway 19. Nineteen then swung northeast again all the way to Bluefield and then across the state line to Princeton, West Virginia, where it turned directly north into central West Virginia.

Carr may have been surprised by the time he'd driven a few hours that Hank had made no sound. The injections should have worn off by now, shouldn't they? Still, he'd driven that ol' boy on lots of trips where he'd done a lot of sleepin'.

It probably took Carr three or four hours to make it into West Virginia. Still no movement or sound in the back seat.

He drove on another fifty-six miles from Princeton northward to Oak Hill, West Virginia. It would be getting light before too long—better check on Hank. He pulled the Cadillac into a Pure Oil Station and reached for Hank's hand to shake him. The hand was cold. Hank wouldn't wake up.

Now Carr barreled the car to the Oak Hill Hospital. It was too late. Hank Williams was pronounced dead on arrival there. The time of that pronouncement is not in the hospital's records, but it probably occurred at about 6 A.M. If Swann Kitts' opinion is right, Hank was dead hours before that.

Charles Carr called Lilly in Montgomery and broke the news to her. Hank's body, she said, should be brought back there. Then Carr talked to Billie Jean. "Mrs. Williams, what do we do with the car?" he asked.

13

Aftermath—The People and the Legend

Don Helms ("Shag"): Steel guitar player, Drifting Cowboys. Nashville, Tennessee

Don Helms and Autry Inman arrived with their musicians in Canton early in the morning that New Year's Day of 1953. They went directly to their hotel and went to bed until time for that evening's show at the Canton Memorial Auditorium. When they arrived, A. B. Bamford met them at their dressing room. "I don't guess you've heard the bad news," Bamford told Helms and the boys, "Hank passed away." Though Helms had felt it was a possibility, he said later, "We were astounded."

So was the audience that night in Canton. When local disc jockey Cliff Rodgers announced that Hank Williams had died, the place was swept by a wave of sorrowful emotion; many people wept openly. Most felt that Hank would have wanted the show to go on, so it did. But not before the assembled cast did a tribute rendition of "I Saw The Light" from behind the curtains, while the audience rose to its feet and hundreds of people sang through their tears.

"Some of the people cried all through the show," Helms remembers. Helms played an instrumental version of "Cold, Cold Heart" and "barely got through it." He, too, was almost overcome.

Three days later Don, along with the rest of the Drifting Cowboys, attended Hank's funeral in Montgomery. What they found in Hank's home town was an outpouring of public sentiment that has few parallels in American history.

213

Don Helms continued then to work for Ray Price, and he played with several other great names, becoming one of the best-respected musicians in Nashville. In the late sixties he played four and a half years with Hank Williams, Junior, and now tours the country with some men he knows pretty well: Jerry Rivers, Hillous Butrum, and Bob McNett. There are a lot of people who want to listen to Hank's great songs played by the men who played them first and played them best.

"Hank wasn't perfect," Helms says straightforwardly. "I've never found anybody else who was, either. I've never found the perfect man. There's only One of them."

Lillian Skipper Williams (Mrs. W. W. Stone): Mother of Hank Williams. Montgomery, Alabama

Lilly's first action after Hank's death was to handle his wake, which was to take place at her boardinghouse on McDonough Street. Two factions had quickly grown up: the Lilly-Irene-Audrey faction and the Billie Jean and Her Family faction. The undertaker arranged for each group to view the body separately, taking no chances. They took turns sitting in the room with the silver casket.

Lilly also received thousands of cards and letters of sympathy from all over the country. But there was barely time to mourn; the legal confusion was already getting sticky. Hank's real and personal property was valued at only about $13,000, but everyone knew the royalties would be quite valuable. Lilly, Irene, Audrey, and Billie Jean all entered the fray. Since Hank was divorced from Audrey, and since it turned out there was a question of the legality of his marriage to Billie Jean, Lilly filed a petition seeking to be named administratrix of the estate. Billie Jean contested this action, but Lilly and her lawyers arranged to buy Billie Jean's legal claims to the estate. The sum finally agreed upon was $30,000.

Lillian lived to see her dead son mourned by well over 20,000 people on the day of his funeral. She lived for the first annual Hank Williams Memorial Day in Montgomery on September 21, 1954, where she rode in the robin's-egg-blue convertible through a parade crowd of 60,000. She converted Hank's old room on McDonough Street into a shrine honoring his memory, with Hank's costumes, guns, guitars, and sheet music decorating it.

Then Lilly died in February, 1955, at the age of 57, and Hank's sister Irene became the legal administratrix of his estate.

Jerry Rivers ("Burrhead"): Fiddler, Drifting Cowboys. Goodlettsville, Tennessee

Jerry Rivers traveled with some other Opry musicians to Montgomery for Hank's funeral, which was to be held on Sunday, January 4, 1953. As they approached the city by car, they became involved in the biggest traffic jam any of them had ever seen. Somehow they made it to the boardinghouse. The black Cadillac hearse was already drawn up in front of the old frame building, and the onlookers were standing in the streets, the sidewalk, the yard. Rivers and the other Drifting Cowboys had been named honorary pallbearers, while the active pallbearers came from the ranks of Hank's business associates. Two of the active pallbearers got caught in the traffic snarl, however, and Rivers was asked to help move the silver casket from the house to the Municipal Auditorium where the funeral would be held. At 1 P.M. Hank's body was carried to the foot of the auditorium stage, and at 1:15 the casket was opened and the doors were opened to allow a line to pass by for one last look at Hank Williams.

Jerry Rivers later worked with other Opry stars, then formed his own group, the Homesteaders, with whom he traveled the world for many years. In 1967, Jerry wrote his personal tribute to Hank Williams, his book entitled *Hank Williams: From Life to Legend.*

Jerry now is part of the re-formed Drifting Cowboys, keeping alive the music of Hank Williams. "If there will be an end to the Hank Williams legend," Jerry has written, "it isn't in sight yet."

M. C. Jarrett: Musician, sign painter. Montgomery, Alabama

Jarrett and his wife went to visit the Williams home on Friday, January 2, at about four in the afternoon. They had known Lilly and Irene as well as they'd known Hank.

"There was nobody there but Lilly and Irene," says Jarrett. "Hank's body was lyin' in the vestibule of the old house. We talked awhile. Mrs. Williams wanted me to be a pallbearer. She wanted me to get some of the other boys from town. . . .

"But along about six o'clock, trucks started driving up with flowers from Nashville," Jarrett continues. "Big arrangements in the shape of guitars and the like. Then the curiosity-seekers started comin' in." There got to be too many people for M. C. and he left.

The next day it began to mushroom. First the funeral was to be held at the Dr. Henry L. Lyon's Highland Baptist Church, but as the city filled with people, Pastor Lyon and A. B. Bamford decided they'd better move it to the Municipal Auditorium. The move was announced that Saturday.

Jarrett tried to get downtown Sunday for the funeral. "Twenty thousand people?" He laughs. "It was more like two hundred thousand! I walked downtown and there were so many people that I turned around and went home."

Billie Jean Jones (Eshlimar, Williams, Horton, Berlin): Wife of Hank Williams at the time of his death. Shreveport, Louisiana

Billie Jean's family joined her in Montgomery and they all stayed in one hotel room, because they couldn't afford more. She wanted to have a say in the arrangements for the funeral, but felt that Lilly was "running the show." On the day of the funeral, the young widow went with her family to the auditorium. "It was the first funeral I'd ever been to," Billie said later, "and when I came in with my family we sat down in the middle of the audience. Finally the undertaker came back and asked if I wanted to sit with the family."

The undertaker gave Billie Jean a seat in the front row right next to Audrey, and the younger woman was greatly distressed. "I felt like any minute someone was going to say, 'Will the real Mrs. Hank Williams please stand up?'" she remembered.

Billie recalled that the long service included "everybody who could croak a note." The funeral started at 2:30 P.M., when the doors were sealed up. Twenty-seven hundred people watched the ceremony.

First, there was singing. The performers stood on the stage above the casket, which was surrounded by huge floral wreaths and arrangements. One piece was in the shape of a Bible and carried the first few notes to "I Saw the Light" across its cover.

Backstage, Little Jimmy Dickens wept while Ernest Tubb sang "Beyond the Sunset." Roy Acuff then sang "I Saw the Light" with Red Foley, Carl Smith, Webb Pierce, and others helping out on the choruses. Finally Red Foley rendered his "Peace In The Valley" as tears coursed down his face. Hank had loved the song, and had asked Red to sing it at his funeral if he "went" first. Billie felt that many of the Opry stars were merely looking for exposure, but certainly Foley was not. The message, a simple and short one, was delivered by Doctor Lyon. "His life," said Lyon, "is an example of what can happen in this country to one little insignificant speck of humanity."

The graveside rites were, in Roger Williams' words, "mercifully brief," as again thousands jammed the ceremony to view the interment. Billie Jean was among the family members who received a rosebud at the close of the service.

For a few months following Hank's death, Billie Jean Williams was one of *two* "Mrs. Hank Williams" touring the countryside to sympathetic and well-paying crowds. At first, she was able to prove herself the "real Mrs. Hank Williams" and once had papers served on Audrey to stop her show in New Orleans. Later, though, Billie Jean took the $30,000 settlement from Lilly and gave up her legal rights to Hank's estate, and her legal right to use the name "Mrs. Hank Williams" was also given up as part of the deal at Audrey's request.

She kept her widow's Social Security rights, however, and filed a joint Federal income-tax form for 1952 for herself and Hank. But her story had really only begun.

In 1954, she met and married another country singer, another Hayride performer, named Johnny Horton. "I guess I married him on the rebound," she later commented, "but I needed any love that anyone would give me . . . Johnny's love was genuine." She struggled along with Horton's slow-starting career until 1959, when he became an overnight sensation with his "Battle of New Orleans." A year later, when his follow-up, "North to Alaska" was one of the biggest songs of the year, Horton was killed in an automobile accident en route to a show date in Texas. For the second time, Billie Jean received bad news at dawn. The two-time widow, now in her late twenties, had grown wiser with her years. She collected the hundreds of tape recordings her husband had made of himself and began taking them to Nashville where she hired Nashville musicians to back them up. Her arrangement with Columbia records sold Johnny Horton a million records a year every year for ten years after his death, and Billie Jean Horton Enterprises is still a lucrative company today.

In 1969, Billie viewed for the first time the M-G-M movie, *Your Cheatin' Heart*, and came out of the theater fighting mad. In the movie, Hank Williams never married a second time, and the only female who might be Billie is portrayed as a rather loose, vampy type. Billie Jean then went to work to make things right. She filed a $1.1 million suit against M-G-M and eventually cleared her name, though no malice by M-G-M was proven. Along the way, in a 1971 court decision, she established herself as Hank Williams' legal wife at the time of his death.

It was only a matter of time until this led her into court over her share of Hank's copyright renewal rights, which she had never relinquished. In 1975, Billie Jean and Hill and Range Music of New York won the right to half of all royalties paid for Hank's songs whose copyrights are renewed. Fred Rose Music hotly contested this action and appealed the court's decision, but the appeal was turned down.

Billie Jean is now divorced from N. Kent Berlin (her fourth husband was an insurance executive) and she enjoys a quiet life in South Shreve Island, a Shreveport suburb somewhat removed from Bossier City, the far less prosperous area of town where Billie grew up with her family.

Irene Williams Smith: Businesswoman, sister to Hank Williams. Dallas, Texas

Hank's sister, "Hank's first booking agent," Irene, claims to have known through a kind of mystical experience that Hank was dead. She was living with her husband in Virginia at the time, and when a highway patrolman knocked on her door the morning of January 1, 1953, Irene reportedly called a relative as the patrolman had told her to and asked immediately, "Where did Hank die, and where is my mother?"

Through the tense days surrounding the funeral, Irene acted as a peacemaker between Audrey, Billie Jean, and her mother. She encouraged Billie not to let Lilly do anything Billie objected to, and she turned up at one point on the funeral day with a widow on each arm.

When Lilly died in 1955, it was Irene who became the administratrix of the estate, a post she held until 1969. At that point, subsequent to a conviction for possession of illegal drugs, Irene moved out of the legal picture, both as administratrix of the estate and as legal guardian of Hank Junior. At that time Irene was a successful real estate broker in the Dallas area.

After serving several years in prison, Irene returned to the business world as an office manager for a Dallas firm and plans a book of her own someday on her brother. She says she has about 30,000 words of childhood memories written down already.

Elonzo H. (Lon) Williams: Locomotive engineer, farmer, father of Hank Williams. McWilliams, Alabama

Lon Williams lived in McWilliams for the rest of his life, with a houseful of mementoes to remind him of his son. Lon, as Roger Williams has noted, assumed a kind of dignity in the way he stayed completely away from the legal scratching and clawing for pieces of Hank's estate.

He died in McWilliams in 1969 at the age of 78.

James (Jim) Denny: Talent promoter, booking agent. Nashville, Tennessee

Jim Denny went into a partnership with Webb Pierce in a booking agency of his own shortly after Hank's death. He felt, along with Pierce, that the Opry was often too restrictive in its management dealings with artists.

Denny's agency became very successful and was a pioneer

institution that would inspire many other similar ventures in Nashville, changing the complexion of the entire artist-management model in that city forever.

Jim Denny died in 1957.

Audrey Mae Williams: Singer, promoter, ex-wife of Hank Williams. Nashville, Tennessee

Once Billie Jean had gone on her way in 1953 with her $30,000 settlement, Audrey quickly assumed the role of being Hank Williams' true widow, just as if they had never been divorced. (She also claimed that Hank had asked her to remarry him shortly before he died.)

Though Lilly was doing the consulting with Willie Gayle, the representative from the Henley Memorial Company of Montgomery, Audrey persuaded Hank's mother to allow her to have her poem, "Thank You Darling," etched into the Vermont granite of Hank's tall, striking memorial. In the poem, she thanks Hank for his love, for his care of the children, and ends with the words,

> There are no words in the dictionary
> That can express my love for you
> Someday beyond the blue
> —Audrey Williams

Audrey, according to a *Billboard* report on November 29, 1952, had already been in California before Hank's death seeking to put together an all-girl band. After his death she decided to call the band the Drifting Cowgirls, in honor of her husband.

Audrey toured the country off and on for well over a decade as Mrs. Hank Williams, with various bands and supporting acts. She sang Hank's songs, her songs . . . and she shaped her entire presentation toward the appearance that she had been Hank's one and only.

As soon as Hank Junior was able to sing, he did, by golly, as part of Audrey's traveling shows.

In 1956, Audrey went into the recording studio to record "Let Me Sit Alone," a song written by Jimmy Rule, family friend to Hank and Audrey years before and coauthor with Hank of "How to Write Country and Western Music to Sell." The song was an impassioned piece of morbidity whose message was that no one could take Hank's place in Audrey's life, aimed at the cry-along market.

That same year, Audrey was in consultation with M-G-M pictures, and announced that June Allyson and Jeff Richards would star in the film version of Hank's life to be titled "Your Cheatin' Heart." The year before another announcement had said Kay Starr would have the female lead in "Cold, Cold Heart."

By 1960, Audrey had groomed Hank Junior so that he was ready to sing "Lovesick Blues" at the Opry. Of her travels with Hank Junior, Audrey was quoted about that time as saying, "In fairness to Hank, I can't say I need the money, but I love to sing and it's all I know."

No, she didn't need the money. She received her half of Hank's future royalties as granted by their divorce settlement for the rest of her life, plus whatever she made on her tours and concerts. But she did, like her ex-husband, need love.

Hillous Butrum recalls one conversation he had with Audrey in 1954. She was concerned that people thought she "ran around," and assured Butrum she did not. She merely had a difficult time staying home alone in the house she had built with Hank.

Audrey never remarried. The Nashville rumor mill linked her with various lovers from time to time, but there is no more reason to believe these stories than to disbelieve them. The common cast of the rumors usually had Audrey "keeping" some up-and-coming young talent.

The big house on Franklin Road was remodeled and re-modeled again, enlarged several times, with all the amenities added, including a pool and a guest house done Polynesian style.

But Audrey remained an unhappy person. "Sometimes she'd say something like, 'I was married to Hank Williams, and I lost him! He was here and then gone,' as if she was trying to think how it could have been avoided," Hank Junior remembers.

Audrey had her own problems with alcohol and drugs as the

sixties wore into the seventies. In 1972 she was arrested in Defuniak Springs, Florida, on charges of drunk driving, resisting arrest, and destroying county property. A law officer reported he had to forcibly take her out of her car after getting a complaint from a tavern owner. Then, according to police, Mrs. Williams broke some windows in the county jail while waiting for a bondsman to post bond.

In 1974, Audrey was in on plans in Montgomery to erect an elaborate Hank Williams museum-tomb-memorial, plans that were aborted after getting to the blueprint stage. Perhaps it was because the memorial's proponents were asking people to donate $750,000 for a structure that was to resemble an eighty-foot-high cowboy boot.

Audrey also tried in vain to get her Franklin Road house approved as a museum, but she never got through the Nashville zoning restrictions. She compromised in 1974 by "cleaning out her attic" and selling some of her memorabilia at a well-publicized sale, at which she charged admission to get into the home.

By this time Audrey's health was not good, and all her public appearances were made in various blonde wigs which did little to flatter her features. In 1975, the lady suffered several setbacks. The lawsuit won by Hill and Range (and Billie) cut in half her earnings from Hank's royalties, and some of her real estate was seized by the IRS. That was also the year that Hank Junior fell off a mountain up on the Idaho–Montana border and was next to death for many weeks.

Audrey died on November 4, 1975, of "natural causes." She was fifty-two. Her body lies in the Oakwood Cemetery Annex just a few feet away from her ex-husband's gravesite at the foot of the granite monument she had helped to design. Audrey was buried in a fringed cowgirl outfit she'd worn many years before when performing happily with Hank.

Randall   Hank   Williams   (Hank   Williams,   Junior/
"Bocephus"):   Progressive   country   music   writer/per-
former.   Cullman, Alabama

"People always told me, 'You're gonna be just like Hank,'"
says Hank Williams, Junior, "and at some points in my life, I've
almost proved them right.'"

The fact that Randall Hank Williams *didn't* turn out to
imitate his father's self-destructive life is a credit to this young
man, because many parts of his growing-up years were not
taken from *anybody's* book on How to Raise A Normal Child.
As a schoolboy, he did manage to have hobbies and friends like
any boy, but it wasn't long until his momma had him out on the
road with her. At age eleven he began drinking in the near-
perverse adulation that his father could never figure out.

He once told an interviewer about a time he was signing
autographs, "and this woman whips out $100 and gives it to this
man for a pen I used. Believe it or not, that doesn't give a
person a good feeling inside."

By his mid-teens Audrey and promoter Buddy Lee had
formed Aud-Lee Productions, whose main attraction was Hank
Williams, Junior, and his band, the Cheatin' Hearts. Raised
into adolescence in such an atmosphere, with almost stifling
expectations of grandeur and glory, young Hank seemed to
take it all in stride. He casually drove the '52 convertible to high
school.

As he sang his father's songs and learned to play guitar,
banjo, and piano, he grew into manhood. In the early seventies
he married a Nashville beauty named Gwen Yeargain. They
soon had a son whom they named Shelton Hank Williams III,
but their marriage didn't last. While waiting for his divorce,
says Hank Junior, he began to "feel Daddy's songs when I sang
'em." He spent some time drunk, some times depressed, trying
to get through it by joining other people in similar situations—
George Jones, for one.

In 1973, he took an overdose of barbiturates, but some
friends managed to get his stomach pumped in time. It was at
that point young Hank realized he needed a change. He said
good-bye to the rhinestone suits and the Songs Daddy Sang and

planted himself down in Cullman, Alabama, to regroup. In 1974, he released his last album on Daddy's old label, M-G-M, and it was a *zinger*. It didn't sound like anything he'd ever done. The songs told of the load he had to carry trying to be his daddy's son, and the *music*, well, the music kinda *rocked* along, y'know? Hank had some new friends helping him on that album, "Stoned At the Jukebox:" Charlie Daniels, of the Charlie Daniels Band, and Toy Caldwell, of the Marshall Tucker Band. And it turned out quite well.

Then just as things were starting to go right—he'd even met this great girl named Becky White—it happened. He was on top of a mountain up near the Continental Divide in western Montana, enjoying a beautiful climb with a rancher friend and his son. Hank put his foot down on some snow that the others had just walked across, and his foot caused the snow to give way. The next thing he knew he was plunging straight down a mountainside. He landed 500 feet below on a boulder that smashed his skull open between his eyes.

"I was holdin' one side of my face on," he remembers. Hank Junior says he "made his peace" while he was waiting there in the snow, but God wasn't comin' down the road yet.

He lived. And though his face was horribly torn up, one eye pulled out of its socket, today he performs again for enthusiastic crowds. So far there've been eight operations, including one where he says they had to "fill up a hole" between his eyebrows. But the girl Becky sat through it all by his side. And he knew if she loved him when his head was the size of a pumpkin, she must love him for sure. With her and his new life, he says he's found contentment.

Hank and Becky were married on June 18, 1976. He is fully recovered now. With beard, dark glasses, and cowboy hat, he looks more wacked-out than wounded, but without the glasses you can notice the scar tissue around the right eye, and without the hat you see the scars in the forehead as well.

Hank is a sportsman, a down-home boy who likes to walk the streets of Cullman unnoticed with his hunting buddies, a one-woman man in love with a one-man woman. It may take him a while yet to be completely understood, he may never (though he is a *very* talented man) reach the pinnacle of success reached by his daddy. But he's got a lot of treasures his daddy never owned.

"One thing I know," says young Hank. "He don't need me to make him any more than he already is."

Fred and Wesley Rose: Executives of Acuff-Rose Music. Nashville, Tennessee

Fred and Wesley Rose watched the awesome year of 1953 together, when Hank Williams won everything in the Country Music world posthumously, including a *Cash Box* award for "Your Cheatin' Heart" that Hank Junior accepted at age four on the Grand Ole Opry stage. The estate made $73,000 on royalties that year, and the next year was even bigger.

Fred Rose died in 1954 of a heart attack. (He had had one attack during a Hank Williams recording session, but true to his Christian Scientist philosophy, he'd walked out to a lounge, rested a few minutes, and returned to finish the session.)

In 1961, Fred Rose, Hank Williams, and Jimmie Rodgers were the first three men inducted into the Country Music Hall of Fame.

It was Wesley Rose who watched the Hank Williams legend grow into the gigantic thing it is today. And he watched the royalties grow too. In 1973, they topped $500,000.

Wesley had to replace Hank Williams if his company was to have a future. He came up with people like Marty Robbins, Felice and Beaudeleaux Bryant ("Bye-Bye Love"), and a veritable truckload of other songwriting talent which has kept Acuff-Rose on the top of the publishing world in Nashville.

The silver-haired executive has weathered the lawsuits with as much grace as he can muster. He feels the last round of suits, in which Hill and Range (along with Billie Jean Horton) won the right to split the publishing royalties with Acuff-Rose "will ruin Hank's catalog." The reason being that when a new song or album is released, publishing companies usually help promote the record to help make themselves money. But now, with the publisher's percentage on Hank's songs split in half, Rose feels such promotion efforts by Acuff-Rose or Hill and Range would not be worth the return on the investment. Thus record companies would be forced to spend dollars *they* may not want to spend.

In the meantime, Rose would rather talk about the old days. "Hank was from the people. He enjoyed entertaining. He was a throwback to Cantor and Jolson. He liked to entertain. *He liked people.*" And nobody knows better than Wesley Rose that people liked, still like, Hank.

Epilogue: The Tragic Legacy

The legend would have been there anyway. Nobody promoted the 1953 poll that named Hank Williams as "the most popular hillbilly entertainer of all time." But a circus-act atmosphere has always tainted the Hank Williams legend. First there was the rash of memorial records made after his death, most notably "The Death of Hank Williams" by Jack Cardwell, which sold several hundred thousand copies after being rushed into wax during those first weeks of 1953.

There were the allegations that Hank had fathered an illegitimate child. At one point in the long legal Gordian knot, it was feared the child might step forth to claim its share of the estate. As far as I know, that never happened. Several sources have told me, though, that there was a child; one woman offered the mother's name. I do not know.

There were the women who screamed and fainted at Hank's funeral, and the women who still carry a torch for the man these long years later. Some of them trying to readjust their torches to burn near his son have been turned away. More power to his son.

There was the way Audrey roamed the country (and Billie Jean too, for a while) nurturing and then harvesting pity like it was cotton, while for many years the Car, the Death Car, was displayed in downtown Nashville right next to Minnie Pearl's doll collection.

Like Hank Junior, one wants to see the man and his music

left alone to stand against the ages without the greasepaint and the cheap postscript eulogizing.

It looks like people are always going to love Hank Williams. There's no worry about that. In 1977, a national organization of CB truck drivers voted "Your Cheatin' Heart" as their favorite record of all time. Let the popularity roll.

But let it be for the right reasons. Let it be for Hank's pacesetting talent, giving inspiration to people like Bill Haley and Buddy Holly. Let it be for his songs, which may someday stand next to those of Stephen Foster to represent American grassroots-popular music for this century as Foster's songs do for the last century.

In years to come, the genius of Hank Williams may be more fully recognized than ever—genius that knew no social boundaries, that no amount of deprivation could keep imprisoned.

But leave the man a man. As Jerry Rivers had said, "We all excuse ourselves from the room once or twice a day; so did Hank." Hank Williams was an enormously talented man who lived a life of good deeds and bad, who was sensitive and lonely, often generous, sometimes selfish, usually stubborn. And under the sun there have been many other such men who along with Hank will be judged by One who has told us not to judge.

Hank was not an "alley cat," to be cut down or perhaps built up for his sexual behavior. He was a man who cheated sometimes, but loved one woman until she divorced him and then loved another woman. Neither was he a god, who carried superhuman blood in his veins and the weight of the world on his shoulders. No. He was an artist—a man who could express universal feelings with uncanny accuracy and insight. And he was a performer. Like Wesley Rose said, "He loved to entertain." He was a genius at that too.

Some have said "Hank was just an ol' boy who didn't give a damn about nothin'." And that's not true either. He came to a place where he no longer cared much about what happened to Hank Williams, but despair does not come from not caring. It comes from caring about something one cannot find or achieve.

Hank could not find inner peace. He never got in tune with the universe he could describe so beautifully. But there's more to it than that. He never found the love of God, which he deeply believed existed somewhere but thought he was not good enough for. And because he believed his search would be futile, he never looked too hard for God.

Hank the hell-raiser, Hank the drunken genius, Hank the womanizing wild man—all are myths due for reevaluation. Hank Williams could not write when he drank, and he suffered self-torture in guilt feelings for every woman with whom he ever adulterated himself. *Now* who wants to be just like him? Maybe we're already more like him than we thought.

Chet Atkins, who grew from a young studio guitarist in Hank's time into a great artist and a powerful Nashville recording executive with RCA, has a good saying about the young men who come to Music City and make their bids for stardom thinking that such attempts should necessarily include Hank Williams' style of drinking, drugs, and carousing.

"I like to think," says Atkins, "that Hank Williams accomplished what he did not *because* of his drinking, but *in spite* of it."

What killed Hank Williams? The autopsy performed on his body showed evidence that alcohol had certainly taken its physical toll on him. In Hank's stomach and intestines, the coroner found linings inflamed and shredded from the years of digesting liquor. Hank's lungs contained excessive fluids and his liver was contaminated with fatty deposits—he was on his way to cirrhosis.

Roger Williams and his medical counsel say that Hank probably died of "alcoholic cardiomyopathy." That is, heart disease caused by too much drinking for too long a sustained time. Williams notes that new medical research shows how prolonged ingestion of alcohol can lead to "the presence of small foreign bodies within the cells of the heart and to irregularities of heartbeat." Thus a person's heart may stop functioning at some time after this condition has been reached, even if he or she is not overly intoxicated at the time of death.

However, Hank's friend Corky Adams, himself a heart specialist, looks at the evidence of what Hank had taken into his body on the night he died and concludes that anyone might have died from such a combination of ingested chemicals. The alcohol, the chloral hydrate or Demerol probably added to that, plus the two injections of morphine could well have combined to bring about a "respiratory depression."

Adams believes that an alcoholic myopathy would have "put the patient in severe congestive failure, where at the time of his death he would not have been able to breathe hardly at all and would have required oxygen." Most likely, according to Adams, this kind of death would not have been a sudden thing. He does not discount, however, the possibility of a fatal arhythmia—of death due to an altered heart rhythm as also suggested by Roger Williams' research.

"But if he did receive an injection that night," concludes Adams, "if he had that plus alchohol plus any sleeping pills, it could easily have built up enough sedative effect to depress the respiratory center . . . and he could have just stopped breathing."

In any case, Hank never meant to kill himself. Alcoholism has been called a means of self-destruction, a slow suicide, by some psychologists; but Hank didn't consciously want to die. He just didn't know how to go on living.

Some other-worldly shadow may have generated the undercurrent of intense despair Hank could feel but neither chart nor name. Yet he held no Satanic delusions about an easy escape into an alluringly peaceful realm of death. He only knew he'd had to escape from life, from the pain in his back, from the pain in his heart, from the pain he felt every time he looked for light and found only darkness.

Hank had failed as a husband, as a father, and finally even as a performer. The shame of these shortcomings was immense. Here was a man who had prided himself on his mastery of things. Music, lyricism, audiences, women—all had been as clay in his gifted hands. Now he'd lost his touch.

Hank never perceived how people loved him. In Don Helms' words, "he never knew how big he was." What good was the adulation anyway? What was it worth to him as Hank brooded over his list of entrapments through that last long winter ride up from Montgomery to the West Virginia foothills? He was still alone, wasn't he?

God Almighty watched Hank. From as close as the Cadillac's rear seat ashtray and as far away as the farthest flung galaxy, He watched Hank Williams take his solitary ride into eternity. But there was nothing more God could do. He had said "Come to Me," but Hank had chosen not to. He had said "Seek Me out," but Hank had given up. Only God and Hank know where Hank's soul was transported when he departed his vehicle that night and left his body lying on the chilly black leather Hopefully God's mercy and Hank's heart had sometime been introduced.

If his soul traveled upward, Hank may have noticed as never before the way the dark Appalachian mountains appeared from several thousand feet up, and how quaintly and touchingly the light gleamed yellow from the few farmhouses whose lamps were lit. He may have been surprised as he was drawn upward at how fragile was this mist that appeared as solid puffs of cloud below in the starlight. Traveling higher, he may have seen the jagged eastern edge of the continent, and the curve of our planet itself, phosphorescent with the coming dawn.

It was all so different from up here. The big towns were so small . . . why, Montgomery and Nashville weren't even flyspecks, much less all the people he'd hoped to please. But it wasn't just the distance making Hank's perspective a new one. There was this sense of, of *glory* Hank could feel around him. There was a magnetic presence, an energizing aliveness to the space he floated in, yet the perfection he felt was still nothing he could see—it merely affected the way he saw everything else. Now finally it was making sense; the curious predicament of that painful orb down there was opened to his eyes.

Hank may have guessed, too, that the planet would—must— soon burn out in much the same manner he had: feeling a senseless urgency, seeing no constructive alternative to decline, and unable to make meaningful contact with the perfect universe surrounding its despair nor with that universe's Guardian.

And now, lifted out of the oppressive atmosphere he had so recently been subject to, Hank may have wished—as many of us might wish—that he could have seen as clearly long before this night.

Selected Bibliography

BOOKS

Bock, Al. *The Gospel Life of Hank Williams*. Nashville: Green Valley Record Store, 1977.

Gentry, Linnel. *A History and Encyclopedia of Country, Western, and Gospel Music*. Nashville: McQuiddy Press, 1961.

Horstman, Dorothy. *Sing Your Heart Out, Country Boy*. New York: Dutton, 1975 and New York: Pocket Books, 1976.

Hurst, Jack. "Hank Williams." *Nashville's Grand Ole Opry*. New York: Harry N. Abrams, Inc., 1975.

McDaniel, William R. and Seligman, Harold. *Grand Ole Opry*. New York: Greenberg, 1953.

Pleasants, Henry. *The Great American Popular Singers*. New York: Simon & Schuster, 1974.

Rankin, Allen and Williams, Lillian. *Our Hank Williams*. Montgomery: Philbert Publications, 1953.

Rivers, Jerry. *Hank Williams: From Life to Legend*. Denver: Heather Enterprises, 1967.

Shelton, Robert and Goldblatt, Burt. *The Country Music Story*. Indianapolis: Bobbs-Merrill Co. Inc., 1966.

Shestack, Melvin. *The Encyclopedia of Country Music*. New York: Thomas Y. Crowell, 1974.

Williams, Roger. "Hank Williams." *The Stars of Country Music*. Edited by Bill C. Malone and Judith McCulloh. Chicago: The University of Illinois Press, 1975.

Williams, Roger. *Sing A Sad Song, The Life of Hank Williams*. New York: Ballantine, 1973, 75.

MAGAZINES AND ARTICLES

Gleason, Ralph. "Hank Williams, Roy Acuff, and then God!!". *Rolling Stone*. June 28, 1969.

Linn, Ed. "The Short Life of Hank Williams". *Saga*. January, 1957.

Waldron, Eli. "The Death of Hank Williams". *Reporter*. May 19, 1955.

Waldron, Eli. "The Life and Death of a Country Singer". *Coronet*. January, 1956.

Newsweek. January 12, 1953.

Time. January 12, 1953.

"Sadly The Troubadour". *Newsweek*. January 19, 1953.

The March 1975 issue of *Country Music* is a "Hank Williams Special" and includes two articles entitled "Hank: The Music" by Nick Tosches and Dave Hickey respectively, "Remembering Hank" in which Hank Williams, Jr. interviews friends of his father, and "Hank: The Relics." The issue also includes an advertisement for full color reproductions of an oil painting of Hank.

Serious collectors should refer to the Jerry Rivers book, *Hank Williams: From Life to Legend* for a long list of old magazines, journals, and song folios which feature Hank Williams.

Discography

Courtesy of Jerry Rivers with update by the author

The first records made by Hank Williams were on the Sterling record label. Since there were no professional recording studios in Nashville, Tennessee, at the time (about 1946) these were all cut directly onto acetate discs at the WSM radio studios and were released on 78 RPM, 10″ shellac records. The musicians were basically the Oklahoma Cowboys (now the Willis Brothers) Guy, Vic, and Skeeter Willis, and Chuck "the Indian" on bass. At times other musicians were added to this basic group.

Following are the four Sterling releases:

S-201	Never Again (Will I Knock On Your Door)
	Calling You
S-204	Wealth Won't Save Your Soul
	When God Comes and Gathers His Jewels
S-208	I Don't Care (If Tomorrow Never Comes)
	My Love For You (Has Turned To Hate)
S-210	Honky-Tonkin'
	Pan American

When Hank Williams went to MGM records, MGM also took the Sterling masters which were later included in MGM albums. Most of the first MGM records were recorded in a Cincinnati studio, except those which were already on Sterling masters. Hank recorded his first session after he formed his Drifting Cowboys band in Nashville, and all following sessions at Castle Recording Studios in the old Tulane Hotel at Eighth Ave. and Church St. (Now removed.) Before forming his Drifting Cowboys, the following musicians were used on various early record sessions:

Tommy Jackson—fiddle
Chubby Wise—fiddle
Dale Potter—fiddle
Don Davis—steel guitar
Jerry Byrd—steel guitar
Jack Shook—rhythm guitar
Zeb Turner—lead guitar
Zeke Turner—lead guitar
Ernie Newton—bass
Fred Rose—piano
Owen Bradley—piano
Bill Drake—rhythm guitar
Brownie Reynolds—bass

Following are Hank's first 78 RPM, MGM records:

10033	Last Night I Heard You Crying In Your Sleep
	Move It On Over
10073	Fly Trouble
	On The Banks Of The Old Ponchartrain
10124	Rootie Tootie

234

	My Sweet Love Ain't Around
10171	Honky-Tonkin'
	I'll Be A Bachelor Till I Die
10212	The Blues Come Around
	I'm A Long Gone Daddy
10226	Pan American
	I Don't Care (If Tomorrow Never Comes)
10271	I Saw the Light
	Six More Miles
10328	I Can't Get You Off My Mind
	Mansion On The Hill
10352	Lovesick Blues
	Never Again
10401	I've Just Told Mama Good-bye
	Wedding Bells
10434	Dear Brother (with Audrey Williams)
	Lost On the River (with Audrey Williams)
10461	Mind Your Own Business
	There'll Be No Teardrops Tonight
10506	Lost Highway
	You're Gonna Change Or I'm Gonna Leave
10560	I'm So Lonesome I Could Cry
	My Bucket's Got A Hole In It
10609	I Just Don't Like This Kind of Livin'
	May You Never Be Alone

All the records after this point (except previous releases included in albums) were recorded by the Drifting Cowboys formed by Hank Williams in Nashville in July of 1949. The original group consisted of: Don Helms—steel guitar, Jerry Rivers—fiddle, Hillous Butrum—bass, Bob McNett—lead guitar. After about one year, two of these were replaced by Sammy Pruitt—lead guitar and Howard Watts (Cedric Rainwater) on bass. On most sessions, additional rhythm guitar and piano were added to the group. Also, some philosophical songs and recitations were released under the name of Luke the Drifter, and an organ was added to some of these sessions.

10630	Beyond the Sunset (Luke the Drifter)
	The Funeral (Luke the Drifter)
10645	My Son Calls Another Man Daddy
	Long Gone Lonesome Blues
10696	Why Don't You Love Me Like You Used To Do
	A House Without Love
10718	Everything's O.K. (Luke the Drifter)
	Too Many Parties (Luke the Drifter)
10760	Why Should We Try Anymore
	They'll Never Take Her Love From Me
10806	Help Me Understand (Luke the Drifter)
	No, No, Joe (Luke the Drifter)
10813	I Heard My Mother Praying For Me
	Jesus Died For Me
10832	Nobody's Lonesome For Me
	Moanin' the Blues
10904	Cold, Cold Heart
	Dear John
10932	Just Waitin' (Luke the Drifter)
	Men With Broken Hearts (Luke the Drifter)
10961	I Can't Help It
	Howlin' At the Moon
11000	Hey, Good Lookin'
	My Heart Would Know
11017	I Dreamed About Mama Last Night (Luke the Drifter)

	I've Been Down That Road Before (Luke the Drifter)	11861	I'm Satisfied With You The Angel of Death Sing, Sing, Sing
11054	Lonesome Whistle Crazy Heart	11928	Faded Love and Withered Roses
11100	I'd Still Want You Baby, We're Really In Love		Please Don't Let Me Love You
11120	Ramblin' Man (Luke the Drifter)	11975	Message To My Mother Mother Is Gone
	Picture From Life's Other Side (Luke the Drifter)	12029	A Teardrop On A Rose Alone and Forsaken
11160	Honky Tonk Blues I'm Sorry For You My Friend	12077	The First Fall Of Snow Someday You'll Call My Name
11202	Let's Turn Back the Years Half as Much	12127	The Battle of Armageddon Thank God
11283	Jambalaya Window Shopping	12185	California Zephyr Thy Burdens Are Greater Than Mine
11309	Why Don't You Make Up Your Mind (Luke the Drifter)	12244	I Wish I Had A Nickel There's No Room In My Heart For The Blues
	Be Careful Of Stones That You Throw (Luke the Drifter)	12332	Blue Love Singing Waterfall
11318	Settin' the Woods On Fire You Win Again	12394	The Pale Horse and His Rider (with Audrey Williams)
11366	I'll Never Get Out of This World Alive		Home In Heaven (with Audrey Williams)
	I Could Never Be Ashamed Of You	12438	Ready To Go Home We're Getting Closer To The Grave Each Day
11416	Kaw-Liga Your Cheating Heart	12484	Leave Me Alone With The Blues
11479	Take These Chains From My Heart Ramblin' Man		With Tears In My Eyes
11533	My Love For You I Won't Be Home No More	12535	Waltz of the Wind No One Will Ever Know
11574	Weary Blues From Waitin' I Can't Escape From You	12611	I Can't Help It Why Don't You Love Me
11628	Calling You When God Comes And Gathers His Jewels	12635	My Bucket's Got A Hole In It We Live In Two Different Worlds
11675	You Better Keep It On Your Mind	12727	Just Waitin' Roly Poly
	Low Down Blues	13489	You Win Again (Re-recorded with new backing)
11707	How Can You Refuse Him Now A House Of Gold		I'm So Lonesome I Could Cry (Re-recorded with new backing)
11768	I Ain't Got Nothin' But Time		

13630   There'll Be No Teardrops Tonight   (Re-recorded with new backing)
There'll Never Take Her Love From Me (Re-recorded with new backing)

All of the following "300" series taken from albums:

30453   Lost Highway
I've Just Told Mama Goodbye
30454   I Saw the Light
Six More Miles
30455   Mansion On the Hill
Wealth Won't Save Your Soul
30456   A House Without Love
Wedding Bells

The following were taken from Luke the Drifter albums:

30755   Be Careful of Stones That You Throw
I Dreamed About Mama Last Night
30756   Pictures   From   Life's Other Side
Men With Broken Hearts
30757   The Funeral
Beyond the Sunset
30758   Help Me Understand
Too Many Parties

Following are 45 RPM "KGC" series:
KGC-107 Lovesick Blues
Your Cheatin' Heart
KGC-108 Why Don't You Love Me
Hey, Good Lookin'
KGC-109 Honky Tonk Blues
Half As Much
KGC-110 Jambalaya
I'll Never Get Out of This World Alive
KGC-111 Ramblin' Man
Kaw-Liga
KGC-112 Moanin' the Blues
You Win Again
KGC-113 Cold, Cold Heart

I'm So Lonesome I Could Cry
KGC-127 My Bucket's Got A Hole In It
We Live In Two Different Worlds
KGC-128 I Can't Help It
House Of Gold
KGC-134 Long   Gone   Lonesome Blues
My Son Calls Another Man Daddy
KGC-142 Roly Poly
Just Waitin'
K-107   "Hank Williams Sings"— 45 album:
30455   Mansion On The Hill
Wealth Won't Save Your Soul
30456   A House Without Love
Wedding Bells
30454   I Saw the Light
Six More Miles
30453   Lost Highway
I've Just Told Mama Goodbye

45 EP Albums:
X-168   "Moanin' the Blues"
X-1216 Moanin' the Blues
I'm So Lonesome I Could Cry
My   Sweet   Love   Ain't Around
Honky Tonk Blues
X-1217 Lovesick Blues
The Blues Come Around
Long   Gone   Lonesome Blues
I'm A Long Gone Daddy
X-202   "Memorial Album"
X-1612 Your Cheating Heart
You Win Again
Settin' the Woods On Fire
Hey, Good Lookin'
X-1613 Cold, Cold Heart
I Could Never Be Ashamed Of You
Kaw-Liga
Half As Much

X-242   "Honky-Tonkin'"
X-1317   Jambalaya
         I Won't Be Home No More
         Honky-Tonk Blues
         I'll Never Get Out of This
           World Alive
X-1318   Honky-Tonkin'
         Howlin' At the Moon
         My Bucket's Got A Hole In
           It
         Baby, We're Really In
           Love
X-243   "I Saw The Light"
X-4110   Dear Brother
         Wealth Won't Save Your
           Soul
         I Saw the Light
         Calling You
X-4111   Jesus Remembered Me
         A House Of Gold
         How Can You Refuse Him
           Now
         When God Comes And
           Gathers His Jewels
X-291   "Ramblin' Man" (Also re-
           leased as two records):
X-1135   Ramblin' Man
         My Son Calls Another Man
           Daddy
         I Can't Escape From You
         Nobody's Lonesome For
           Me
X-1136   Lonesome Whistle
         I Just Don't Like This
           Kind Of Livin'
         Take These Chains From
           My Heart
         Why Don't You Love Me

45 EP Records:
X-1014 "Crazy Heart"
  Crazy Heart
  Baby, We're Really In Love
  My Heart Would Know
  I Can't Help It
X-1047 "Luke the Drifter"
  Pictures From Life's Other Side
  Help Me Understand
  Men With Broken Hearts
  Too Many Parties

X-1076 "Move It On Over"
  Move It On Over
  Fly Trouble
  Window Shopping
  Pan American
X-1082 "There'll Be No Teardrops
    Tonight"
  There'll Be No Teardrops Tonight
  You're Gonna Change
  Nobody's Lonesome For Me
  Mind Your Own Business
X-1165 "Luke the Drifter"
  Why Don't You Make Up Your
    Mind
  Just Waitin'
  I've Been Down That Road Before
  Everything's O.K.
X-1215 "Moanin' The Blues" (see
    X-168 for two more volumes in
    this set):
  Lowdown Blues
  Someday You'll Call My Name
  Alone and Forsaken
  Weary Blues From Waitin'
X-1218 "I Saw The Light" (see X-243
    for two other volumes in this
    set):
  Sing, Sing, Sing
  Message to My Mother
  Thank God
  The Angel of Death
X-1319 "Honky-Tonkin'" (see X-242
    for two other volumes in this
    set):
  Mind Your Own Business
  Rootie Tootie
  I Ain't Got Nothin' But Time
  You Better Keep It On Your Mind
X-1491 "Sing Me A Blue Song" Vol. 1
  Wedding Bells
  May You Never Be Alone
  Lost Highway
  Why Should We Try Anymore
X-1492 "Sing Me A Blue Song" Vol. 2
  I Heard You Crying In Your Sleep
  Blue Love
  Mansion On the Hill
  They'll Never Take Her Love
    From Me
X-1493 "Sing Me A Blue Song" Vol. 3

I've Just Told Mama Goodbye
A House Without Love
Six More Miles
Singing Waterfall
X-1554 "The Immortal Hank Williams" Vol. 1
There's No Room In My Heart
Waltz Of the Wind
Pan American
With Tears In My Eyes
X-1555 "The Immortal Hank Williams" Vol. 2
I Wish I Had A Nickel
Fly Trouble
Please Don't Let Me Love You
I'm Satisfied With You
X-1556 "The Immortal Hank Williams" Vol. 3
No One Will Ever Know
Faded Love and Withered Roses
First Fall Of Snow
California Zephyr
X-1636 "Memorial Album" (see X-202 for two other volumes in this set):
Crazy Heart
Move It On Over
My Heart Would Know
I'm Sorry For You My Friend
X-1637 "The Unforgettable Hank Williams" Vol. 1
I Can't Get You Off My Mind
I Don't Care
Dear John
My Love For You
X-1638 "The Unforgettable Hank Williams" Vol. 2
On The Banks Of The Old Ponchartrain
We Live In Two Different Worlds
I'll Be A Bachelor Till I Die
Let's Turn Back The Years
X-1639 "The Unforgettable Hank Williams" Vol. 3
I'd Still Want You
Never Again
Blue Love
Leave Me Alone With The Blues
X-1643 "Luke the Drifter" Vol. 2
Pictures From Life's Other Side

Men With Broken Hearts
Help Me Understand
Too Many Parties
X-1644 "Luke the Drifter" Vol. 3
Be Careful Of Stones That You Throw
I Dreamed About Mama Last Night
The Funeral
Beyond The Sunset
X-1648 "I Saw The Light" Vol. 2
I Saw The Light
Calling You
Dear Brother
Wealth Won't Save Your Soul
X-1649 "I Saw the Light" Vol. 3
How Can You Refuse Him Now
When God Comes And Gathers His Jewels
Jesus Remembered Me
House Of Gold
X-1650 "Ramblin' Man Vol. III"
I Can't Help It
There'll Be No Teardrops Tonight
My Heart Would Know
You're Gonna Change (Or I'm Gonna Leave)
X-1698 "Lonesome Sound of Vol. I"
It Just Doesn't Matter Now
First Year Blues
Cool Water
Dixie Cannonball
X-1699 "Lonesome Sound of Vol. II"
I'm Free At Last
Roly Poly
The Old Home
Rock My Cradle
X-1700 "Lonesome Sound of Vol. III"
Sundown And Sorrow
Rockin' Chair Money
Tennessee Border
Swing Wide Your Gate Of Love

10" LP Albums:
E-107 "Hank Williams Sings"
A House Without Love
Wedding Bells
Mansion On the Hill
Wealth Won't Save Your Soul

I Saw The Light
Six More Miles
Lost Highway
I've Just Told Mama Goodbye
E-168 "Moanin' The Blues"
  Moanin' The Blues
  I'm So Lonesome I Could Cry
  My Sweet Love Ain't Around
  Honky Tonk Blues
  Lovesick Blues
  The Blues Come Around
  I'm A Long Gone Daddy
  Long Gone Lonesome Blues
E-202 "Memorial Album"
  Your Cheating Heart
  You Win Again
  Cold, Cold Heart
  I Could Never Be Ashamed Of You
  Settin' The Woods On Fire
  Hey Good Lookin'
  Kaw-Liga
  Half As Much
E-203 "Luke the Drifter"
  Pictures From Life's Other Side
  Men With Broken Hearts
  Help Me Understand
  Too Many Parties
  Be Careful Of Stones That You
    Throw
  I Dreamed About Mama Last
    Night
  The Funeral
  Beyond The Sunset
E-242 "Honky-Tonkin'"
  Jambalaya
  I Won't Be Home No More
  Honky Tonk Blues
  I'll Never Get Out of This World
    Alive
  Honky-Tonkin'
  Howlin' At The Moon
  My Bucket's Got A Hole In It
  Baby, We're Really In Love
E-243 "I Saw The Light"
  I Saw The Light
  Calling You
  Dear Brother
  Wealth Won't Save Your Soul
  How Can You Refuse Him Now
  When God Comes And Gathers His
    Jewels

Jesus Remembered Me
House Of Gold

12″ LP Albums:
E-3219 "Ramblin' Man"
  Ramblin' Man
  Lonesome Whistle
  My Son Calls Another Man Daddy
  I Just Don't Like This Kind Of
    Livin'
  I Can't Escape From You
  Nobody's Lonesome For Me
  Take These Chains From My
    Heart
  Why Don't You Love Me
  I Can't Help It
  There'll Be No Teardrops Tonight
  You're Gonna Change Or I'm
    Gonna Leave
  My Heart Would Know
E-3267 "As Luke The Drifter"
  Pictures From Life's Other Side
  Help Me Understand
  Be Careful Of Stones That You
    Throw
  The Funeral
  Why Don't You Make Up Your
    Mind
  Just Waitin'
  Men With Broken Hearts
  Too Many Parties
  I Dreamed About Mama Last
    Night
  Beyond The Sunset
  I've Been Down That Road Before
  Everything's O.K.
E-3272 "Memorial Album"
  Your Cheating Heart
  You Win Again
  Cold, Cold Heart
  I Could Never Be Ashamed Of You
  Crazy Heart
  My Heart Would Know
  Settin' The Woods On Fire
  Hey Good Lookin'
  Kaw-Liga
  Half As Much
  Move It On Over
  I'm Sorry For You My Friend
E-3330 "Moanin' The Blues"

Low Down Blues
Someday You'll Call My Name
Alone And Forsaken
Weary Blues From Waitin'
Moanin' The Blues
I'm So Lonesome I Could Cry
My Sweet Love Ain't Around
Honky Tonk Blues
Lovesick Blues
I'm A Long Gone Daddy
Long Gone Lonesome Blues
The Blues Come Around
E-3331 "I Saw The Light"
I Saw The Light
Calling You
Dear Brother
Wealth Won't Save Your Soul
How Can You Refuse Him Now
When God Comes And Gathers His
 Jewels
Jesus Remembered Me
A House Of Gold
Sing, Sing, Sing
Message To Mother
Thank God
The Angel Of Death
E-3412 "Honky-Tonkin'"
Jambalaya
I Won't Be Home No More
Honky Tonk Blues
I'll Never Get Out of This World
 Alive
Honky-Tonkin'
Howlin' At The Moon
My Bucket's Got A Hole In It
Baby, We're Really In Love
Mind Your Own Business
Rootie Tootie
I Ain't Got Nothing But Time
You'd Better Keep It On Your
 Mind
E-3560 "Sing Me A Blue Song"
Wedding Bells
May You Never Be Alone
Lost Highway
Why Should We Try Anymore
I Heard You Crying In Your Sleep
Blue Love
Mansion On The Hill
They'll Never Take Her Love
 From Me

I've Just Told Mama Goodbye
A House Without Love
Six More Miles
Singing Waterfall
E-3605 "The Immortal Hank
 Williams"
There's No Room In My Heart
Waltz Of The Wind
Pan American
With Tears In My Eyes
I Wish I Had A Nickel
Fly Trouble
Please Don't Let Me Love You
I'm Satisfied With You
No One Will Ever Know
Faded Love And Withered Roses
First Fall Of Snow
California Zephyr
E-3733 "The Unforgettable Hank
 Williams"
I Can't Get You Off My Mind
I Don't Care
Dear John
My Love For You
On The Banks of the Old
 Ponchartrain
We Live In Two Different Worlds
I'll Be A Bachelor Till I Die
Let's Turn Back The Years
I'd Still Want You
Never Again
Blue Love
Leave Me Alone With The Blues
E-3803 "The Lonesome Sound of
 Hank Williams"
It Just Doesn't Matter Now
First Year Blues
Cool Water
Dixie Cannonball
I'm Free At Last
Roly Poly
The Old Home
Rock My Cradle
Sundown and Sorrow
Rockin' Chair Money
Tennessee Border
Swing Wide Your Gate Of Love
E-3850 "Wait For The Light To
 Shine"
Wait For The Light To Shine
Jesus Is Calling

Ready To Go Home
Last Night I Dreamed Of Heaven
When The Book Of Life Is Read
Devil's Train
Thy Burdens Are Greater Than Mine
Are You Building A Temple In Heaven
The Prodigal
Are You Walkin' and Talkin' With The Lord
The Battle Of Armageddon
Going Home
E-3918 "Greatest Hits"
Cold, Cold Heart
Jambalaya
You Win Again
Kaw-Liga
Your Cheating Heart
Hey, Good Lookin'
Half As Much
Take These Chains From My Heart
There'll Be No Teardrops Tonight
Settin' The Woods On Fire
Honky-Tonkin'
I Can't Help It
Why Don't You Love Me
I'm So Lonesome I Could Cry
E-3923 "Hank Williams Lives Again"
Your Cheating Heart
You Win Again
Cold, Cold Heart
I Could Never Be Ashamed Of You
Crazy Heart
My Heart Would Never Know
Settin' the Woods On Fire
Hey, Good Lookin'
Kaw-Liga
Half As Much
Move It On Over
I'm Sorry For You, My Friend
E-3924 "Sing Me A Blue Song"
Wedding Bells
May You Never Be Alone
Lost Highway
Why Should We Try Anymore
Last Night I Heard You Crying In Your Sleep
Blue Love (In My Heart)

Mansion On The Hill
They'll Never Take Her Love From Me
I've Just Told Mama Goodbye
A House Without Love
Six More Miles
Singing Waterfall
E-3925 "Wanderin' Around"
Ramblin' Man
My Son Calls Another Man Daddy
I Can't Escape From You
Nobody's Lonesome For Me
I Can't Help It
There'll Be No Teardrops Tonight
I Just Don't Like This Kind Of Living
Lonesome Whistle
Take These Chains From My Heart
Why Don't You Love Me
My Heart Would Know
You're Gonna Change Or I'm Gonna Leave
E-3926 "I'm Blue Inside"
Low Down Blues
Someday You'll Call My Name
Alone And Forsaken
Weary Blues From Waiting
Lovesick Blues
The Blues Come Around
I'm A Long Gone Daddy
Long Gone Lonesome Blues
Moanin' The Blues
I'm So Lonesome I Could Cry
My Sweet Love Ain't Around
Honky Tonk Blues
E-3928 "First, Last, And Always"
(Same titles as E-3605)
E-3955 "The Spirit Of Hank Williams"
Window Shopping
Wearin' Out Your Walkin' Shoes
A Teardrop On A Rose
Lost On The River
Jesus Died For Me
A Home In Heaven
Fool About You
The Pale Horse And His Rider
If You'll Be A Baby
Mother Is Gone

Dear Brother
When You're Tired Of Breaking Other Hearts
E-3999 "On Stage"
Note: These numbers were recorded live during transcribing of fifteen-minute radio shows for the Hadacol Corporation. Originally recorded on large acetate discs for distribution to radio stations around the nation, MGM obtained rights to release the material in album form after Hank Williams' death. Called Health and Happiness shows by the sponsor, and recorded in Castle Studios with the Drifting Cowboys, there was originally a considerable amount of dialogue between Hank, the musicians, Grant Turner (announcer) and Audrey Williams, some of which was left in the finished album. This album closely reflects Hank's "on the road" sound with his own group.

 I'm A Long Gone Daddy
 Rovin' Cowboy
 I'm Telling You (Audrey Williams)
 Bill Cheatam (Jerry Rivers, fiddle)
 When God Comes And Gathers His Jewels
 The Blues Come Around
 I Want To Live And Love (Hank and Audrey)
 Rovin' Cowboy
 Wedding Bells
 Lovesick Blues
 I'll Have A New Body (with group vocal)
 Where The Soul Of Man Never Dies (with group vocal)
E-4040 "Greatest Hits, Vol. II"
 Crazy Heart
 Move It On Over
 Honky Tonk Blues
 I'll Be A Bachelor Till I Die
 My Sweet Love Ain't Around
 They'll Never Take Her Love From Me
 Mansion On The Hill
 Window Shopping
 Nobody's Lonesome For Me

I'm Sorry For You, My Friend
I Just Don't Like This Kind Of Livin'
Ramblin' Man
Howlin' At The Moon
Baby, We're Really In Love
E-4109 "On Stage, Vol. II" (see Note at E-3999)
 Rovin' Cowboy
 You're Gonna Change Or I'm Gonna Leave
 Settin' The Woods On Fire
 There's A Bluebird On Your Windowsill (Audrey Williams)
 Old Joe Clark (Jerry Rivers, fiddle)
 I Saw The Light (group vocal)
 Rovin' Cowboy (used as theme)
 The Tramp On The Street
 Lovesick Blues
 Help Me Understand
 The Blues Come Around
 Fingers On Fire (Bob McNett, lead guitar)
 Rovin' Cowboy
E-4138 "Beyond The Sunset"
 Beyond The Sunset
 Pictures From Life's Other Side
 Men With Broken Hearts
 Help Me Understand
 Too Many Parties
 Why Don't You Make Up Your Mind
 I've Been Down That Road Before
 Be Careful Of Stones That You Throw
 I Dreamed About Mama Last Night
 The Funeral
 Just Waitin'
 Everything's O.K.
E-4140 "Greatest Hits, Vol. III"
 Long Gone Lonesome Blues
 Let's Turn Back The Years
 Rootie Tootie
 Mind Your Own Business
 My Heart Would Know
 I Won't Be Home No More
 On The Banks Of The Old Ponchartrain

May You Never Be Alone
Lost Highway
I've Just Told Mama Goodbye
I'll Never Get Out Of This World
  Alive
The Blues Come Around
I'm A Long Gone Daddy
You're Gonna Change Or I'm
  Gonna Leave
E-4168 "Very Best"
  My Heart Would Know
  Lovesick Blues
  Cold, Cold Heart
  Hey Good Lookin'
  Kaw-Liga
  Ramblin' Man
  Jambalaya
  Half As Much
  Why Don't You Love Me
  Wedding Bells
  I'm So Lonesome I Could Cry
  Honky-Tonkin'
E-4211 "Great Country Favorites"
  There'll Be No Teardrops Tonight
  Move It On Over
  (Also various selections by other
  artists)
E-4227 "Very Best" Vol. II
  My Heart Would Know
  Lost Highway
  Howlin' At The Moon
  Mind Your Own Business
  Mansion On The Hill
  You Win Again
  Settin' The Woods On Fire
  Window Shopping
  Honky Tonk Blues
  May You Never Be Alone
  They'll Never Take Her Love
  From Me
  Half As Much
E-4254 "Lost Highway"
  Lost Highway
  Be Careful Of Stones That You
  Throw
  Jambalaya
  Ramblin' Man
  I've Just Told Mama Goodbye
  Long Gone Lonesome Blues
  My Bucket's Got A Hole In It

Six More Miles
Thy Burdens Are Greater Than
  Mine
Kaw-Liga
Pictures From Life's Other Side
Cool Water
E-4267-4 "Hank Williams Story" set
  of 4
  (Combination of previous albums)
E-4300 "Humorous Songs"
  Howlin' At The Moon
  Just Waitin'
  Honky Tonk Blues
  Mind Your Own Business
  I'll Never Get Out Of This World
  Alive
  Nobody's Lonesome For Me
  Move It On Over
  Everything's O.K.
  Fly Trouble
  I've Been Down That Road Before
  Please Make Up Your Mind
  Kaw-Liga
E-4377 "Legend Lives Anew, With
  Strings"
S-4377
  Kaw-Liga
  House Without Love
  I'm Sorry For You My Friend
  Lovesick Blues
  Let's Turn Back The Years
  Men With Broken Hearts
  I'm So Lonesome I Could Cry
  Wedding Bells
  Pictures From Life's Other Side
  You Win Again
  They'll Never Take Her Love
  From Me
  I Don't Care If Tomorrow Never
  Comes
E-4380 "Movin' On—Luke The
  Drifter"
S-4380
  Pictures From Life's Other Side
  Help Me Understand
  Please Make Up Your Mind
  Be Careful of Stones That You
  Throw
  The Funeral
  Just Waitin'

Men With Broken Hearts
Too Many Parties
I've Been Down That Road Before
I Dreamed About Mama Last
  Night
Beyond The Sunset
Everything's O.K.
E-4429 "More with Strings"
S-4429
  Dear John
  Your Cheating Heart
  Long Gone Lonesome Blues
  Lonesome Whistle
  Jambalaya
  Ramblin' Man
  Howlin' At The Moon
  There'll Be No Teardrops Tonight
  Settin' The Woods On Fire
  Half As Much
  Cold, Cold Heart
  Someday You'll Call My Name
E-4481 "I Won't Be Home No More"
  I Won't Be Home No More
  Lost Highway
  Mind Your Own Business
  My Heart Would Know
  Nobody's Lonesome For Me
  May You Never Be Alone
  Mansion On The Hill
  Move It On Over
  Honky Tonk Blues
  I Just Don't Like This Kind Of
    Livin'
  Baby, We're Really In Love
SE-4529 "Hank Williams And
  Strings—Volume III"
  Window Shopping
  My Bucket's Got A Hole In It
  Just Waitin'
  (Last Night) I Heard You Crying
    In Your Sleep
  Why Should We Try Anymore
  Be Careful of Stones That You
    Throw
  I'll Never Get Out Of This World
    Alive
  Moanin' The Blues
  My Sweet Love Ain't Around
  Why Don't You Love Me
  Crazy Heart

SE-4576 "Hank Williams In The Be-
  ginning"
  Calling You
  Honky-Tonkin'
  I Don't Care (If Tomorrow Never
    Comes)
  Never Again (Will I Knock On
    Your Door)
  My Love For You Has Turned To
    Hate
  Pan American
  Wealth Won't Save Your Soul
  When God Comes And Gathers His
    Jewels
  Move It On Over
  (Last Night) I Heard You Crying
    In Your Sleep
  On The Banks of The Old
    Pontchartrain
SE-4561 "The Essential Hank
  Williams"
  My Bucket's Got A Hole In It
  Honky Tonk Blues
  May You Never Be Alone
  Lovesick Blues
  Kaw-Liga
  I'm So Lonesome I Could Cry
  Move It On Over
  Ramblin' Man
  Honky-Tonkin'
  Long Gone Lonesome Blues
  Howlin' At The Moon
SE-4680 "Life To Legend"
  Move It On Over
  Mansion On The Hill
  Lovesick Blues
  Cold, Cold Heart
  Hey, Good Lookin'
  I Can't Help It
  Jambalaya
  Half As Much
  Your Cheatin' Heart
  Kaw-Liga
SE-4755 "24 Of Hank Williams
  Greatest Hits"
  Your Cheatin' Heart
  Move It On Over
  I'm So Lonesome I Could Cry
  Honky Tonk Blues
  My Heart Would Know

Kaw-Liga
Cold, Cold Heart
Lovesick Blues
Ramblin' Man
Honky-Tonkin'
There'll Be No Teardrops Tonight
Mind Your Own Business
Jambalaya
Wedding Bells
Hey, Good Lookin'
Window Shopping
Settin' The Woods On Fire
I Can't Help It
Half As Much
Why Don't You Love Me
You Win Again
May You Never Be Alone
Baby, We're Really In Love
Take These Chains From My Heart
3E2 "36 of Hank's Greatest Hits" (3-record series)
(Combination of three previously released title combinations)
3E4 "36 More Of Hank's Greatest Hits" (3-record series)
(Combination of three previously released title combinations)
M-509 "Hank Williams"
Alone And Forsaken
Beyond The Sunset
Wedding Bells
Rockin' Chair Money
Rock My Cradle
Tennessee Border
Too Many Parties
I'll Be A Bachelor Till I Die
I'm Free At Last
Lonesome Whistle
M-547 "Mr. and Mrs. Hank Williams"
Dear Brother
Lost On The River
I Dreamed About Mama Last Night
Jesus Remembered Me
The Pale Horse And His Rider
(No Hank Williams vocals on flip side—Devoted to Audrey and band)
M-602 "Immortal"
Never Again

Pan American
My Sweet Love Ain't Around
I Don't Care If Tomorrow Never Comes
May You Never Be Alone Like Me
Sundown And Sorrow
Lovesick Blues
Nobody's Lonesome For Me
Hey Good Lookin'
Last Night I Dreamed Of Heaven
M3HB "Insights Into Hank Williams In Song And Story"/Hank Williams and Hank Williams, Jr.
Jambalaya (On The Bayou)
Why Don't You Love Me
Men With Broken Hearts
A Picture From Life's Other Side
Nobody's Lonesome For Me
My Bucket's Got A Hole In It
I Dreamed About Mama Last Night
I Just Didn't Have The Heart To Say Goodbye*
When He Sang*
Hey, Good Lookin'
(I'm Praying For the Day That) Peace Will Come*
Half As Much
Wedding Bells
There'll Be No Teardrops Tonight
Standing In The Shadows*
*Sung by Hank Williams, Jr.
M3G 4991 "A Home In Heaven"
Help Me Understand
Jesus Is Calling
When The Book Of Life Is Read
Jesus Remembered Me
A Home In Heaven
Beyond The Sunset
Where The Soul Of Man Never Dies
Jesus Died For Me
Thank God
I'm Going Home
MG-1-5019 "Live At The Grand Ole Opry"
Moanin' The Blues
Nobody's Lonesome For Me
I Just Don't Like This Kind Of Livin'
Why Don't You Love Me

(talk with Minnie Pearl)
They'll Never Take Her Love From Me
Lovesick Blues
Long Gone Lonesome Blues
Cold, Cold Heart
(talk with Minnie Pearl)
Dear John
Hey, Good Lookin'
You're Gonna Change (Or I'm Gonna Leave)
MG-2-5401 "Hank Williams, Sr. 24 Greatest Hits Vol. 2"
My Bucket's Got A Hole In It
Crazy Heart
I'll Never Get Out Of This World Alive
Moanin' The Blues
I Could Never Be Ashamed Of You
Lost Highway
You're Gonna Change (Or I'm Gonna Leave)
A House Without Love
I'd Still Want You
Dear John
Let's Turn Back The Years
Howlin' At The Moon
Mansion On The Hill
I Saw The Light
(I Heard That) Lonesome Whistle
I'm A Long Gone Daddy
Why Should We Try Anymore
Long Gone Lonesome Blues
Nobody's Lonesome For Me
They'll Never Take Her Love From Me
My Sweet Love Ain't Around
I Just Don't Like This Kind Of Livin'
I Won't Be Home No More
I'm Sorry For You, My Friend

Jerry Rivers acknowledges and appreciates assistance in compiling this discography from The John Edwards Memorial Foundation at U.C.L.A., from Lou Deneumoustier of "Disc Collector," and Elizabeth Schlappi.

Tribute Records on Hank Williams

Decca 28584 Single by Jimmie Logsdon
Hank Williams Sings The Blues No More
The Death Of Hank Williams
Ranch House 10419 Single by Cal Shrum
That Heaven Bound Train
MGM 11433 Single by Arthur Smith
In Memory Of Hank Williams
Republic 100 Single by Joe Rumore
Tribute To Hank Williams
MGM 11450 Single by Jimmy Swan
The Last Letter
King 1172 Single by Jack Cardwell
The Death Of Hank Williams
Victor 20-5164 Single by Johnnie and Jack
Hank Williams Will Live Forever
King 1174 Single by Hawkshaw Hawkins
The Life Of Hank Williams
Coral 60148 Single by Johnny Ryon
That Heaven Bound Train
Decca 28630 Single by Ernest Tubb
Hank, It Will Never Be The Same Without You
Coral 64150 Single by Little Barbara
(I Would Like To Have Been) Hank's Little Flower Girl
Capitol 2397 Single by Ferlin Husky
Hank's Song
Capitol 2401 Single by Jimmie Skinner
Singing Teacher In Heaven
Trumpet 184 Single by Luke McDaniel
A Tribute To Hank Williams My Buddy
Rosemay 1 & 2 By Virginia Rounders
Hank Williams Meets Jimmie Rodgers
There's A New Star In Hillbilly Heaven

Index

249